CHANNELING MOROCCANNESS

Channeling Moroccanness

LANGUAGE AND THE MEDIA OF SOCIALITY

Becky L. Schulthies

FORDHAM UNIVERSITY PRESS NEW YORK 2021

Fordham University Press gratefully acknowledges financial assistance and support provided for the publication of this book by the Rutgers University Research Council.

Fordham University Press also publishes its books in a variety of electronic formats. Some content that appears in print may not be available in electronic books.

Visit us online at www.fordhampress.com.

Library of Congress Control Number: 2020919016

Printed in the United States of America

23 22 21 5 4 3 2 1

First edition

for all the Fassis who shared their lives with me

Contents

Note on Transcription and Translation

I owe a great debt to my many Fassi colleagues and friends for allowing me to record, assisting me with transcription, and clarifying my understanding of many hours of recordings and observations. I based the transliterations in this text on my understanding of Moroccan ways of speaking, using the International Journal of Middle East Studies (IJMES) transliteration key. However, the transcriptions are my Moroccan contributors' understandings of how to write Moroccan spoken and written forms, and as Chapter 4 of this book points out, orthographic heterogeneity was common in everyday Fassi practices of writing their ways of speaking. So don't be surprised if you find variability in the transcriptions—it reflects the writing practices of the Fassis I wrote about in this ethnography.

An Arab student of mine pointed out that the use of the term "Modern Standard Arabic" (MSA) vs. *alfuṣḥā* was an educational shibboleth; it demonstrated what kind of Arabic training one had. Instead of using my own terms, I opted throughout this book to use Fassi terms for the main language forms I analyzed: *l'arabīya* (Arabic) often contrasted with *français* (French), *darīja* (Moroccan Arabic) often contrasted with *fuṣḥā* (formal "literary" Arabic). But these were not fixed registers: they were classifications that did important social work, as you will soon read.

Arabic Letters	IJMES Transliteration	Phonetic Value (IPA)
ء	'	[ʔ]
ا	ā	[æ:]
ب	b	[b]
ت	t	[t]

Arabic Letters	IJMES Transliteration	Phonetic Value (IPA)
ث	th	[θ]
ج	j / g / ğ	[ʒ] / [ʤ] / [g]
ح	ḥ H	[ħ] [']
خ	kh / x	[X]
د	d	[d]
ذ	dh	[D]
ر	r	[r]
ز	z	[z]
س	s	[s]
ش	sh / š	[ʃ]
ص	ṣ	[ṣ] [s≥]
ض	ḍ	[ḍ] [d≥]
ط	ṭ	[ṭ] [t≥]
ظ	ẓ	[ð] [D≥]
ع	' ' / '	[ʕ]
غ	gh / ġ	[ɣ]
ف	f	[f]
ق	q / ḳ	[q]
ك	k	[k]
ل	l	[l]
م	m	[m]
ن	n	[n]
ه	h	[h]
و	w / u:	[w] / [u:]
ي	y / i:	[j] / [i:]

CHANNELING MOROCCANNESS

Introduction

Moroccan Channels, Channeling Moroccanness

الحلقة ١: التسبيح الالكتروني

Episode 1: Remote Control Prayerbeads

I daily found myself part of early evening assemblages in Fassi homes,[1] *gathered around a table with partially consumed flatbreads, jam, cheese, sweets, boiled eggs, half-full tea glasses, and a television. My Fassi interlocutors called this routinized event* casse-croute,[2] *or* التاي, atāy—*a time to unwind from the day's labors and reaffirm sociality bonds with family, neighbors, and friends through food and conversations about any- and everything. Though anthropologists have written how French colonial work schedules (Kapchan 1996, 154–55), café culture (Graiouid 2007), media technologies (Davis and Davis 1995), and citizen-consumer aspirations (Newcomb 2017, 116–20) have shaped Moroccan tea gatherings, some Fassi families preserved this as an important vestige of Moroccan heritage—how their mothers, grandmothers, and aunts cared for and facilitated their social networks (Fernea 1975; MacPhee 2004; Mernissi 1994; Newcomb 2009). Since my first Moroccan fieldwork ventures in the early 2000s, the profound everyday quality of this recurring sociality ritual had piqued my ethnographic interest in the connections between electronic mass mediation of Moroccanness and talk about it. I learned the way to make and pour tea so that the bubbles foamed properly in the glass; the respectful ways to reach across the table and tear off appropriate bread pieces to dip in olive oil or spread with* Le Vache Qui Rit *cheese; how many sweets or boiled egg halves to take so as to not appear greedy; what kinds of television programs backgrounded the relaxed teatime atmosphere; and the patterns of talk that could accompany these domestic interactions.*

During one particular teatime gathering I recorded and transcribed, a mother, her two teenage daughters, their male cousin, and female neighbor had been flitting across television channels and chatting for the better part of an hour. The daughters had just returned from school, the women were resting from domestic responsibilities, and the cousin was taking a break from studying for his university classes. The remote was in the hand of the fifteen-year-old daughter, who continually moved between transnational satellite stations. She had been flipping between an Egyptian music video station and a Bollywood movie channel. Her sister, mother, and older cousin each asked her to change to a different station, but she ignored their requests. No one immediately protested her disregard, conveying a sense of languid ease—being together was the purpose of watching, no matter the programming. At one point the younger sister began singing the song attached to one of the videos flashing by, and the mother clicked her tongue in exasperation. She followed this with a critique couched in a religiously significant metaphor: لا حولا ولا قوة إلا بالله (lā ḥawlā walā qūwat īlā bīllah, "*There is no power or strength except in God.*") *I often heard this phrase used in Fez and Morocco more generally to express awe, frustration, empathy, encouragement, anxiety, piety—a range of sentiments that could only be fixed in the context of the utterance. In this instance, the mother's voice quality began with a breathy intake and dropped pitch rapidly as she expelled the phrase, signaling repetitive use and a tone of resignation tinged with sarcasm. She was mildly frustrated with the lack of a specific program. The younger sister further affirmed her mother's evaluative stance toward this practice of montage viewing, extending the critique with the commonly accompanying phrase* إلا بالله العلي العظيم (īlā bīllah āl'alī āl'aḍīm, "*except in God the High and Great One*"). *She added her own subtle adjustments to meaning by furthering the downward pitch plunge and inserting a breathy mimicry. Her playful mocking of her mother's regular use of this phrase to express frustration further layered the critique to include the speaking practices of her mother and channel surfing of her sister.*

At nearly the same moment, her older male cousin jumped in with a one-word phrase telegraphing previous discussions about the media practice of flipping through stations: التسبيح *(tasbīḥ). This described a religious practice whereby one continuously and repetitively moved beads,* التسابيح (tsābīḥ), *through one's fingers and recited/remembered the names of God. Each movement of the hand was coordinated with praise pronouncements in the form of descriptors of God's qualities, reinscribing the relationship between believer and worshipped. While it was not uncommon for Moroccans, especially those seeking a more expansive religious life, to fill their spare moments with the supplicatory motions of* tasbīḥ, *it was sometimes disparagingly regarded as perfunctory rather than refining. In other words, one could go through the motions without the practice having the right kind of transformative effects. This description of channel surfing as* tasbīḥ, *the cousin later informed me, he had learned from this same aunt, so he knew at least some of those present would understand his one-word evaluation. For his aunt, the thoughtlessness of devotional bead practices was doubly damaging at this moment. She quickly added that those who turn the beads say* سبحان الله (subḥān āllah, *"glory to God"), sometimes spending the whole day in that motion without going out of the house—just like they were doing with the remote control at that moment. The neighbor agreed with a quiet "ah." The mother saw their repetitive motions of pressing the remote as an embodied, merely going-through-the-motions practice without intent. Here the mother also indexed how performing* télécomonde tasbīḥ *(prayerbead-like television remote finger motions) reproduced a relationship between believer and worshipped, between her daughter and entertainment television. This was not a passive acceptance of the practice. I understood her double-edged critique to flay both unconscious going-through-the-motions of religious practice as well as unthinking engagement of media that failed to facilitate the right kinds of sociality.*

Lamenting the Failure of Communicative Channels

As I repeatedly listened to my recording of this teatime interaction and other Fassi media engagements, I began to see this as a pattern of lamenting the failure of things designed to connect people.[3] The mother, her nephew, and neighbor created a sameness between two practices: the likeness of familiar embodied hand motions (channel surfing and prayerbead supplication) across different kinds of routinized sociality encounters (between Muslim worship of God and Moroccan domestic media viewing). In doing so, they foregrounded one aspect, repetitive hand motions, to lament problematic relations to mediums designed for connection: prayerbeads and remote control televisions.[4] This wasn't just a familial critique of communicative failure; rather, they directed their lament both to themselves in that moment and to Fassis and Moroccans more broadly.

What does it mean to relate as Moroccans when there is widespread feeling of communicative failure? This book approaches the question by exploring how laments of communicative failure tied to language and media generated unrecognized projects of relational reform in urban Fez. Over the last decade, failure laments in Fez have focused on communicative channels, such as television or Whatsapp, mediums that they expected to bring people together in appropriate ways. But these mediums also included the language forms in which the media operated, such as standard Arabic (*fuṣḥā*), Moroccan dialect Arabic (*darīja*), French, and Tamazight, as well as ways of speaking like a storytelling rhymed prose register and collective Qur'anic recitation. Both media and language shared some of the same qualities as channels: they were to connect speakers and addressees, and they only became visible when they failed to connect Moroccans in the right ways. The Fassis among whom I worked had ideas about what social relations should be, based on a nostalgic view of what had been lost, but also what ought to be and had yet to be realized. You may think the opening episode was just language play and improvisation, a moment when a Fassi family marked similarities of troublesome practices to pass the time. After a decade of doing fieldwork in Morocco, I look back at this interaction as part of a larger pattern, one in which laments about loss of, or longing for, more effective communicative channels actually generated multiple projects of making Moroccanness, a sense of how they should relate as Moroccans. They also evoked ideologies about how communicative channels should work. These channels, or mediums, that they expected to connect people could range from objects such as devotional beads and remote controls to interactional forms such as languages and dress styles, media platforms like television news or WhatsApp group chats, and institutions such as public or Qur'anic schools. Although they viewed the mediums as forms of connection, they did not see them as unencumbered channels. They focused on the problematic aspects of the ways television or prayerbeads operated as channels in order to reform relationality. I argue that communicative laments about the failure of mediums to connect people properly have become key to Moroccanness.

In this introduction, I introduce why Fassis linked language mediums and mass media channels to social relationality, national identity, interactional work, and political projects. To do so, I explain how Fassis understood ideas such as Moroccanness, media, language, sociality, and politics and how that differs or overlaps with the ways scholars of language and media have been writing about these concepts. In the process I briefly introduce the Fassi perspectives of communicative channel failures I examine in the chapters of this book: both their ideas about the already realized breakdown of Fassi sociality and the anxiety-producing specter of future consequences. These perceptions of failure seem to have motivated multiple uncoordinated practices of communicative renewal, reform, and rejection. Chapter 1 introduces the Fassi linguistic soundscape, giving a sense of the context in which laments about communicative failure arose. Chapter 2 explores competing Fassi perspectives on what it meant to engage in public life through "literate listening" to news in Morocco and introduces the practice of distributed literacy. The language of news and literacy in Morocco is standard Arabic (*fuṣḥā*), which is different from everyday forms of Arabic. Despite modernist claims that literacy is reading and writing that leads to a secularized reasoning through individually acquired set of skills, some Fassis critiqued this visual path to reasoning and pooled the oral literacy skills of multiple family members in making sense of broadcast news. In Chapter 3 I continue to analyze how Fassis understood moral literacy through an oral storytelling register of rhymed prose revamped for civic education via television. Instead of relying on *fuṣḥā*, standard Arabic, to convey moral civic values such as gender equity, Moroccan television producers valorized a *darīja* (Moroccan Arabic) way of speaking, storytelling rhymed prose, to educate viewers. I demonstrate a channel and relationality ideology that shaped why viewers embraced the rhymed prose medium, but not the gender equity message. Chapter 4 examines the moral loading of connecting through written *darīja* (Moroccan Arabic) speech in media platforms such as billboards, books, social media, and newsprint. Until 2011, standard Arabic was the official language of Morocco according to the constitution and ideologically the variety to be used in written genres.[5] In practice, Fassis wrote Arabic using a variety of linguistic forms and heard the relationality effects and politics of *darīja* writing differently depending on the media platform/channel in which they encountered it. In Chapter 5 I bring morality, literate listening, and sonic reading together to explore Fassi responses to the relationality of "Moroccan Islam," a state-sponsored effort to reshape religious discourse and practices via language and media channels in the wake of "extremism." Each of these chapters show that Fassis had different ideologies about how to relate, the role of channels in connecting Moroccans, and what practices they understood as the right kind of Moroccanness relationality.

I use the term "Moroccanness" instead of Moroccan identity to highlight the interactional process of negotiating and debating what it meant for Fassis to connect as Moroccans. Why do I analyze Moroccanness, a sense of appropriate relationality, instead of individual identity work? Because the Fassis among whom I lived viewed Moroccanness as the contested labor of defining what kinds of social connection mattered. Rather than foregrounding their individual subjectivity, sense of self, or socialization into structures of feeling, I explore the ways communicative laments focused on their concerns about *how* failures were affecting their relationality—*how* they should relate as Moroccans. Fassis have long encountered other kinds of social connection through pilgrimage, migration, trade, colonialism, and tourism and have debated what kinds of connectedness to adopt or reject to be Moroccan (see Messier and Miller 2015 for a description of thirteenth-century traveler Ibn Battuta; Zhiri 2001 and Davis 2006 on the sixteenth-century writer al-Hasan al-Wazzan; Burke 2014 on nineteenth-century French colonial ethnographic writing; Bazzaz 2010 on early twentieth-century religiopolitical conflicts emerging from Fez; and Newcomb 2009 on Fassi women). Scholars have argued that social movements seeking to define Moroccanness, or renewal campaigns, have been central to the history of Morocco (Pennell 2013). There was nothing new in this concern, even if Fassis evoked a "tradition vs. modern" dichotomy to situate it. What I explore in this book is the focus, in the last decade, on appropriate use of communicative channels to influence Moroccan relationality in media, education, and religion contexts (see also Schulthies 2014a).

Perhaps this has emerged because Morocco's past two kings have repeatedly emphasized Morocco's social relatedness to multiple worlds: Morocco is a tree with African roots, its trunk in the Arab-Muslim world and its branches in Europe. This framing of Moroccanness as tied to African peoples, the Muslim *ummah* (community), Arabness (see Schulthies 2015), and European influences was often evoked in my fieldwork, but often as a point of debate rather than a consensus (see Episode 2 of this chapter). Fassis I encountered were also anxious about the failures of appropriate social connectedness and violence tied to North African migration to Europe, Syria, and the Arab Gulf. They keenly lamented the troubling transnational outcomes of communicative channel failure, even if they didn't agree about them: terrorism, hooliganism, immorality, extremism, intolerance, endemic corruption, apathy, depression. And those laments generated political projects of Moroccanness, not just how to be a certain kind of person, but how to relate to each other within a nation-state sociality as lived in the specific urban context of Fez.

My training is in linguistic anthropology, which assumes that communication is always about something other than referring to things as they are in the world. Communication, like language, is multifunctional, doing many things at the same time: transferring information, creating a social relation, calling attention to itself, marking identities. Hence when I use the term "connection," I don't mean neat and tidy information transfer in an equal exchange sense. Instead, I explore kinds of contested socialization and intersubjectivity linked to a widespread ideology of nationwide communicative failure. Moroccanness, as I am using it, is not subjectivity as in the senses of self (perception, affect, thought, desire, fear) animating action (Ortner 2005, 31), but rather the ideologies and practices of social relatedness emerging from anxieties about the failure of communicative channels. In other words, I'm interested in how they practiced relatedness via communicative channels, or thought it should be practiced, not just what identity work was being done.

Communication, as understood by my Fassi friends, was not just social connection facilitated by linguistic and media technologies. The Fassis among whom I worked viewed communicative media and language as central elements of social relations on multiple scales: familial, interpersonal, intraurban, national, coreligionist, and transnational. Communication was tied to moral ways of knowing and being through social interaction (see Chapters 2, 3, and 5). However, they didn't agree about what moral ways of knowing, and being connected as Moroccans, meant. Fassis shared with me various perspectives: that media was a tool of consumerism, secularist politics (see Episode 2 in this chapter), Muslim extremism, or state-directed political apathy (see Episode 2 in this chapter). Each of these critiques evoked an embedded assumption that media should connect Moroccans. Even the state-run media and its quasi-privatized stations articulated an explicit connection ideology: media and modernization or development ideology, in which communicative channels should be mobilized to create modern citizens (Lerner 1958). After the 2004 media reform law, designed to shift national media from state to private control and expand independent television and radio domains, media production continued to operate with state political oversight (Zaid 2015): media should educate the public as much as entertain; media should promote state policies for the listening/viewing Moroccan public; and commercial advertising should be clearly articulated as separate from informational and entertainment programming. Whether seeking to promote consumer-citizens, civic engagement, or literacy, maintaining political power, or providing leisure, media was about moral relationality.

Many communication scholars have critiqued this ideal of media as social connection. Mattelart argued that the field of communication technology was born within European nation-state "modernizing" projects, striving to create a universal social bond, enlightened rationality, social regulation, and technosocial development in the service of capitalism (Mattelart 1996).[6] Latin American theorist Jesús Martín Barbero has argued that even the terms "media," "communication," and "information" have become objects, powerful entities with mystical powers to dupe the masses, extend state and corporate power, or liberate through active reception practices (Barbero 1987; see Zaid 2015 for an analysis of Moroccan media ideologies). In each of these scholarly frameworks, communication was a medium for connection, though not a neutral channel. The term had problematic baggage. Briggs and Hallin have labeled these ideologies about the relationship between discursive practices and social relations "communicability" and argued that we need to explore the everyday ideological explanations of how communication is produced, circulated, and received in order to understand the way power works (2007, 45). This book is one such attempt to explore everyday Fassi understandings of communication as failing to connect Moroccans appropriately and how that shaped political and social projects. As I hope to show, their notions of what that meant varied quite a bit.

The Fassi perspectives about communicative failure I describe in this book could be viewed as reproducing these state-led modernizing ideologies of communication and language as social connection and "modernization" tools or handmaids of capitalist elite control. That certainly appears in some perspectives expressed by Fassis when they criticize "the media" for failing to make good Moroccan citizens. But the kind of social connection Fassis described did not always fit the modernist models of societal progress, consumer citizens, or universal rationality described in European and American media and communication scholarship. In fact, they often sought to articulate themselves in opposition to notions of universal rationality (Schulthies 2013), or an inevitable march toward social progress (Schulthies 2014a; see also Newcomb 2017). Certainly, they had idealized models of sociality that informed their laments of communicative failure (which I describe in more detail throughout this book). Their lived understandings of mediated connection both engaged and reworked modernist ideas, through which emerged critiques such as distributed literacy (Chapter 2), wisdom of the unschooled (Chapter 3), graphic-sonic social mediascapes (Chapter 4), and Moroccan Islam as tolerant social progress (Chapter 5). They engaged and evoked multiple communicative ideologies in their efforts to shape Moroccanness. As presented in Chapters 2 and 4, there were different kinds of "listening subjects": people who set themselves up as critics of communicative channel failure in order to advance their notion of appropriate moral relationality. Moroccan listening subjects drew on aspects of European communication and media ideologies, but also incorporated other media and relationality traditions. This was not a straightforward process of identifying a communicative theory origin, but rather a selective appropriation and deployment, what I like to call a calibration, of multiple rationales in the practice of social relating in a climate of perceived communicative failure.

You might ask why I am focusing on a national relationality (Moroccanness) rather than a religious (Muslim or Jewish), ethnic (Amazigh or Arab), or situationally salient connection (such as neighborhood, hometown), especially since my research was in a specific context: Fez. All of those kinds of sociality occurred in the interactions I analyzed, but during the last decade, Fassis evoked the national scale as a ground within or against which they related other kinds of social relatedness in my study of media interactions. This was partially because most of the Fassis among whom I worked engaged national media outlets and press agencies regularly, despite widespread access to transnational media for more than three decades (see Abu-Lughod 2005 for a similar argument with regard to Egyptians), and local radio, newspaper, and internet sites since 2004. Even if they rejected the assumptions of colonial nation-state formations embedded in national media outlets (identifying themselves within the Muslim, Arab, Amazigh, and African worlds), Fassis still expressed themselves in relation to the nation-state framing of Moroccanness. We'll see this clearly in the chapters that follow, where Fassis debate what kinds of listeners can participate in civic life via news consumption; whether gender parity as a civic virtue can emerge from a rhyming register of old folks; what forms of writing Moroccan Arabic (notice the national framing) in social media and books are doing politically; and what kinds of clothing, speech, and comportment bundles should be adopted as the Moroccan model of Islamic practice.

It may seem like a contradiction that a widespread pattern of lamenting communicative channel failure led to multiple politically uncoordinated Moroccanness relationality projects—but that is the core set of practices and perspectives I explore in this ethnography. These laments didn't follow a scholarly-identified genre of "song punctuated with sobs and words . . . to evoke audience sympathy" at moments of shock and sorrow (Wilce 2007, 124). Instead, I came to recognize these longing and loss expressions as calibrations of Moroccanness.[7] They also evoked media ideologies (expectations about what media is or should do, Gershon 2010b), and communicative ideologies (modalities of connection, Keane 1995) in their laments of what was and should be.

These social acts of Moroccanness in Fez were both conscious, mundane, and routinized. In her study of the social work of talk among clients in an urban Chicago addiction recovery program, Carr noted that social workers taught participants to use specific ways of speaking to demonstrate their sobriety. Only when they used language properly did therapists view clients as honest in their recovery; the clients subsequently were granted access to critical legal services and economic aid. In the process, clients' heightened awareness of what some forms of speaking could do improved their performance skills so that they could flip the script and use it against the system (Carr 2011, 196). This meta-awareness was not about the clients' abilities to articulate or describe the social work of sobriety talk, but rather a conscious, acquired, embodied practice like manual muscle memory of riding a bicycle—the ability to adjust their talk to do things.

I viewed Fassi communicative laments as similarly conscious, mundane, embodied efforts to shape Moroccan relationality and ways of being by attending to connective mediums—modes of language use (such as listening and writing), ways of speaking associated with specific kinds of persons (registers), and ways to engage the more widely known electronic and print media channels. Rather than furthering the discourse about Morocco's conflict between liberal secularists and religious conservatives, this ethnography shows the subtle range of ideologies and practices evoked in Fassi homes to calibrate appropriate Moroccan relationality and political consciousness. In these laments of communicative failures, Fassis linked medium deficiencies (whether human or electronic) to specific kinds of connectedness and sociality. Many Moroccans lamented communicative failure as a social problem, as I will describe in episodes throughout this book, but they did not always mean the same things. The sedimentation of these similar though slightly different social acts of connection gave the appearance of a unitary phenomenon: Moroccanness. In practice, it permitted a range of connection work to be recognized as Moroccan and the furthering of conscious yet sometimes unrecognized forms of relationality projects in Fez. My interlocutors didn't call their comments about communicative failures laments in the sense of a speech genre, but rather a longing for better times, better skills, and better interactions that had been lost or somehow never developed during their lifetime.[8] Specifically, I understood these laments as pointing toward Fassi perceptions of communicative channel failures and important ways ideologies about media and language shaped Moroccan relationality projects.

In this book, I explore Moroccan engagements with media channels and phatic labor, the layering of mundane social action designed to strengthen social bonds with earnest critique, affective reasoning, and emergent, negotiated ways of knowing. In each chapter, I introduce laments about communicative channel failures that precipitated Moroccanness projects by the state and several Fassi calibrations of those Moroccanness efforts. I saw these laments as ways of speaking, listening, and being that created Moroccanness, the feeling of participating in the ongoing formations of Moroccan public relationality, even when my Fassi interlocutors differed considerably in their expressions of what connecting as Moroccans was or should have been. Nevertheless, I make the case that in the aggregate, these laments allow a range of connection forms to be recognized as Moroccan, and indeed for a quasi-unitary phenomenon of Moroccanness to cohere.

Moroccanness and Channel Failures

Moroccanness connection laments were not always a complaint, an argument, a political position, or a critique—though they could be. In the following episode, concern about the failures of a state television channel as a medium designed to connect Moroccans overlapped with ideologies about the linguistic medium through which that relationality should occur. It illustrates the focus on channels as sociality mediums foregrounded in Moroccanness expectations and practices.

الحلقة ٢: كنگولها حنا ماشي دولة عربية

Episode 2: "I'll Say It: We Are Not an Arab Country"

I awoke one morning in March 2016 to find a firestorm in the Moroccan press and social media about comments on Moroccan identity made by Samira Sitail.[9] *She was the Information Director for 2M, Morocco's quasi-public second television station located in Casablanca, and a vocal opponent of the current government, headed by a self-proclaimed pro-monarchy Muslim political party. She had been invited to appear on a video-recorded Radio Aswat live radio interview with well-known host Rachid al-Idrissi on International Women's Day. 2M, and Samira as one of the channel directors, had been attacked in previous months for programming practices, such as promoting Moroccan Arabic-dubbed foreign dramatic serials, which critics claimed were part of a campaign to distract and deaden the intellectual life of Moroccans. She had also publicly supported the Amazigh movement's demands for greater government recognition and presence of the indigenous languages and customs in parliament, public media, and law. These and other comments had drawn the attention of public intellectuals concerned about what they viewed as attacks on Morocco's Arab and Islamic identity.*

Samira was a controversial figure among some of my Fassi interlocutors, though most knew little about her professional history. They knew her as a director of 2M and a key Moroccan media producer for three decades. She was born and educated in France to Moroccan parents, returning in the late 1980s to Morocco when offered a journalism position at the Moroccan National Radio and Television Company, RTM. At the time, Morocco only had one television station. She moved to 2M when the state took over majority share in the struggling private cable venture in 1996. Throughout the 2000s, she was vocal in her opposition to what she viewed as troubling "Islamist government policies" that she saw as a threat to Moroccan media and universal human rights efforts. While serving as 2M's news director, Prime Minister Abdelilah Benkirane accused Samira of actively erasing mentions of him from broadcasts as a protest against his government's policies and political orientations.[10]

One of the popular innovations of Moroccan radio stations around 2012 was to post video recordings of radio interviews on YouTube, extending their audience access and medium durability. Invited guests and the interviewers sat with headphones and large recording microphones around a table in a radio sound booth. Video cameras from different angles captured the "unscripted" interview as it aired on the radio. Viewers could see the facial expressions, gestures, and bodily comportment of the interviewer and interviewee once links to clips of this interview were embedded in online news articles, circulated through Facebook links, and posted on Whatsapp group messaging.[11]

Samira Satail was asked to respond to critics of 2M's programming choices, especially the channel's investment in Moroccan Arabic (الدريجة [darīja]*)*[12] *dubbed Turkish, Mexican, and Indian dramatic serials. Despite constitutional assertions of formal Arabic (الفصحى* [fuṣḥā]*)*[13] *as the language of the state, television and radio broadcasts had long been a mix of* fuṣḥā *for news and* darīja *in entertainment and talk shows (Ennaji 1995; C. Miller 2012; Zaid 2013). In the 1990s, Moroccan television produced plays and serials in* darīja, *purchased Mexican television serials dubbed into* fuṣḥā *from other Arab countries, Japanese anime cartoons dubbed into* fuṣḥā, *and Bollywood movies with* fuṣḥā *subtitling, and broadcast Egyptian dramas in Egyptian Arabics.*[14] *By the mid-2000s, state channels had added Lebanese-dubbed Turkish melodramas, and by 2009, they began producing* darīja*-dubbed dramatic serials they had purchased from Brazil, Mexico, Turkey, and India. As mentioned previously, some Moroccans (called the conservative Arab nationalist or Islamist discourse pole) had published criticisms of this programming trend, while others (a progressive wing) both celebrated Moroccan Arabic dubbing as a mark of cultural diversity and bemoaned the problem of poor cultural production (C. Miller 2012, 171–72).*

During the interview, Samira stated in a mix of darīja, fuṣḥā, *and French that Morocco was not an Arab country, but Maghribi. "Maghrib" is the Arabic name for Morocco, meaning the place where the sun sets, the west, and often elaborated as the Arab West (المغرب العربي* [al-maghrib al-ʿarabī]*) or* المغاربية (al-maghāribīya), *the region including Tunis, Algeria, and Morocco. The French word for Morocco is* Maroc, *and* maghébines *has come to mean North African immigrant populations in France (Rouighi 2012, 110–12). In Samira's response to a question about 2M's promotion of Moroccan-dubbed foreign serials and the linguistic bases for national identity, she chose to foreground the Maghrib aspect of the historical name. She did so to highlight the non-Arab contributors to the country's political and social life. "We are not an Arab country. I'll say it and I'll say it, I assume we are a Maghribi country, we are a Maghribi country. Historically, we look at our origins, in terms of our Berber origins, and we see all the confluences, the influences we have received. We are a Maghribi country, and we ought to see [this diversity] as a tool of power and pride, not an object of totally useless debates" (see Appendix 1 for transcript).*

For Sitail, Moroccans should consider being Maghribi, a historically multilingual and multicultural mix, as a source of pride. She started with a firm negation of Arab nationalism, putting stress on the darīja *negation form (ماشي* [mashī]*) in the declarative statement, "We are not an Arab country." Rachid, the interviewer, interjected with an elongated* "haaa," *as though she had finally* *come to the main point. His wordless utterance was a metapragmatic sign, conveying his evaluation of her utterance, but also his stance toward what her statement was doing. He had been waiting for her to say something that would allow him to position her in the debate about Moroccan national identity. Sitail went on in* darīja, وكنگولها (.) كنگولها (kangūlhā (.) kangūlhā, *"I'll say it (.) and I'll say it,") and then switched to French:* et je l'assume nous somme un pays maghrébin (.) nous somme un pays maghrébin, *"and I assume we are a Maghribi country (.) we are a Maghribi country." Rachid co-constructed this utterance with her but in* darīja, *as she was speaking French:* حنا دولة مغاربية (ḥnā dūla maghāribīya, *"We are a country of Maghribis"). Sitail responded with reduplicated* darīja *(agreement vocables) to sediment the force of the two statements:* إييه إييه (īyeh īyeh, *"yes, yes"). Another person in the sound booth jumped in with a formal Arabic statement to clarify her claim:* تاريخا مغاربيية (tārikhīyān maghāribīya, *"historically Maghribis"*),[15] *which Sitail echoed,* تاريخا (tārikhīyān). *She then switched to French again:* en vois nos origins sur le, nos origines berbères on voit toutes les confluences les influences nous avons reçu, nous somme un pays maghrébin, et il faut que nous assume encore une fois, il faut que se soit l'objet d'une force d'une fierté et non pas l'objet des débats qui sont totalement inutiles aujourd'hui *(translated in the previous paragraph). As she spoke, Rachid responded with mmm and the French* oui, *"yes," to encourage her talk and perhaps as an agreement with the inclusionary public discussion she was advocating.*

In this interaction, Samira Sitail used declarative statements to affirm what kind of country Morocco is, was, and should be socially. For her, Morocco had always been a multilingual and multicultural mix of influences. She embodied that ideology in the mixing of languages she used (French, darīja, *and formal Arabic) as they emerged through the interaction. She did not include any Amazigh linguistic forms despite her mention of Amazigh cultural influence on Moroccans. She could have employed the widely known* تامغربيت *(tmaghribīt),*[16] *a Tamazight-encased Arabic word incorporated into* darīja *celebrating Moroccan cultural and linguistic pluralism. In addition, she didn't explicitly mention French colonial influence as a positive force, despite its obvious traces on the discussion. Even though she argued that Moroccan national identity had always been pluralist, her assertion that Moroccans should cease debating their identity and accept diversity as a strength affirmed what she disavowed—that Morocco wasn't quite as pluralist for others as it was for her.*

♣

In this highly publicized moment, Samira Sitail employed a claim of cultural and linguistic pluralism in arguing that Moroccan national connectedness was not Arab but Maghribi, its own unique brand. The way she did so implied Moroccans had once been more pluralist than they were now, and the medium of that pluralism was a fluid multilingualism of nonstandard (*darīja*), indigenous (Tamazight), colonial (French), and globally circulating standard (*fuṣḥā*) language forms. She framed her media production policies at 2M, as well as her personal interventions in public debates, as motivated by this longing for a Moroccanness that once was and should be. In her argument, 2M, as a national television channel, had expanded its programming to include more kinds of Moroccanness (*darīja*-dubbed Indian serials, *fuṣḥā* and French news and political talk shows, French-dubbed American movies, documentaries and social talk shows in *darīja*, and Tamazight-subtitled Moroccan movies) in order to reflect Moroccans' core pluralist identity. She wasn't trying to change something but to connect Moroccan viewers to their plurilingual past in order to build a more inclusive future. Her nostalgia was future-facing even as it evoked a moral critique of present Moroccan social connections via an idealized and elitest past.[17]

Wilce has argued that lament, in the sense of ritual mourning, has been a metaphor for modernity (2009, 158). In this view, modernity is not a new era, but rather a set of political projects seeking to mark something as distinct from tradition. As part of that process, talk about the present can index what had been lost to progress (traditional lament), and iconically mimic lament. Yet lament, in the sense of metadiscursive calibrations I explore here, can include a longing for what has not yet come. In this case, I saw Sitail insisting on an equivalence between a plurilingual historical Maghrib and a social pluralism she sought to promote. Even so there were Moroccan challenges to her commensurability lament. As viewed through the wide circulation of this video online and in everyday discussions, her comments incensed those concerned about neocolonial European forms of cultural and linguistic encroachment on Moroccan social relations. This was not because they didn't recognize the cultural pluralism she advocated, but because they saw her statement—largely in French and *darīja* without any use of the Tamazight languages—as a medium for a project to import and impose European values into Moroccan relationality (see Campaiola 2014). Importantly, this critique was not just from "Islamist"-inclined writers (those advocating a greater role of Islam in governance), but also those involved in liberalizing projects. In his commentary response to Samira Sitail's interview, Taoufik Bouachrine criticized her simplistic reduction of Moroccan identity to geography (Maghrib was a geographical adjective rather than an ethnic identity) and the Amazigh movement seeking to extend the role of Tamazight peoples and language in Morocco. Yet another "progressive" publication criticized Sitail's advancement of a neocolonial French ethnic terrorism-informed Islamophobia, one that sought to curtail "troubling" religious-political relationalities, indexed by *fuṣḥā* and Islam, in public life.[18] Each of these public respondents calibrated Moroccanness by responding to Sitail's characterization-turned-lament.

Other ethnographies have beautifully explored the role of nostalgia talk, celebratory or mournful, in the formation of Moroccan social life and collectivities (Boum 2013; Crawford 2014; Eickelman 1985; Glasser 2016; Hoffman 2006; Kapchan 1996; Levy 2015; MacPhee 2004; McMurray 2001; Newcomb 2009; Pandolfo 1997; Shannon 2015; Spadola 2014). I focus, in this ethnography, on the various responses and social action that emerged from a specific kind of nostalgia, an ideal of connectedness not just about past sociality, but also Fassi futures. I do so by tracking laments about medium failures: communicative channels and language codes that were supposed to connect Moroccans, both my interlocutors' embodied neighbors and imagined co-citizens. Channels I analyzed include mediums such as oral languages of civic instruction and news broadcasts, writing orthographies in online interactions, heritage speech genres employed in television dramatic serials, and multimodal bundles mediating orientations to Islam. I saw these laments as ways of speaking that created Moroccanness, the feeling of participating in the ongoing relationality of Moroccan public life, even when my Fassi interlocutors differed considerably in their expressions of how and over what Moroccans should connect.

So how did I see this working? I understood these laments about medium failure as generating Moroccanness in Fez through commensurability of indexical feeling rather than shared genre lament forms or content. Indexicality is the way in which an utterance points to something about the context or the way participants view the utterances as relating to other contexts (Silverstein 1976; Wortham and Reyes 2015, 11–12). When I asked some of my Fassi contacts about both the previous episodes, they viewed them as indexing failures in ways that Moroccans relate, either in the home or nationally. In their comments, they talked about the wider contexts that these accounts were connected to, and in doing so they confirmed the indexical feel of longing and concern with forms of interactional contact, different kinds of channels, mediums, and sign codes; what scholars have identified as expressions of phaticity (Elyachar 2010; Hymes 1962; Jakobson 1960; Kockelman 2010; Lemon 2017; Malinowski 1936 [1923]; Nozawa 2015). My analysis throughout this book will not just focus on the ways Fassis I worked among described their relationality concerns, but also how they responded to them; how their expectations about how Moroccans could or should connect shaped their responses; and the sociality forms that emerged from phatic (channel, relationality) attention.

As the previous episodes demonstrated, the stylistic forms and content of lamenting could vary. They could be about opposing projects and yet still affirm the existence of ways of being Moroccan that the speakers disavowed. I heard this longing for more effective communicative mediums expressed by self-identified Moroccan liberals, secularists, leftists, religiously minded, so-called political Islamists (those wanting to organize political life using Islamic principles), and *salafis* (those seeking to return Muslims to practices of early Islam), Islamic philosophy-inspired intellectuals, and the disillusioned among my Fassi interlocutors. What was as important, I argue, were the different kinds of participant uptake, or responses, that emerged in relation to these longing and loss utterances. In other words, I trace their often-uncoordinated efforts at connective repair or social renewal that were more about the production of moral relationality and intersubjectivity than the failure of communicative channels. Specifically, I explore some of the social actions and medium ideologies that didn't fit into binary liberal-Islamist framings in Morocco, but rather precipitated what Bayat called nonmovements, a politics of undirected yet socially organizing practice (Bayat 2010). He argued against the force of political ideology in driving change throughout the Middle East. Instead he focused on the everyday efforts of those who felt ambivalent about current political ideologies, yet nonetheless created phenomena that states eventually had to address. His view of ideology was classic political philosophy even if it had new iterative guises: neoliberal capitalism, Marxist socialism, Islamic republicanism, Islamist democracy. Rather than leaving ideology aside, I want to pay attention to more mundane yet pervasive kinds of ideologies. I see these Moroccan social nonmovements of communicative renewal as mediated through communicative ideologies about channels and codes. All Moroccans evoked semiotic ideologies, understandings of what made something language, a channel, or meaningful (Keane 2003). These ideologies could be multiple, partial, positioned, and contested depending on the context (Kroskrity 2000). Language and media ideologies were part of the ongoing formations of Moroccaness that arose in everyday responses to laments about communicative longing and loss. Whether it was the failures of Moroccan education to teach the languages employed in national civic and news media effectively; the problems of formal Arabic as the medium of Moroccan educational instruction; the revitalizing of specific Moroccan heritage speech genres in historical melodramas; the reclaiming of a proper multimodal array for socializing citizens into the Moroccan pattern of Islamic practice; or the lack of standardized ways of writing Arabic in online and social media contexts—Fassis participated in the ongoing practices of making Moroccanness, of relationality, through their responses to these laments. The nonmovements I observed were not named phenomena such as secularist or Islamist; rather, discursive fields materialized as intersubjective personas to which Fassis could calibrate themselves in specific moments: listening critic, educated and aware, morality advocate, reading public, Moroccan Muslim. Paying attention to the interactional, shifting nature of these nonmovements can help understand the unpredictable half-lives of political relationality.

Media and Relationality

Mass media in Morocco, like much of the world, was everywhere—but not because I encountered the sights and sounds of televisions perched on walls and shelves in Fassi homes and corner grocery shops, newspapers strewn across tables in Fassi cafes, books bouncing in the backpacks of students headed to school, mobile phones that had privatized Fassi neighborhood internet café access, or shepherds wandering hills with their sheep and handheld radios.[19] When I first starting coming to Fez, I thought I was there to learn about Arabic change, but found that the complex debates about language and media I encountered captured my intellectual fascination. The English word "media," with its sonic and etymological resemblance with the word "medium," can feel like a container, a transmission vehicle in which messages move untouched through the channel. In Fez, my interlocutors used the word الاعلام (*ali'a'lām*) to reference the kinds of media I just described. Arabic noun and verb forms build from triliteral or quadriliteral roots, and *al'a'lām* was tied to the root form for "knowledge" and "knowing." In a decontextualized dictionary sense, it pointed to both the sources of knowledge and the means of conveying that knowledge—its mediums. For Fassis, it also meant media producers and financial backers that used mass media as a not-so-transparent vehicle for their political projects.

I encountered media talk everywhere—even when there was no television, newspaper, book, radio, computer, or phone in sensory proximity. Talk about media channels, content, affective modes, and morals was the stuff of everyday sociability—to talk about media was to recognize and create a mutual lived experience, one saturated by mass mediations of electronic, print, vocal, and visual kinds (Gillespie 1995). While there was the perception of sharedness, Moroccan media talk was not always cordial or harmonious. It involved animated evaluative work: assessing whether one should align with or amass against the messengers, messages, and mediums—all while sipping tea, enjoying lunch, visiting neighbors, catching a ride, studying for class, making a sale, buying bread, or walking through Fez with friends. In other words, I encountered a great deal of media talk that involved communicative work: the labor of worrying about, weighing, identifying, critiquing, lauding, and lamenting the failures of connectedness and its conduits.

الحلقة ٣: نسافرو العالم بالتلفزة

Episode 3: We Travel the World through Television

Selma's ḥabib,[20] *her maternal uncle, had gathered us all on Sunday to enjoy a meal together in the village on the outskirts of Fez where he lived and operated a public communal bath house.*[21] *Sunday, persisting in as a vestige of French colonial bureaucratic structuring, was the primary day off during the Moroccan work week. Most public employees and many in the private wage-labor sector lived and worked in the populist neighborhoods of the* ville nouvelle, *"new city" French-designed urban quarters away from the centuries-old walled medina of Fez. They enjoyed only one full day off on the weekend: Sunday. I was staying with Selma's family, and so accompanied them to the family feast.*

Selma's mother was divorced and raising her three teenage children on whatever income she could gather as a housekeeper—which included taking in me, a foreign boarder. Selma was eighteen and finishing up her baccalaureate (high school) education. I had come to know Selma through a mutual friend who knew both of us were looking for a place to live. We were all living temporarily at the mercy of this mutual friend, whose father had died and left the family villa[22] *vacant while siblings disputed how to divide their inheritance. The friend offered to let us stay in the house until it could be sold. This makeshift domestic space immediately included satellite television serving as a significant contributor to family routines, discussions, and perceptions. It was on most of the time, before everyone left for school or work and as soon as anyone returned, adding to the soundscape streaming through the open windows: cars in the street, Arab music videos, kids playing soccer in the alley, Arabic-dubbed Mexican dramatic serials, neighbors chatting over afternoon tea, Moroccan talk shows, the hiss of a pressure cooker preparing a Ramadan meal on the gas stove, French-dubbed Hollywood and Arabic-dubbed Bollywood films, impassioned laments about the latest political issue, the cascading echoes of the Maghrib (sunset) call to prayer from surrounding mosques alerting us it was time to gather and break the fast—echoed a few minutes later by the call to prayer on national television.*[23]

Of course, Selma's home was not the only household in which satellite television served as a key family interaction member. On this Sunday gathering at her uncle's small apartment, most of the family lounged on salon couches circling the walls, renewing the everyday conversational ties and emotional bonds contributing to their relationships—with the television as background member. There were about twenty-five members of the extended family there gathering to celebrate the end of Ramadan, Eid al-Fitr. *Some of the younger children sat on the floor, watching the television or playing among themselves. Other family members moved back and forth between the salon, the kitchen, and the bath house next door. We were watching Moroccan state television known as* الاولى (al-ūla), *"the first" of Morocco's two television channels (2M being the other state-private venture channel). A religious cartoon in Arabic came on about the life of the prophet Joseph, and Selma's uncle commented to all present how few Moroccans actually knew anything about the prophets without television. While we waited for the chicken tagine to be served,*[24] *Selma's mother introduced my research by saying, "She's studying how Moroccans talk about media." Selma's uncle offered his observation about the role of television in their homes: "Television is how we stroll the world while sitting in our living room."*

♣

I heard this idea many times throughout my fieldwork: that television and other forms of mass media facilitated mobility and the kinds of knowing that came from contacts with other people and places for those unable (or unwilling) to learn through travel and book-study. Selma's uncle was a generous man, and I understood his comments as both social commentary and gentle attempts to instruct me as the inexperienced and ill-informed foreigner as the family gathered that day. He appreciated that television extended his knowledge of things he couldn't encounter because of his social, economic, and political obligations and constraints. At the same time, he was concerned that his extended family were lulled into letting television impart knowledge rather than making the effort to learn through study and interaction.[25] He echoed a wider critique that Moroccan national television spent far more programming hours on music, movie, and dramatic serial programming than religious programs—even though the call to prayer was broadcast five times a day on *al-ūla*. Yet television was not the only failed medium—the public educational system was regularly implicated in failing to teach Moroccans about Islam, leading to complacency and immorality or radicalization, according to several of my Fassi interlocutors. In May 2003, just a few months before my Sunday lunch with Selma's family, Morocco had experienced a major religiously motivated attack in which thirty-seven Moroccans were killed. Extremist Islam, learned through foreign media, was blamed. In particular, people claimed satellite television and small portable media (like audio cassette and VCR tapes, as well as VCD and DVD disks and more recently internet videos) had corrupted and confused Moroccans about proper Islam. One of the Moroccan state responses was to recultivate what they called the Moroccan model or pattern of Islam, نموذج المغربي (*namūdhaj almaghribī*), a historically "moderate" Islam, which they would spread via modern radio and television stations, training institutes, and global dissemination of training materials. The Moroccan pattern of Islam included a bundle of semiotic forms promoted as uniquely Moroccan:

clothing, Qur'anic recitation styles, writing scripts, textual reasoning patterns, and communicative channels for connecting to appropriate Islam. I examine Fassi responses to the state media efforts at shaping Islam in Morocco in Chapter 5. The uncle's comment about learning Islam was set within this context. What was being learned through specific kinds of interactional mediums shaped the kinds of relationality emerging from education about Islam.

Set adjacent to his lament about the forms of contemporary Islamic education, the television as mobility metaphor served both as a longing for other ways of knowing and a critique of passivity that television as a knowledge medium generated. In other words, there was an implicit media ideology embedded in the uncle's critique: electronic media opened some kinds of social relations and foreclosed others. When I first began fieldwork a decade ago, one Fassi taxi driver told me that television had replaced the tea serving tray, السنية (*ssinnîya*), as the symbol of Moroccan family gatherings. He explained that prior to the spread of television, families used to gather around the *ssinnîya* in the evenings, visiting each other, sharing tea and conversation as related in Episode 1. This was the time set apart for collaboratively discussing daily happenings and issues of familial and community interest, as well as local, national, and international events. Now, he continued, people gathered around the television and limited their conversation to commentary on programs and commercials. In this anecdote, the taxi driver framed television and tea serving trays as the same medium, something that would draw Moroccan families together. Yet he also understood this as a frame for sociality across Morocco: Morocco was connected as iterations of families gathering to discuss matters of interest in their lives. The television had replaced the tea tray medium in creating a purpose for relationality and social interaction reduced to programming comments rather than strengthening their interpersonal ties.

What mattered for the taxi driver and Selma's uncle were the kinds of relationality that emerged from those mediations. All these interactions were shaped by my presence, as the American researcher, and what they thought I knew and should know about Moroccan media and social connection. None of these Fassis knew each other and yet echoed each other's longing for other kinds of relationality. In making these iconic (sameness) links between sociality and media, they foregrounded some things: televisions replacing teatime connections; passive reception replacing embodied mentoring. In order to do so, they had to background other things: tea sociality was part of television sociality, as in Episode 1, and media reception was rarely a passive, solitary event—illustrated by Episodes 1 and 3. I find these likeness-linking and erasure processes key to the undirected, everyday phatic making of Moroccanness explored throughout this book.

The Linguistic Labor of Relationality in Fez

Phaticity, or ideologies about mediums of social connection, have relied on infrastructural conduits (channels and communicative modalities such as speech and writing), psychological attachments (relationality), and sociality conventions (see Kockelman 2010, 408). The concept has a long genealogy in anthropology but has been arguably undertheorized until recently (Nozawa 2015; Lemon 2017). Anthropologist Bronislaw Malinowski labeled the purpose of talk designed to foster social relations as phatic communion. It was his critique of referentialism, a European Enlightenment ideology in which the primary purpose of language was to refer to or reflect things as they are in the world (Malinowski 1936 [1923], 315; see also Bauman and Briggs 2003). For Malinowski, the main function of everyday talk in small-scale societies, like the Trobriand Islands where he lived for several years, was to create and maintain social relationships in a ritualized fashion (hence the communion metaphor). Since their primary purpose was connectedness, everyday talk was really the medium for building relationships. Jakobson also thought sociality was a key function of communication in all societies. Interaction did more than refer to things or convey information (referential function). It also expressed aspects of a sender's identity or affective state (emotive function); recognized and invited addressees or interlocutors (conative function); called attention to the form of the message (poetic function); reflexively evaluated the grammar and social meanings of the code itself (metalingual function); and included the maintenance of relationality through spoken, whistled, signed, drummed, sung, and written channels (phatic function). Jakobson expanded Malinowski's idea that phatic communication served a psychosocial bond. He included the signaling of interactional openings and closings, as well as the materiality of visual/aural perception and attention in his "Hello, can you hear me?" and "Are you listening?" examples (Jakobson 1960, 355). Phaticity was about channels, perception, and sociality.

Both Malinowski and Jakobson saw phatic function as routinized, repetitive, and socially significant yet unremarkable for participants. Small talk, greetings, leave-takings, chatting, rapport talk were important for relational work. For analytical purposes, the scholars separated phaticity, connection mechanisms, from referential meaning, the information bearing part of communication. Subsequent linguistic anthropologists demonstrated the ways that interactions can layer sign modes and functions (Hymes 1962, 32; Silverstein 1976, 24; Briggs 1986, 53): a bit of talk could be metalinguistic (talk about talk) and expressive (indexing something about the speaker's identity) or phatic (doing relational work) and referential (stating how media conveys messages).

Importantly, the phatic function involved work, the labor of connecting signers and interpreters (Elyachar 2010, 455). As Elyachar noted, phatic connectivity in urban and transregional Arab contexts did not rely on direct proximity or one-to-one psychological models of contact, but rather "a generalized disposition to create, maintain, and extend communicative channels" through exchange of affect, money, information, and faith (2010, 458). Like Elyachar, I trace the relationality labor of Fassi channel ideologies, but do so through their responses to laments of communicative failure that precipitated reform work.

Channels in Fez were diverse but significant infrastructures. They could be electronic media, named languages, written or spoken language modalities, ways of practicing Islam. They could also be neighbors couriering news; colleagues posting a religious video on Facebook and precipitating on- and offline comments; a friend triangulating a loan for a relative living in another country through a Moroccan friend of a friend they knew living there. People served as channel nodes who sent, received, interpreted, and reshaped messages, belief, currency, and sentiment. Throughout this book, I analytically track the moments when Fassis served as channels themselves by foregrounding or erasing classic phatic media such as language code modalities (written, spoken, aural, visual, Moroccan Arabic, formal Arabic) and ideologies about mediation devices and their failures. For example, in Fez television was cast as an interlocutor or background noise, when in practice it could be both. I tend to highlight phatic labor specialists, individuals who inserted nodes into the connectivity webs of these communities by making legible channel infrastructures and translating their meaning for others. In the following episode, I describe one such example of phatic labor.

الحلقة ٤: مداكرة على السياسة الفرنسية

Episode 4: Interpreting French Politics

Friday afternoons were quiet and slow in the Fez medina, the old walled city. The normally bustling commerce and tourist venues stood shuttered and locked so people could rest and attend the communal Friday noon prayer. Even those in the populist neighborhoods of the ville nouvelle *would gather for a longer lunch break after the Friday prayer—often over couscous. Toufiq had invited me to lunch with his family that afternoon. While changing work and school schedules did not allow the whole family to gather for lunch every day (Newcomb 2017), the television was an important contributor to the social gathering. We had all just leaned back into the couches surrounding the table, with a large half-eaten couscous platter resting in the center. The television had been on throughout lunch, but we only turned our attention to watching al-Arabiyya news after eating. Al-Arabiyya satellite station had been created by Saudi businessmen in 2003 as a counter to Qatari-managed al-Jazeera, started in 1996. Interest in both news stations waxed and waned in the Arabic-speaking world depending on events (Cherribi 2017; Darwish 2009; El-Nawawy and Iskandar 2003; Khalil and Kraidy 2009; Lynch 2006; Rinnawi 2006). Most Fassi families channel-surfed between news stations, including French and English programs, in order to triangulate perspectives. Toufiq's father, Mohammed, followed the news out of habit rather than real interest in events. Discussing current events was part of his sociality outside the house as well as within it. The current al-Arabiyya report was about the Saudi foreign minister visiting France and showed an image of the newly elected French president at that time, Nicolas Sarkozy.*

The family had worked in the Fez medina for generations. The grandfather operated several communal bakeries and supplied bread (and smuggled guns) during the French occupation. The father, Mohammed, broke into the tourist trade in the 1970s, learning conversational French, English, Spanish, Italian, and German as he bartered Moroccan handwoven carpets, antiques, and hospitality. The eldest son, Toufiq, followed his father's craft, selling carpets in the plurilingual enclaves of a medina bazaar. He had learned formal French and Arabic in school and English as a third language up through the first year of university. The bazaar where he worked contracted with tour guides to bring both large bus groups and smaller private tours to the three-hundred-year-old historic house, to see the marble and tile mosaics, water fountains, gypsum wall carvings, painted woodwork ceilings—and carpets for sale. In the small talk moments after Toufiq answered their questions about Moroccan aesthetics and customs, he plied these potential clients with questions of his own about their politics, sports, and life.

As we languidly listened to the news after lunch, Toufiq launched into a commentary about French tourist responses to their May election.[26] *He said most of them claimed it was the youth who voted the president into power. Some of these tourists didn't like their president because they feared he would change everything. As he was recounting their views Toufiq mixed French and Arabic in a common form of urban* darīja, *mostly when he was quoting the tourists or paraphrasing their positions. This led his sister Loubna to jump in, opining in French why she thought a majority supported the president. Although she had studied Spanish as a third language in high school, she worked at a service call center for a French telecommunications company that had outsourced its labor to Morocco, where they didn't have to pay as much for French-speaking employees. Her interactions with French clients were about media promotions and telephone plans, but to build rapport with her clients she tried to keep abreast of French social life via French media programming. As she spoke, Toufiq translated a few of the French political words in Arabic for his mother, whose schooling was limited to Qur'anic classes at the local mosque, and a younger sister, whose French knowledge primarily covered phrases that had entered into everyday Moroccan use or the conversational domains she was just learning at school. His father regularly interjected with jaded jabs about the corruption of elected officials. This precipitated agreement through slight nods by the mother, a resigned* darīja vocable, *ايوا*, īywā, *"well . . ." that trailed off into a sigh by Loubna, and Toufiq's counternarrative of youth civic projects inspired by Egyptian religious television figure Amr Khaled.*

♣

In this episode, Mohammed's family illustrated phatic communion, the ritual after-meal conversations of relational work. I had observed this Fassi family, as well as many others, engaging in this kind of activity over the last decade. It did not qualify, however, as gossip or small talk, but—spurred by the news broadcast—political commentary imbedded in the connectivity webs of Moroccanness. Toufiq's family called it لاحتكاك (*liḥtikāk*): associations and knowledge that came from regular contact, mingling, and friction (in the sense of heated and generative exchange). Morocco has a long history of contact with French tourists, missionaries, ethnographers, militaries, and administrators (Burke 2014), as well as French language and policies (Ennaji 2005). Traces of French influence continued in the bilingual Moroccan educational system (Boutieri 2016), French-language tourism relations described earlier, but also in the naturalized use of French language forms among seemingly illiterate and unschooled Arabic speakers. The news broadcast was in the transnational standard Arabic, *fuṣḥā*, a written and spoken language acquired primarily through formal schooling. Spanish and French were also acquired primarily in schools, though also through contact with tourists and broadcast media, as related in this account. The linguistic code they associated with everyday Fassi interactions was *darīja*, which included regional and social variants such as Toufiq's unmarked French-Fassi Arabic urban way of speaking.

On the surface this appeared as a story of linguistic mediators, in which Toufiq rendered standard Arabic news and French conversational interactions meaningful for family members who hadn't acquired those language skills (Wagner, Messick, and Spratt 1986). My Fassi interlocutors, however, viewed these interpretive events as collaborative relationality and knowledge making. For Toufiq, contact could create impassioned critique and disagreement even as it affirmed social connection. It involved friction: repeated contact, a labor of distributed literacy (see Chapter 2), and ideologies of languages as channels that connect—however imperfectly—signers and interpreters.

In anthropological theorizing, channel and code have been described using a similar analytical metaphor (or trope): language codes (the speech habits of a population however understood) and channels (socially recognized communicative mediums such as writing, speech, gestures) are bridges that facilitate or filter interpretation and circulation. They connect signers and interpreters physically and perceptually through channels, cognitively and socially through codes (Kockelman 2010, 406). The bridge trope occurs in discussions of media as language channels:

> Spoken utterances mediate relations among co-present communicators, print artifacts at greater remove in time and space, electronic technologies at varying degrees of mutual awareness, directness of contact, and possibilities of reciprocation. To speak of communicative mediation is to observe that communicative signs formulate a bridge or connection among those they link, mediating social relations through activities of uptake and response at different scales of social history. (Agha 2011, 163)

In this quote, Agha explicitly linked linguistic codes with media channels. They served as social bridges between signers and interpreters, though "receivers" shaped those collectivities by the ways they responded to the messages across contexts. Agha viewed spoken, print, and electronic media as all material channels mediating social relations: "Utterances and discourses are themselves material objects made through human activity—made, in a physical sense, out of vibrating columns of air, ink on paper, pixels in electronic media—which exercise real effects upon our senses, minds, and modes of social organization" (Agha 2007, 2–3). As recounted in Episode 4, linguistic codes (urban French-infused *darīja*, French, and standard Arabic) mediated the family's relations as channels for renewing their family closeness as well as transnational politics they connected to their own lives (telecommunications and tourist clients).[27] Importantly, I explore the social-material effects of these phatic moments, when Fassis foregrounded or erased language forms and channel affordances.

I will argue that Fassis see codes and channels as partaking of some of the same qualities. They are both tools of connectedness, both susceptible to hidden agendas (parasites), invisible when they work well and troublesome when appropriate connection fails. More importantly, when channels (whether language forms or media) become visible because of their supposed failure or backgrounded because they are working well, they change the participant structures of media engagement and thus relationality (Gershon and Manning 2014, 544–45). Situating how Fassis understood them at any moment may help understand how these language codes and media channels mediated Moroccanness. My Moroccan interlocutors slipped between lamenting codes and channels as troublesome bridges and taken-for-granted mediums for bringing them together. In other words, they regularly critiqued the idea that language and media were designed to bring people together, even as in other contexts they expected language and media channels to do so. As Eisenlohr noted, both linguistic codes and media channels move between highly visible elements of communication and disappearing in moments of mediation (2011, 267). Gershon and Manning argued that language codes and media channels were distinguished analytically when scholars moved away from co-present interaction and viewed media's materiality as different from language (2014, 539). Shaping this distinction was the ideology of spoken language as a default, immaterial medium for meaning (a widespread Enlightenment idea; see Irvine 1989) and media as the various material and technological extensions that facilitate meaning's circulation (Eisenlohr 2011, 267). Other scholars didn't make this distinction: "media" included mediums, communicative channels, technologies, platforms, genres, and products (Spitulnik 2000, 148). It was a shifter, referring to whatever the users meant. In this way, media could be both an intermediary and a mediator, a medium and an actor. Language and media forms could be the means to connect Moroccans, but also shape and even constrain what it meant to connect as Moroccans in Fez.

I adopt Kockelman's blend of Peircian semiotic theory (Peirce 1955 [1897–1910], 80) and actor-network mediation (Serres 2007 [1980], 65; Latour 2005, 39) to suggest how this might work (Kockelman 2010, 413). When Toufiq spoke French-influenced *darīja* at home, he was employing it as a channel connecting himself to his family and other *darīja* speakers. This was *darīja* as intermediary. Samira Sitail employed *darīja*-dubbed serials as part of a pluralism project to decenter formal Arabic's hold over Moroccanness. Critics viewed Samira Sitail's *darīja* television programs as serving a different kind of purpose—diverting Moroccans both through bad programming and by darijization of public life. This was *darīja* as mediator. In this way, 2M's urban French–influenced *darīja* mediated Moroccans through form and content, leaving material effects on social relations. Kockelman called this the parasitic function, when codes become troubling mediators of Moroccanness (because of associations linked to the channel), rather than an intermediary conduit connecting Moroccans. To be clear, French-influenced *darīja* mediated social relations in Toufiq's family as well, but less visibly and explicitly. The family did not see *darīja* at that moment as a problematic channel in the ways Samira Satail and her critics did in their interactions. French-influenced *darīja* was both code and channel, parasite and facilitator, medium and mediator, material and nonvisible—depending on the context. Making a channel visible as a problematic mediator of relationality was key to Fassi sociality reform projects.

I explore Fassi responses to other examples of mediation/intermediary labor of communicative reform in Chapters 3 and 4. From the late 2000s to 2016, a group of Moroccan cultural producers repurposed a rhymed prose form of *darīja* (هدرة الميزان [*hadra lmīzan*]) associated with grandmothers and street performers to convey "modern" Moroccan civic values. Most often this involved promoting equality for women. In doing so, they sought to make a linguistic form, rhymed prose, into a mediator of Moroccanness, shaping viewers' perceptions of civic engagement through a nostalgic medium primed with equality content. As I ethnographically followed the social life of this register through everyday media practices, I recognized the way phaticity shaped the actor possibilities of rhymed prose. The kinds of phatic communion described in Episodes 3 and 4 didn't always involve focused attention to programming content. I track the ways my Fassi interlocutors nostalgically appreciated the reproduction of *hadra lmīzan* on television but seemed to miss entirely the "modern" civic values content. They did so because of implicit and explicit media consumption and relationality ideologies embedded in their webs of everyday phatic connectivity.

Building from the moral relationality of the rhymed prose in heritage television programs, in Chapter 4 I analyze the ways laments about Arabic writing have shaped practices of phatic connection in Fez. I look at the ways Fassis engaged *darīja* writing as a blending of multisensory channels tied to specific media platforms: folklore books, WhatsApp, advertising billboards, and newsprint. Merging the aural/spoken soundscape (Hirschkind 2006) and the visual/graphic linguascape (Blommaert 2013), I examine the intertwining of these sensorial channels in the sounding of *darīja* script and scripting of *darīja* sounds by reading subjects (see Inoue 2006), everyday Moroccans who authorized themselves to weigh in on the politics of writing. In the face of debates about the role of language in Moroccan relationality, Fassi everyday scriptic heterogeneity pointed to a practice of ambivalence toward written *darīja* in specific media platforms, but not others. The platforms of writing mattered to the phatic work of connecting Moroccans in Fez.

This is an ethnography about the ideologies and anxieties Fassis shared with me about the mediums of that connectedness: spoken and written language forms, electronic and print media, and the personas indexed by them. More significantly, it is about how Fassis connected, identified each other, and failed to relate. It is about the mediating of overlapping and differentiated Moroccanness projects in urban Fez and describing the phatic communion rituals that furthered the political productivity of communicative failure. The constant critique of failed connectivity evidenced Fassis investment in communicative reform, both as a reviving of "lost" sociality and a recalibrating of future relationality forms. As carefully cultivated relations, the everyday work and pleasure of media talk (talk during and about media events) facilitated access to and participation in Moroccanness projects as conversations unfolded. While there were many participant frameworks, or configurations of interactional roles and statuses (Goodwin and Goodwin 2006), that I participated in throughout my fieldwork, the primary location for much of my research was Fassi homes. I conducted interviews with Moroccan media producers, public school teachers, and public intellectuals, as well as observing countless everyday interactions spanning a decade—some of which I audio-recorded and others about which I took detailed observational fieldnotes. This book includes a very small portion of all these interactions, but ones I feel give a sense of relationality labor in Fez.

Mediating Me

While my research began with an interest in the linguistic mechanisms families in urban Fez employed to make sense of media in their homes, my ideas about this project changed over the years. During twenty-eight months of fieldwork dispersed over a decade, I saw channels and codes cast as actors as much as relationality mediums in these Moroccanness projects. But I also was cast as a participant in these mundane moments of meaning-making. There was no part of Morocco where Moroccans were unaware of how my presence shaped interactions or their expressions about events. Perhaps it was my own physical and economic mobility made possible through research grants, my Arabic language skills, my American citizenship, or my embodied semiotics of foreignness that raised these issues to the fore. Regardless, I was ever available for my Moroccan interlocutors as an object of discussion, a foil for political frustrations, a catalyst for critical counter narratives, an emissary for discontent.

الحلقة ٥: مولاي التهامي

Episode 5: Writing Tuhami

My introduction to the dialogic of fieldwork came in a rather abrupt and telling encounter during pilot fieldwork. As a pre-fieldwork venture, I was afforded a scholarship to study Arabic in Morocco during the summer of 2001.[28] *This was two months before 9/11, before studying Arabic by Americans was commonplace and the U.S. security demand for "Arabic linguists" (more accurately defined as dragomen; see Colla 2015) heightened to desperate. The institute catered to both non-native students of Arabic and Arab students of English and boasted a large shaded garden with green metal tables and benches for studying outdoors in the waxing summer heat. Moroccan high school and university English students would spend hours "studying" in the garden, in the hopes of a chance meeting with foreigners trying to learn Modern Standard Arabic (MSA). Foreigners eagerly struck up friendships with Moroccans who they imagined would offer intimate views into Moroccan lives. I'm certain the administration saw this as a great opportunity for Moroccans and Americans, Germans, and British students to practice their speaking skills. More was anticipated by students, who sought deeper relationships as a means for privileged access into the world of the other, with language as vehicle and rite of passage.*

I was forcefully reminded of this about two months into my stay. At the time I was studying Fassi darīja *and trying desperately to connect the years of Modern Standard Arabic instruction in the U.S. with the embodied language styles of Moroccan youth. I forged friendships with several young Moroccan women in their third year of English at the public university, Sidi Mohamed Ben Abdellah. They helped me with* darīja, *and I explained more arcane nuances of Shakespeare and American poetry. I was trying to locate and define my dissertation research interests and was thus open to everything. I asked and received permission to record the girls' conversations as a means to enhance my language acquisition through repeated playback. I placed my bulky DAT player on the metal table, adjusted the microphone, and began recording. The microphone picked up the clank of books on the table, the scrape of clothes as bodies moved to make space for newcomers, the wind in the trees, and the ebb and flow of conversation that included hushed social commentary and greeting routines to passersby. At one point another university student came up and addressed herself to the group. I had met her previously, and the young women at the table had informed me that she was a married student in the English program. As I listened to the tape later in repeated playback, I was struck by how telling it was of our positionality. She greeted the group with a standard Fassi greeting,* السلام عليكم (ssalāmu ʿalaykum *[peace be upon you]), then asked me in English, "How are you, Becky?" I responded in* darīja, بخير لا باس (bikhīr, lā bās, *"Fine, how are you?") At this point she noticed the recorder and microphone on the table and asked in English if I was doing interviews, to which I responded, in* darīja, *that I was just recording. She seemed confused momentarily, commenting again that it seemed I was doing interviews. When I clarified in English that I was just recording conversations, she finished my sentence by saying, "In order to write another*

Tuhami." I laughed nervously and said in Arabic, لا لا لا (lā lā lā, *"no, no, no"*), *and again tried to explain my use of the recording was personal, for learning the dialect.*

My personal initiation into anthropology as a suspect discipline was highlighted that summer. When students asked me about my interest in Morocco and Arabic, I tossed off a well-rehearsed mantra about being an anthropologist interested in language and culture. Interestingly enough (and contrary to many university students in the U.S.), anthropology is known to Moroccan university students through their exposure to French colonial history in North Africa and the role of ethnology in the civilizing mission (Malika Khandagui personal communication, September 2004). English students were acquainted with ethnography as a writing genre, since they were required to read sections of Vincent Crapanzano's Tuhami: Portrait of a Moroccan *(1980) in their Cultural Studies course. Invariably, when students would find out I was an anthropologist, they would tell me how much they disliked and distrusted the one example of American ethnography about their society they had encountered. Some felt it was terrible to write a book about someone clearly marginal within society and pass it off as representative, explicitly citing the subtitle,* Portrait of a Moroccan, *as misleading. Others resented the idea that an outsider appropriated the experience and voice of a Moroccan in order to advance his own theories, misunderstandings, and projections about the Moroccan Other. In either criticism, the students rejected an anthropological representation and inherently problematized my own project by choosing to alert me of my sketchy associations. Shaykh Abdessalam Yasin, deceased leader of one of the most influential Islamic movements in Moroccan universities and a self-taught reader of English, remarked to another anthropologist after reading* Tuhami, *"How could anyone publish such a book?" (Munson 1993, 191).*

♣

Even though Crapanzano's experimental book *Tuhami* was designed to challenge ideas about objective knowledge in ethnography, Moroccan students disagreed with representing Moroccanness in this way.[29] That afternoon, as I sat trying to straddle my own positionality as a student of Fassi lives and language, an ethnographer trying to insist on my intersubjective commitments, I was reminded of how easily my actions were linked to misrepresentation based on methodological channels. The recording microphone indexed my unproven credibility and held me accountable for representations of Arabic, Morocco, Fez, and Islam in a mediatized decolonizing world. Unlike other anthropological accounts of entering the field that led literarily to enlightenment (Geertz 1973; Abu-Lughod 1997), my fieldwork experience was a steady stream of subtle and explicit challenges to my authority as a (seemingly independently wealthy) researcher and to my position as an Arabic-speaking American. These challenges were not simply of sentiments against American international actions, but part of larger processes of critique and credibility present in Morocco arising in part because of distrust of political, educational, and economic systems generally (see Chapters 2 and 3).

Thus, I offer this ethnography as a series of discursive snapshots I observed and contributed to make, in which my training and positionality contributed to a slightly different vantage on language and media in Fez Morocco. I recommend throughout this book other ethnographies, analyses, memoirs that will give a sense of other encounters (researchers, tourists, migrants, pilgrims, traders, explorers, politicians, neighbors, laborers) that shaped Moroccanness projects. This book is mine and yet not mine. The Fassi communities I affiliated with shaped (and continue to shape) my interpretations.

Media, Politics, and Publics

Numerous studies of Arab media have analyzed communicative technologies such as newspapers, cassette tapes, television channels, blogs, and Facebook to understand Arab publics, social and political subjectivities, and Muslim movements in the Arabic-speaking world (Abu-Lughod 2005; Armbrust 1996; Bishara 2013; Crawford and Hoffman 2000; Dwyer 2004; Eickelman and Anderson 2003; Hafez 2008; Hirschkind 2006; Khalil and Kraidy 2009; Kraidy 2009; Kraidy 2016; Lerner 1958; Lynch 2006; Miles 2006; Rugh 2004; Salamandra 2008; Spadola 2014). Language scholars have viewed mass media as a tool for exploring language change and perceptions about language and social classification (Al-Batal 2002; Bassiouney 2010; Caubet 2017; Hachimi 2013, 2017; Hoffman 2006; W. F. Miller 2007; C. Miller 2012, 2017). I build on these studies, describing the ways language and multimodal media ideologies influence how reception happens: the social productivity and politics of communicative failure as renewal of sociality ties, as well as the bringing to bear of linguistic anthropology theory on the analysis of media. In addition, I engage current scholarly interest in semiotic multimodality to bring together soundscape literature (Hirschkind 2006) with linguistic landscape scholarship (Blommaert 2013). Writing, reading, and listening are separated analytically in much scholarship, despite the embodied sensorium experience of everyday mediation. To this end, I explore the listening ideologies shaping television news reception in a context where formal reading literacy is assumed for understanding; the moral properties and civic effects of revitalizing an oral storytelling register for public service television; the sonic qualities and ideologies informing public writing of Moroccan Arabic "dialect" on billboards, social media, and newsprint. Last, I bring these channel and multimodality perspectives to bear on "Moroccan Islam," a state-sponsored effort to moderate religious communicative failures, model appropriate connectedness, and export that connectedness to Europe and West Africa.

Most of the Fassis among whom I worked did not engage the idea of a public sphere as understood in the scholarly literature: arenas where people of a given collectivity identify, discuss, and politically mobilize in relation to social issues. That does not mean they were unconcerned about Moroccanness as a political project, as the vignettes throughout this book demonstrate. They would talk about educated/noneducated distinctions but classified them differently (see Chapter 2) and divided political movements on moral grounds as often as policy distinctions (see Episode 2). In fact, I rarely heard notions of working or middle class used to reference themselves or others. This was not because they didn't know these ideas—they knew the terms when I asked about them—but because they had a different conceptual frame for thinking about sociopolitical formations. The classification of collectivities most often divided along the lines of those who had more resources than they needed (لا باس عليهم [*lā bās ʿalayhum*, "the ones with no worries"]), normal folks (الناس العاديين [*annās alʿadīīn*]), and those who needed help (المساكين [*lmsākīn*, "the poor"]).[30] Their alignment within these collectivity frames was situationally evoked—what I've been calling a calibration of Moroccanness, everyday phatic processes of connecting and disconnecting central to relating in Fez.

In linguistic anthropology, knowledge circulation about social issues (the core of public sphere discussions) has not been viewed as a simple matter of production, transmission, reception. Instead, analysts pay attention to how actors frame one "text," message, bit of talk, kinds of persons, as related to another; a process of entextualization (Briggs and Bauman 1992; Silverstein and Urban 1996; Agha 2007). Circulation, as an explanatory concept for how knowledge and people move, relies on processes that involve framing two or more things as the same in some way (Hankins 2012, 204). As Gal noted, "in 'circulation,' texts, messages, utterances, ideas, and practices are not physically or spatially displaced, nor do the semiotically relevant aspects of people and things 'travel.' Rather, the effect of movement is a social achievement of interaction; it arises from a perceived repetition and hence a seeming linkage (across encounters) of forms that are framed, reflexively, as being the 'same thing, again,' or as yet another instantiation of a recognized type in some cultural framework" (Gal 2018, 2). Framings of similarity, transformation, or rupture are achievements, and it takes work to produce an ideological frame as much as a thing framed (Hankins 2012, 206). I provide a look at these calibrations throughout this book. I explore in Chapter 1 some of the sign systems in Fez (phonological, morpho-syntactical, lexical, discursive, semantic, pragmatic, gestural, orthographic, sartorial) that shaped specific linguistic genres (Chapter 2: news talk), registers (Chapter 3: هدرة الميزان [*hadra lmīzan*, "rhymed prose"]), sociohistorical named languages (Chapter 4: الداريجة [*darīja*, "Moroccan Arabic"]), and Moroccan Muslims (Chapter 5: نموذج المغربي الإسلامي [*namūdhaj almaghribī alīslāmī*, "the Moroccan model of Islam"]) during the last decade.

Perhaps a metaphor may help us think about these calibrations of Moroccanness. One of the most widely known and consumed dishes of Moroccan cuisine has been the tagine. It was named after the cone-shaped clay pot in which the slow-cooked meat and vegetable stew was prepared, with long connectedness to North Africa (Newcomb 2017, 110; Mardam-Bey 2002, 199; Zaouali 2007, 47). Tagines are served regularly in Moroccan homes and are available at roadside cafes for truck drivers and travelers and on every restaurant menu offering Moroccan fare: chicken with olives and preserved lemon rinds; chunks of lamb shank bedded in layers of caramelized onions, topped with honeyed prunes and toasted seasame seeds; nuggets of fall-off-the-bone beef nestled amid an oregano-enhanced sauce of zucchini and okra. Though easily recognizable as part of a Moroccanness framing, the number and variety of tagines have also been central to marking subtle regional and social distinctions, all calibrated as Moroccan tagines: an everyday tagine might include a quarter of a chicken, melted onions, and loads of sliced carrots or the "classic" lamb with potatoes, carrots, and tomatoes served as a staple throughout the Amazigh regions of the Atlas mountains. In Marrakesh Moroccans would seek out the famous *tangia*, a primarily meat tagine with spices and aged butter (*smen*); the southwest Sous was well-known for goat tagines with dried fruits such as apricots or plums; in the north a request for tagine would involve fish, sometimes stacked on slow-cooked potatoes, carrots, and tomatoes; the region of Oujda in the east produced pears and thus was known for its tagine with meat and honeyed pears; and Fez was often linked to the chicken with preserved lemon tagine. An increasingly health-conscious segment of the population might avoid meat in tagines or cook it without salt or garlic. All these variations were prepared throughout Morocco, and despite the different ingredients, spices, and practices of making them, all were recognized as tagines. I suggest that Moroccanness was much like tagines: the laments, ideologies, and practices I explore in this book were varied and debated but were calibrated as significant in the making of Moroccan relationality. Regardless of the locale served, tagines take time to cook, often a couple of hours on very low heat—just as the kinds of equivalences and incommensurabilities I describe involved time to develop as recognizable patterns. And just as decades of preparing tagines can lead a cook to make tagines by muscle memory, so too have some of these Moroccanness calibrations operated without explicit rationales. They have become part of the lived experience of phatic connection.

This is not an ethnography of the connection ideologies of Moroccan oppositional groups, like those aligned with visibly organized protest and reform groups such as the February 20 movement (emerging from the 2011 Arab Spring protests), *hirak* (the 2016 economic development mass protest movement in the Northern Rif region), or *al-Adl wal-Ihsane* (the Justice and Benevolence Muslim opposition group started in the 1970s)—even though these are the kind of Moroccans who garnered the lion's share of investigative interest in news reports. However, it is still an account of language ideologies and practices shaping relations of citizens intensely critical of state institutions and deeply concerned about Moroccanness and morality. The majority of the Fassis I worked among did not view themselves as a counterpublic, a community (imagined and enacted) as against the state. This was because my interlocutors viewed the state as a variegated entity, including the coterie of the king, his family, and advisors; a contentious multiparty parliament; a cabinet of ministers drawn from the political parties with the largest parliamentary blocks and their coalitions with smaller parties; state media run by non-appointed directors with their own political agendas and media ideologies; entrenched shadow state power movers (الدولة العميقة [*addūla al'amīqa*]) with their own economic interests tied to foreign governments and corporations; self-interested local politicians and bureaucrats whose work was to find a way to benefit from their positions; and corrupt police and military personnel who did not enforce the law so much as selectively apply it for their gain. In other words, the state meant different things at different moments, and so their laments of state communicative failures did not always emerge as a sustained movement against the state.

Fassis I worked with were critical of aspects of government, media, education, and language, yet fiercely nationalistic and often defended the king and their country as much as they criticized him and the state. These Fassis, who did not self-identify as part of any given class formation or political movement, seemed to paradoxically hold deep distrust of the state, consistently call for reform, and yet offered widespread support for the king's constitutional referendum in 2011; they constantly critiqued the relationality failures of state media, and yet it continued as a regular presence in their everyday domestic lives. On one hand, we might view them as unreflexive subjects, failures of "modern development" projects in their unflinching support of an outdated political project (Tambar 2012); yet on the other hand they relentlessly critiqued the failures of state projects no matter the political orientation of those in power. I don't offer an objective notion of critique in this book, but rather explore shifting mobilizations of what it meant to engage in laments about the failures to connect appropriately. I hope these chapters will aid us in reimagining critique as a generative tool of both liberal and nonliberal self-identifying Moroccan Muslim collectivities (Asad 2009). My interlocuters challenged assumptions about the role of schooled literacy, presupposed affective personas, and a spoken/written language divide in creating critical, politically conscious, reasoning media subjects. In doing so, they enacted the kinds of unrecognized political projects shaping Moroccan relationality.

My research spans six years before the Arab uprisings and five years afterward. As each of these chapters illustrate, mediational laments and the practices they precipitated involved a great deal of interactional work, the work to calibrate points of similarity and difference, to align or confront, to foreground or background the kinds of work channels should do. Laments of communicative channel failure surfaced when I started asking about social life and media in Fez. This failure focused on aspects of the mediums themselves, the channels connecting interlocutors, whether electronic (such as television stations, WhatsApp, billboards, magazines) or linguistic (spoken standard Arabic, rhymed *darīja* prose, orthographic form, collective Qur'anic recitation). I hope you see how mundane and yet productive of Moroccanness relationality these laments as communicative reform were. اجي تشوف وتسمع (*'ajī tšūf watsma'*: Come, see and hear).

1

A Fassi Linguascape

In 2008, Fez celebrated its founding over 1,200 years ago by Moulay Idriss II, a descendant of the prophet Muhammed whose father, Moulay Idriss I, laid the foundations of the Moroccan state. Arabic of some kind has been a key index of Fez and Morocco since the Idrissi origin story, despite the widespread presence of Amazigh languages. Movement of populations and people, with their language varieties and identities, has been central to the history of Fez, especially its urban life. Moroccans recount and periodize their history as a series of foreign dominations: Phoenicians, Romans, Vandals, Byzantines, Arabs, French, Spanish (F. Laroui 1977). An oft-cited wave of Arab tribal groups in the eleventh century significantly impacted the rural/urban language varieties in the area (Ennaji 2005, 59). In addition, the Maghrib connected West Africa, Europe, and the Arab East through the caravan trade routes (J. Miller 2001), with Arabic as a key lingua franca of those exchanges. Each of these framings has done important work in marking the essence of Moroccanness relationality in Fez.

The city in particular has been oft-characterized as the core founding place of Islam, Arabization, intellectual life, urbanization, and trade in Morocco (Pennell 2003, 33–37). According to nationalist narratives, Fez accommodated refugees from Qairawan (Tunis) in the ninth century and Andalusians, Arabic-speaking Muslims and Jews fleeing the Spanish conquest, from the ninth through the fifteenth centuries. During the twentieth-century French colonial period, administrators attempted a divide-and-rule policy explicitly through educational, linguistic, and legal formulations. They created French schools in Amazigh communities (nominally because they didn't speak Arabic) and developed a "Berber" legal system based on "customary practice" and not connected to the Moroccan Islamic legal codes (Hoffman 2006). The divisions were not just between Amazigh and Arabs, but among Arabs themselves. The French attempted to educate a corps of elite, modern, French-speaking, civilized Arabs to administer the protectorate without reference to dangerous Pan-Arab and Pan-Islamist ideologies emerging from elites studying in the Arab East (Benmamoun 2001, 100). Fez was one of the places from which the French recruited sons of Moroccan elites to "civilize" through a simplified French-language education in an attempt to break the oppositional power of the Arabic-trained Muslim scholars coming out of the networks created by al-Qarawiyyiin University (S. Miller 2013, 122–23). Founded by a woman from Tunis in the ninth century (in the third century of the Muslim calendar), al-Qarawiyyiin had been granting scholarly degrees and training judges, teachers, and local administrators through its network of Qur'anic schools (Eickelman 1985). In addition to the Qarawiyyiin educational network, Fassi scholars such as Shaykh Muhammad al-Kattani were also involved in mobilizing broad-spectrum opposition among elites, merchants, artisans, rural tribesman, and laborers through Sufi الزاوية (*zāwīya*). These worship gathering places, both the *zāwīya* and Qarawiyyiin schools, fostered learning through devotional practices and facilitated social interactions and the discussion of political and religious reform that alternated between supporting and criticizing the sultan (Bazzaz 2010, 4, 9)—all via a mix of orally recited Qur'anic-influenced Arabic and spoken *darīja* (see Chapter 5). While admittedly only a fraction of the Moroccan population received any degree of schooled literacy training before the mid-twentieth century, many of those trained through the Qarawiyyin system became the drivers of political reform. This included Muhammad 'Allal al-Fasi, the force behind the independence political party Istiqlal, and Muhammed al-Fassi, the first minister of education in independent Morocco. Fassis claim the colonial francophone policy was successful enough that the post-independence educational policy designed by French-educated Hassan II included French and *fuṣḥā* Arabic curriculum, despite the protests of Fassi Moroccan nationalists who sought a pan-Arab identity through standard Arabic. In a widely circulated anecdote, one related to me by one of my Fassi colleagues, a member of the committee designated to draft the new curriculum expressed surprise at the changes made to the original draft by Hassan II, especially in regard to the number of Arabic courses replaced by French. When he questioned the king, the response was, "I am bilingual, and I desire all Moroccans to be bilingual like me."

Since independence, the contribution of Fez to the national imaginary continued, but its economic and intellectual life has withered in comparison to other cities, such as Casablanca, Tangier, Marrakesh, and the capital, Rabat. In the last four decades, urban flows have moved old Fassi elites out of their ancestral, "traditional" ornately tiled courtyard homes in the medina to Rabat, Casablanca, and high-rise apartments and villas of the Fez *ville nouvelle* (Hachimi 2005; Newcomb 2009). Fassis who moved out of the medina have lamented that the sounds of the street and neighbors' intimate conversations enter through apartment windows in ways unknown to the quiet interior-facing medina dwellings. They have also decried the rural Arabic and Tarifit (Amazigh language of the Rif mountains) speakers changing interactional space (Porter 2003). Fassis argued that rural folk didn't understand how to dress, move respectfully, or talk appropriately and had corrupted social relations throughout the city (see El Ouardani 2014 for a rural response to this Fassi urban critique). In addition, the soundscape included Amazigh merchants and entrepreneurs from the Rif, Atlas, and Anti-Atlas Mountains as well as Arab and African migrants fleeing conflict and economic challenges in Syria, Senegal, and Mali. Migration to Europe extended Moroccan exposure to German, Spanish, Dutch, and Belgian language varieties (McMurray 2001), as had the tourist economy. French- and English-speaking foreigners had also taken up residence in the Fez medina, not to mention the hundreds of tourists moving through the city and adding to the sonic features. The sounds of apartment construction, the call to prayer, the rumble of trucks/taxis/cars/motorbikes, pressure cookers slowly preparing dinner, children playing street soccer, men socializing in street cafes, and myriad other sounds indexing various kinds of sociality added to the rich complexity of Fassi soundscapes.

As I have written about elsewhere (Schulthies 2015), self-identifying Arabs have historically marked social distinctions through a variety of classification paradigms, or axes of differentiation, that include nation, state, regional, and social registers:

(1) Arab nation ([*al-'umma al-ʿarabīyya*]) versus some Other (Turks, Europeans, Berbers, Armenians, Persians) and that does not equate to the Muslim nation ([*al-ʿumma al-'islāmīyya*]), since it includes Christian, Jewish, and non-Sunni Muslim Arabic speakers as well (Suleiman 2003, 6–15);

(2) Supraregional forms: Maghreb as Arab West (primarily Algeria, Tunisia, and Morocco), Mashreq as Arab East (Syria, Lebanon, Jordan, Palestine), at times including or excluding Egypt, and Khalij as the Arab Gulf, which also either includes or distinguishes Iraq (Hachimi 2013, 270; Holes 2004, 47; and Theodoropoulou and Tyler 2014, 33–35);

(3) Urban-rural divides: *badawī* Arabic glossed by some as rural or tribal and subdivided into nomadic vs. village agriculturalists, and

urban *hadārī* Arabic, at times indexed as civilized, sedentary (Bassiouney 2009, 19);

(4) Postcolonial national varieties: Egyptian, Tunisian, Iraqi, Saudi, Moroccan (Bassiouney 2010; Suleiman 2011, 51–52);

(5) Intranational isoglosses within a state: Fassi (from Fez), Casawi (western Moroccan), Marrakeshi (from Marrakesh), and Shamali (northern) within Morocco (Hachimi 2012; see Haeri 1997 for the Egyptian context);

(6) Socioeconomic and educational registers such as *ʿarabīzī* (mixed Arabic and English), *ʿarnasiyya* (mixed Arabic and French), *fuṣḥā* (Modern Standard Arabic), street talk (*alfahlāwīya, sha ʿbīya, hadra dzanqa*), and polite speech (Bassiouney 2012, 129; C. Miller 2012, 180–82; Suleiman 2004, 29–34);

(7) A theoretical frame found by linguists to reproduce another axis of differentiation: the standard versus everything else. As they studied Arabic, linguists reproduced, amended, and challenged these difference classifications most often within a diglossic theoretical frame in which the transnational standard, known as MSA or *fuṣḥā*, was contrasted with all these other "local" distinctions. These axes of difference, while situationally evoked, did important relationality work.

In addition, when discussing the linguascape of Morocco, multilingualism in some form invariably appeared, as seen in the episodes in the Introduction. The degree of diversity points to the difficulty in calibrating these axes of language difference as channels shaping Moroccanness connection. Multilingualism was decried (A. Laroui 1973; Youssi 1995) and touted as a mark of modern identity (Khatibi 1990), depending on the language ideologies adopted by scholars and citizens alike. As related in Chapter 2, some Fassis viewed the national language of Morocco as French-*darīja* codeswitching, not Arabic. Many scholars extended and simplified Moroccan multilingualism into Standard Arabic, Amazigh/Berber, Moroccan Arabic, and French (Sadiqi 2003, 46; Benmamoun 2001, 97). Elsewhere Ennaji and Sadiqi claimed there were seven languages and dialects interacting in Morocco: Berber, Moroccan Arabic, Classical Arabic, Standard Arabic, French, English, and Spanish (2008, 4). Ennaji (2005), in a volume on education and language policy in Morocco, described the language situation as one of French/Arabic or Berber/Moroccan Arabic bilingualism with Arabic quadriglossia (Classical Arabic, Modern Standard Arabic, Educated Spoken Arabic, and Moroccan Arabic). He further divided Moroccan Arabic into urban and rural varieties with regional variations:

Tanjawi, Casawi, Fassi, Marrakeshi (Ennaji 2005, 59). Yossi argued for trilingualism and triglossia: Berber, Arabic, and French with Arabic broken down into Moroccan Arabic, Middle or educated Moroccan Arabic, and Literary Arabic (Youssi 1995, 34, 41). Hachimi echoed the previous language/dialect formulations and examined the outcomes of contact between women speaking two competing Moroccan urban dialects: an old historical urban prestige variety of Fes and a new Casablancan koine tied to the rapid internal migration and urbanization of the mid-twentieth century (Hachimi 2005). In particular, she explored the variability of two phonological features (the Fassi alveolar trilled /r/ as a uvular /ɹ/ and the uvular stop /q/ as /ʔ/) and the gendered identity work linked with their usage among Fassi women who had moved to Casablanca.

These broad categorizations of language varieties did not quite capture the fine-honed sensitivities Fassis had toward linguistic features and regional identity markings I observed in my own fieldwork. They not only recognized, but regularly deployed regional and social features to play with or mock each other through these recognizable social personas indexed through linguistic features. One extended family with whom I studied and worked in Fez hailed from the Arabic-speaking northern Rif Mountains and were known as *jbala*, mountain folk. The grandfather migrated from the village to Fez in the 1920s and founded a network of communal ovens in the old medina and provided grain from his village during World War II. He married a Fassi woman and had two sons, one of whom grew up speaking old urban bourgeois Fassi and the other a new Fassi koine (Caubet 1993). Both differed in phonological, morphological, and lexical ways from Jebli (mountain *jbala*) speak. Jebli shared the uvular stop /ʔ/ for /q/ as the old Fassi urban dialect (which the new Fassi koine realized as /q/), but old urban Fassis were known to pronounce the vowels accompanying the /ʔ/ as diphthongs /aj/ or /aw/. In addition, the habitual aspect marker in Jebli third person was /m-/ instead of the urban /k-/ or /t-/ (shared by both Fassi urban varieties). The voiced palatal affricate /ʒ/ was pronounced /z/ in old Fassi and /ʒ/ in Jebli and new Fassi. Jebli and the new Fassi koine both used the alveolar trilled /r/ rather than the old Fassi uvular /ɹ/. There were a number of lexical variants among all three as well (see Hachimi 2005 and Caubet 1993).

Each language variety had identity characterizations or personas associated with it. Old Fassi historically was tied to urban, well-connected, bourgeois elites, civilized, proud, and polite, though it had recently been considered feminine because of its preservation among older women (Hachimi 2005, 41). The new Fassi koine was described to me as a modern urban leveling variety, adopted by a new generation of rural migrants interested in disassociating themselves from the stigma of their origins and indexical of a modern neo-urbanity untied to the Fassi old guard elites. Jebli was an *'araba*, "country/ rural" dialect, and linked to illiterate, uncultured, proud mountain-folk. As mentioned, after independence, Fassi elites moved out of the medina and into the *ville nouvelle* or to the coastal political and economic centers promoted by the French (Rabat and Casablanca). Arab Jbala, Berbers from the Rif Mountains, and other migrants from the south and east moved into the homes of the Fassi emigrants and altered the linguistic make-up of the medina.

The family mentioned previously were part of this changing soundscape. They had equal access to all three language varieties (Jebli, Old Fassi, and Fassi koine), and the question arose as to why one son affiliated with the speech of his mother (Old Fassi) and the other opted for a variety not spoken by either parent (Fassi koine). The two brothers themselves politely teased each other, attributing the differences to the *baraka* "blessing" of Moulay Idriss, the founder of Fez. Some family members claimed the old Fassi-speaking son sought to claim an educated bourgeois identity in his social climb out of Jebli origins. By speaking the "feminized" old Fassi, he distanced himself from a rural identity and linked his social connections to old Fassi elites. The other son spoke the new Fassi koine, attaching himself to an urban modernity. Both sons married rural women whose language varieties shifted to the new Fassi koine over time, though they would shift back to their rural forms when interacting with relatives from the countryside. All the children of both families, with the exception of one daughter (of the old Fassi-speaking father), had adopted the new Fassi koine, intertwined with French. In interviews with family members, they were all cognizant of the differences, even teasing each other about their linguistic identities and appropriating Jebli and old Fassi to embody the well-known socially evaluated identity distinctions. To speak, listen, and write in Fez was to calibrate values associated with persona stereotypes of Moroccan relationality, many of which were linked in some way to a form of Arabic. But Arabic was a shifter: it meant different things to different people at different times, as you will read in the coming chapters (see also Schulthies 2015).

2 Literate Listening

Broadcast News and Ideologies of Reasoning

The news might still happen without speech, but it would be difficult to call it news if it were never reported, and this happens only through language and other symbolic media.

(HANKS 1996, 2)

The choice of language restricts access to public television for a large portion of society. For illiterate people, for whom TV remains the main source of information and entertainment, TV programming is not fully accessible.

(OPEN SOCIETY REPORT MAPPING DIGITAL MEDIA IN MOROCCO ZAID AND IBRAHINE 2011, 51)

English Translation	Transliteration	Arabic
What is the illiteracy rate in Morocco??? If I don't include the aware?	*kam nisba al'umīya bilmaghrib??? in lam aqul alwa'ī?*	كم نسبة الأمية بالمغرب؟؟؟ إن لم أقل الوعي؟
Huuuuuge . . . and statistics are imprecise.	*bzaaaaaf . . . wal'iḥṣāī'āt ghīr dqīqa.*	بز فاااااااا. . اولإحصائيات غير دقيقة

Facebook chat comment 2016

One of my Fassi interlocutors shared a screen shot of this Facebook comment from a chat he was having with an online contact—someone who had friended him but who he did not know personally. كم نسبة الأمية بالمغرب؟؟؟ إن لم أقل الواعي (*kam nisba al'umīa bilmaghrib??? in lam aqul alwā'ī*, "What is the illiteracy rate in Morocco??? If I don't include the aware.") Emerging in a discussion about Morocco's educational woes and written in *fuṣḥā* ("literary Arabic"), it reflected a literacy ideology I encountered regularly in Fez: contemporary discussions did not include all salient ways of knowing or being literate. I found this idea recurring in my Fassi encounters and tied to the concept of لقاري (*lqāri*, "one who reads"). So I began to ask, what did it mean to be literate, لقاري (*lqāri*, "one who reads"), and how did that differ from being aware, لواعي (*lwā'i*, "one who is knowledgeable or aware")? Based on my own interests in language and television watching, I also began to ask who felt strongly about making a distinction between kinds of literate listening. Who authorized themselves as listening subjects (Inoue 2006) able to judge others' listening abilities as inferior, and how did that shape Moroccanness projects?

When I asked my Fassi interlocutors to gloss *lqāri*, most everyone used it to define people who learned to read in school, which was predominantly public school (until the push for expanding private schools in 2012) in which the language of instruction was *fuṣḥā*. I became more intrigued when I heard Mohammed's family members use the phrase قاري وماشي واعي (*qārī wamāšī wā'ī*, "literate but not aware") as a moral critique of educated individuals whom the Moroccan education system had failed to socialize into good thinkers. On the other hand, I regularly heard and read Moroccan scholars and media professionals who argued that illiteracy, in the sense of *fuṣḥā* and French listening comprehension, was the greatest impediment to Moroccan media reception. "The choice of language restricts access to public television for a large portion of society. For illiterate people, for whom TV remains the main source of information and entertainment, TV programming is not fully accessible" (Zaid and Ibrahine 2011, 51). In other words, most Moroccans were failing to relate as citizens because they did not command the proper channel: spoken *fuṣḥā*.

What did these Moroccans intend in their framings of (il)literacy, comprehension, and Moroccanness? As one Moroccan language scholar stated, literacy was the acquisition of reading, writing, mathematics, and basic skills (Ennaji 2005, 212).[1] What was (il)literate watching and listening, then? How did one learn literate listening in Morocco? And what kinds of listening did one have to learn in order to be "aware"? This question became increasingly salient as I spent years watching television, reading newspapers, and listening to the radio with Moroccans. I had to ask how language ideologies and literacy practices might have shaped one of the most significant public media genres in Morocco: news.

In this chapter I explore how laments about listening failures by listening subjects (those who authorized themselves to evaluate these failures) allowed Fassis to create competing yet recognizable Moroccan linguistic practices for public participation. From independence in the 1960s to the 2010s, news was broadcast primarily through languages acquired in formal schooling (*fuṣḥā* or French),[2] which many Moroccans, scholars and nonscholars alike, argued were not the spoken languages of Moroccans' everyday lives. Scholars claimed that one had to attend school to acquire the ability to understand the languages of news in analog, print, or digital broadcast forms. Why might this be so? Most of my interlocutors spoke a form of *darījā* at home, sometimes the French-influenced form described previously, but always some form of "Moroccan" Arabic.[3] Folk and academic theories separated Arabic in two: spoken "dialects" and "the standard" used for literate written and official discourse, a language ideology known as diglossia (Ferguson 1959; Brustad 2017). Many Moroccans viewed diglossic linguistic differences as sufficiently separate to seriously affect literacy acquisition. The idea followed a line of thought something like this: no one spoke *fuṣḥā* as a mother tongue, and the linguistic difference between *fuṣḥā* and the Arabic or Tamazight spoken at home, along with language ideologies about *fuṣḥā* pedagogical rigidness and textual stiltedness, impeded student competence and educational success (Wagner 1993; Ennaji 2005; Haeri 2009; Boutieri 2012). Listening subjects who recounted that idea to me mobilized statistics stating that almost half of adult Moroccans were illiterate. They joined the vast majority of Moroccans across all spectrums who regularly decried the failures of the educational system and the state's obligations to its citizenry (Boutieri 2016).[4]

Despite this unity of opinion that Moroccan education needed reforming, I began to identify two patterns, or camps, of listening subjects in Fez that differed in their explanations of (il)literacy's media implications. Some challenged scholarly ideas of what it meant to be literate and by extension a skilled reasoner. They evoked an explicit literate listening ideology: awareness (الوعي [*lwā'ī*]), glossed as keen reasoning skills, came from verbal interaction with a wide range of interlocutors, not just the educated elements of society. Those who questioned the ability of illiterates to understand television programming employed an implicit literate listening ideology: literacy in Morocco was also learning to speak and hear *fuṣḥā* and French correctly. As I aim to demonstrate, a similar literate listening ideology buttressed both arguments about what it meant to reason effectively when evaluating the news and thus to participate in public life (see Errington 2001 and Nevins 2004 for listening ideologies and public participation in other contexts). However, the last argument assumed that literacy was an individual set of interpretive skills, while the former posited literate reasoning as distributed across multiple individuals. Effective listening, whether acquired through schooling or in social interaction, was necessary for Moroccan citizenship, yet each party argued that the other did not know how to reason through listening well. They both lamented that lack of *lwāʿī*, or reasoning awareness, to be a key cause of Moroccan public apathy and sociopolitical stagnation. In other words, failure to listen as "aware" citizens was a failure to relate appropriately with each other. In what follows, I explore the conditions that allowed both these laments to generate vigorous Fassi relationality work surrounding television viewing.

Media Channel Ideologies: Seeing, Hearing, Believing

الحلقة ١: صوت وصورة

Episode 1: Sound and Image

Khadra sat opposite me in the living room of the family's villa, a soccer game playing on the television in the background. Normally she worked six days a week, with Sunday as her weekend, but this Tuesday she could meet with me because they had given her a holiday to celebrate Eid, the Muslim feast of sacrifice. Khadra, aged twenty-eight, lived with her parents, an unmarried aunt, older brother, two younger siblings, and a television they described as being on all day. After attending public university for two years, she opted for a certificate in computing (taught in French) from a private vocational progam, which landed her an administrative secretary position at a local garment factory in an industrial neighborhood of Fez. Her father was a retired state functionary who spent his days reading French-language newspapers listening to Medi1, a private Moroccan news and documentary channel that broadcast in French and Arabic.[5] *Her mother had attended about two years of primary school, but her aunt finished middle school during the period when one could receive certifications in French typing and sewing as part of the curriculum. Khadra's older brother was a chef. After training in Mohammedia, a city on the Atlantic coast, he had worked at hotels for a while but was currently unemployed. She had a sister living in France who had married her French supervisor after working in the garment factory as a clothing designer. Her younger sister was finishing up a certificate in computing and working as an intern tracking demands and outflows of goods at the same factory.*

After eating a prune and lamb tagine for lunch, Khadra and her friend Ayah taught me how to prepare گديد (gdīd): *dried, spiced, preserved meat from the ritually slaughtered ram. We finished putting the marinated strips of lamb out to dry in the bright sun, took pictures of our labor, and returned to the house to enjoy glasses of fresh-squeezed orange juice and Eid cookies. Khadra's brother Hicham relaxed on the couch next to her, enjoying the soccer match and only occasionally weighing into our discussion. Her parents and aunt had retired for a nap in the other room. While we sat, I followed up on questions I had asked about their media practices during a previous interview. While the family had satellite television, they explicitly chose Moroccan stations such as Rabat and 2M because they didn't feel the need to monitor the programming for inappropriate content. That didn't mean they enjoyed the content all the time. Khadra and Ayah both lamented Moroccan television films and dramatic serials:* كل هاد الفلم غير لموت والدباز (kul hād lfilm ghīr mūt wadbāz, *"All those films are just death and quarrels"*). *Khadra and Ayah preferred to watch social and educational programming with their families, but also followed American and French thriller series when they had time. All mentioned news as part of being educated citizens.*

"You must be wary of the news—you have to link events with pictures and make your own judgments based on what is reasonable." Khadra had clearly thought about the truth-value of television messages before this moment and had connected her ideas about meaning to a specific programming genre (television news) and a multi-sensorial epistemology: in order to reason truth, one needed to correlate aural and visual ways of knowing. I had heard this media ideology from other Fassis. She further explained, "When you hear about a car or bus accident, and you see the vehicle in the bottom of a ravine or river, all smashed and curled, and then you hear that only one person died, you know that the pictures show it's impossible. It's important to observe and link what you know to what you see in order to judge what you hear. The news tells you what they want you to see. You must use your own reasoning powers to understand what is true and what is lied about." Ayah, a university graduate in English who also worked at the garment factory, jumped in at this point and confirmed that the pan-Arab news channels lie. Her older brother Mohammed, also a university graduate, told her long ago that she should not trust news without pictures, because there was nothing to confirm what was being said. All felt that you couldn't rely on one sensory or media channel for the truth but needed to compare across modalities and stations.

A few weeks later I sat in another home watching an Egyptian dramatic serial on "Rabat," another Fassi name for "al-ūla," the *national television station. I came with Bouchra, who had introduced me to Sakina, the mother of the family living in this small one-bedroom apartment on the third floor of a building in a Fassi neighborhood known for thug violence and poverty. Sakina's husband worked as an electrician, but he drank and could be mean when he did, so she always had us come when her husband wasn't around. She also struggled to make ends meet and protect her primary school-aged kids from the challenges of their circumstances. Despite these burdens, Sakina's keen tongue and ready laughter always encouraged me to visit. I often found myself on the public bus en route to her house, trudging up the steep hill carrying a bag of oranges or sweets for the kids. That afternoon Bouchra, Sakina, her sister-in-law, and I had lunched on a chicken and carrot tagine, the salon faintly warmed by the heat from cooking the tagine in the adjacent kitchen. Not long afterward, the kids came home from school, and Bouchra helped them finish their homework before the Egyptian serial started. The women and kids had all been following this series and were eager to know what was going to happen next. Like most Fassi families, we draped blankets over our legs in the colder months while sitting on the wall-lined couches facing the television in the salon, which doubled as the children's bedroom and measured four by five meters square.*

When the Egyptian program ended, we visited, recounting the woes of characters in the serial and offering our projections on what would happen in the next episode. Commercials played on the screen as we waited for the Arabic version of the national evening news to begin. Sakina, who had not completed high school, told a story about a recently deceased elderly woman she and her sister-in-law had known who once told them that if they wanted their boys to grow up fast, they should send them to Egypt. Children were born and grew up in the space of a few weeks on Egyptian serials. We all laughed at her media critique of fictionally compressed time just as we heard the musical refrain of the news broadcast. My friend Bouchra had led a peripatetic life and gathered her education in partials: some Arabic public schooling, French from her wanderer father, English from hanging out with missionaries, self-education through listening to radio programs, reading every book she could get her hands on and engaging in online instant messaging friendships with people around the globe. She remarked how much she preferred listening to news rather than watching it on television. "The radio is better because when I watch news the images make me sad, and TV should only be for making one happy." That is why she loved to watch films that made her laugh. Sakina quickly added that one had to be careful about American movies, though, because they often included immoral language, and she preferred to watch something she didn't have to worry about, mostly Moroccan social programming, documentaries, Arabic-dubbed Mexican telenovelas, and Egyptian serials.

A few weeks later I climbed the stairs of a crisp new apartment complex in the center of the ville nouvelle *to meet with Moussa's family. We sat in the family's sejour, the less-formal sitting space with French sofas and a big screen television separated by a low-lying half wall from the formal salon, its brocaded Moroccan banquettes, ornately carved serving tables, and lush salmon and beige-colored Moroccan carpet clearly reserved for special occasions. We sipped fresh-squeezed orange juice and snacked on salted cashews the live-in household servant had brought while we waited for his father to come home.*

*Moussa was a quiet young man, but with clear opinions about language and media. As we sat, he gently but firmly stated there was no future in Arabic. Even waiters these days needed to know English or French to work, and the national language was no longer Arabic but code-switching French-*darīja *bilingualism. In all these examples, he inferred speaking and listening as the primary modalities of interaction. He didn't like the news, and certainly not in Arabic. He was more comfortable with French news, as both his parents were French professors at the university—but he preferred cartoons, comedy shows, and football (soccer) matches. He didn't like to watch television news because it was always about terrible, depressing events. People watched the news as a kind of voyeurism, to look smart, to look interesting because they had something to say, not because of any genuine interest in events. Ramadan television was the best time of the year for Moroccan stations because of the comedy programs they produced, and cartoons the only thing worth watching the rest of the year. Moroccan films were the worst, with the same sad scenarios and ambiguous endings.*

At that point, his father arrived. After greetings in darīja *and a bit of English, his father called the maid to bring mint tea. Moussa explained my research interests, and his father lamented the sad state of both language and media. He himself didn't have time to watch much television, though he was always on his computer and preferred to access his news online, in written and video clip formats. Moroccan television, whether Rabat, 2M, or any of the other stations, didn't actually cover what was happening in Morocco; it was all* makhzen *television, controlled by the state. He searched Belgian, Spanish, and French online reports to know what was going on and preferred the wider range of perspectives. Rabat news was all protocol, detailing the movements of the king and praising government initiatives. If you watched 2M you would think you were living in Palestine, Syria, or Iraq, as they only report on conflict. The news was a distraction from the real problems of the country, and the youth were the victims. Not only did the educational system fail to teach them the languages of the future, the state continued to broadcast news in* fuṣḥā, *a form of speaking no one used natively; not only was the content a diversion from real issues, no one learned Arabic anymore unless they planned to do research, diplomacy, or espionage. I wondered if that last comment was meant for me. In using* darīja *to ask my questions, had I indexed questionable intent or a problematic political alignment? My Americanness and choice of language often raised the specter of suspicion. But the laments about channel failures, whether 2M or Arabic, allowed Moussa and his father to distance themselves from those troublesome mediums. They were tracking the future by triangulating channels and mixing mediums.*

These Fassis displayed a range of media ideologies, or beliefs about the communicative possibilities of channels, which engaged multiple language ideologies. It may appear at first glance that Sakina and Ayah reflected an ocular or visual centric epistemology summed up in the adage "seeing is believing." However, on closer inspection, their media ideology included several sensory channels necessary to interpret the authoritative claims of newsworthy media events. In an explicit critique of media and modernization ideas, they couldn't just accept news accounts. One needed to weigh visual messages and aural content with their own experiences to know if what they heard was plausible or distorted. Appropriate listening was work, the labor of linking sound and images to one's own experience. Khadra and Ayah linked these sensory epistemologies to a particular programming genre, news, suggesting that other types of programming might require a different sensory calculus. Moussa and his father felt that watching the news was ineffective because of the nonmodern linguistic medium for Moroccan stations, *fuṣḥā*. But they also felt the language was instrumentalist, trying to shape kinds of Moroccans they didn't identify with (Arabs oriented toward the Middle East) or believed should be (those focused on a broken past instead of an economic future), by giving them the opportunity to consume news.

Bouchra claimed that television news images were sensory overload and that she preferred aural access to news reports. She and her wandering father were currently living in a small farming village outside of Fez, though she spent several days a week on the couches of friends in the city while she studied English. We would ride a bus for twenty minutes and then walk along a dirt road and farm fence line for another twenty minutes to get to their small two-room cinderblock dwelling. When I stayed with her, we had to take the mule to the communal well to pack ten-liter plastic jugs of water back to the house every day. Yet the tiny courtyard was never silent. A radio kept Bouchra and her father company all day long, and the news was a staple of radio broadcasts. Perhaps that was why she preferred listening rather than watching the news—it was how she was socialized. She had also lived through some very traumatic experiences in her childhood, and novels and movies were a reprieve from her sadnesses. The visuals of television news reinforced for her the injustices she and many others faced. She loved watching American movies to escape the hard realities of life, and we regularly enjoyed pirated DVD versions of the latest film in homes like Sakina's.

While Bouchra preferred visual mediums for entertainment programming, Sakina warned of moral dangers in specific foreign language genres. At that time American movies broadcast on the national stations were dubbed into standard French, usually a more family-friendly "polite" form of French, regardless of the film rating or genre. Moroccans could access American movies in English with *fuṣḥā* subtitles both slightly edited in pan-Arab satellite stations and unfiltered via European channels. With the easy access of satellite television and pirated films, families couldn't guarantee they wouldn't hear something inappropriate, not just in terms of expletives but also with troublesome topics or gender interactions. Perhaps she stated her concerns explicitly because her children were present and she saw it as moment to socialize them into moral media practices. I suspect she also wanted me to know that moral listening was as significant as the cognitive pleasure of watching movies together.

Only Moussa's father mentioned named languages (*fuṣḥā, darījā,* French, English) as a specific impediment to understanding. Others focused on a sensory aspect of channel modality or medium. Each of these accounts included diverse medium ideologies and literacy paths. Despite their differences, they all mentioned listening logics as key to interpretive practices.

Moroccan Literacies and Critical Reasoning

What does it mean to be logical and critical when interpreting the news? Why argue that an individual has to acquire reading and writing in a standard language to reason appropriately? Why focus on writing as the primary medium of abstraction and reasoning rather than speaking genres (Cody 2013, 15; Bate 2009)? Why might critical reasoning necessarily be separate from social functions of reading (Warner 2004)? Why does literacy have to be an individually held set of skills, when they are acquired through socially distributed interactions?

European, American, and Moroccan scholars have long heralded literacy—learning to read and write—as a key linguistic technology for economic advancement, gender parity, and democratic participation (Lerner 1958; A. Laroui 1973; Grandguillaume 1983; Goody 1977; Ong 1982; Ennaji 2005; Ennaji and Sadiqi 2008). In other words, reading/writing literacy was central to national publics and "modern" sensibilities. A key assumption embedded in these development discourses presupposed that citizens needed to read written language for critical thinking (Walters 1990; Warner 2004). In order to use language logically, individuals had to advance from the emotive, rhetorical, and social functions of spoken language to the logical abstractions of written expression. Within this notion was a European Enlightenment-inspired referentialist language ideology—that literacy was primarily about learning to objectify the world through writing and reading: written words became things. Writing created cognitive patterns of abstract reasoning that liberated individuals from the rigid hierarchies of traditional speech. It did so by spatio-temporally distancing them through a visual representational form. This distancing allowed readers to more readily recognize explanations as one representation among many rather than a single received truth from a physically present authoritative patron. Once writing distanced them from social hierarchies of oral interactions, educated individuals were politically, economically, and socially empowered (Cody 2013, 5–14). When one learned to write, that individual acquired the cognitive and civically acceptable tools of full citizenship, unencumbered by nonmodern ways of relating, thinking, and being.[6] This is a simplification of more detailed scholarly analyses, but these are some of the language ideologies tied to literacy. As you might imagine, there have been repeated challenges to these claims (Adely 2009; Cody 2013; Ingold 2007; Walters 1990).

Foucault (1975) pointed out that senses of self in European textual-institutional contexts (schooled literacy) were different than domestic, religious, and workplace contexts because they were tied to state citizen-making projects. He argued that literacy existed before state mandated schooling, but was functional and heterogeneous, a danger to the desire of centralized states for classification, control, and mentoring of its subjects. However, state desires to mold citizens were imperfect because people continued to include non-school literacies in making sense of the world.[7]

Cody summarized some of these contradictions at work in his ethnography of literacy activists in Tamil Nadu India (2013, 14). For political activists, literacy was supposed to be the key to individual empowerment and enlightened citizenship. The activists downplayed the idea that literacy also was accompanied by increasing government control, bureaucratic rationality, and state power. Those who did not read and write did not have social citizenship because they could not participate in the rights and practices of legal citizenship. Yet even when they did acquire the writing skills, villagers in Tamil Nadu did not find that their signatures opened political doors for them. Instead, their momentous achievement, a signed petition for a village graveyard, was shuffled and filed away by technocratic laborers. Even in formal school contexts, such as the secondary school classrooms studied by Adely in Jordan, learning to read and write did not lead to so-called universal ideas of gender economic parity (2009). In the Spanish primary school classrooms studied by Garcia-Sanchez (2014), learning to read and write did not emancipate immigrant Moroccan children from experiencing learning discrimination and translational labor.

Given this fraught relationship between empowerment and literacy acquisition in other contexts, how might we rethink Moroccan scholarly arguments about formal literacy's centrality to the cognitive work of media understanding and national participation? Moha Ennaji, a linguistics professor in Fez, contributed immensely to the English language literature on the political economy of language and education in Morocco. He stated the following in an article analyzing language ideologies in Moroccan media discourse:

> Language can function either as an aid or a barrier to involvement in the national system; that means language can have a unifying or disrupting role, with ramifications for language policy. . . . The use of Modern Standard Arabic as the official language in the media consolidates the domination of the official ideology and widens the gap between this official language and the languages of the masses, i.e., Moroccan Arabic and Berber. (Ennaji 1999, 150–58)

As I read this passage, I noted several implications of Ennaji's argument. He asserted that national unity rested on the languages of the masses, in this case Moroccan Arabic and Amazigh languages. Another was that most Moroccans lacked standard Arabic (*fuṣḥā*) abilities and thus could not participate in national life. An attendant assumption was that Moroccans engaged national media as solitary individuals, even though they were part of public "masses." We don't get a sense of whether the linguistic abilities were reading, writing, speaking, or listening from this quote, but the article specified that the corpus analyzed was television news broadcasts. While not explicitly articulated, he implied that state literacy projects were as much about teaching Arabic listening as reading, writing, and speaking. For Ennaji, the consistent use of *fuṣḥā* in news media privileged it above other languages and excluded most Moroccans who did not command *fuṣḥā*. "It is found that the language of radio and television news is in correlation with language planning and ideology in Morocco. News broadcasts are among the most important means of enhancing the Arabisation policy adopted since the 1960s. Given the formal nature of news discourse, the prestigious place of Modern Standard Arabic is consolidated" (Ennaji 1999, 153). I laud Ennaji's call for linguistic expansion of media programming as a fight against linguistic hierarchies, and fortunately there have been changes that reflect this perspective. National news as of 2018 was broadcast in Tamazight, Tarafit, Tashelhit, French, Spanish, and *fuṣḥā*. The conclusion of his analysis, though, was that the poor or nonexistent *fuṣḥā* listening-reasoning abilities of solitary-media-consuming Moroccans precluded their public participation in national life. While seeking to undermine troublesome hierarchies of Moroccanness based on linguistic variety, Ennaji reinscribed the individualist and modernist ideas about language, public participation, and reasoning (see also F. Laroui 2011). Doing so facilitated movements to introduce more *darīja* television programming (as described in the introduction), promote *darīja* as the language of instruction for schools (Schulthies 2014a), and advocate for *darīja* as the language of public dialogue (as evidenced by the proliferation of mixed *fuṣḥā* and *darīja* internet news websites since 2010).

In order to understand the dynamic linking of language ideologies to media ideologies in analyses like Ennaji's, I think it is important to discuss literacy debates among Moroccan listening subjects—those who authorize themselves to classify Moroccan ways of listening in order to advance their notion of appropriate relationality. Moroccans of all stripes recount the state's poor record, especially in comparison to other Arabic-speaking countries. "Six out of every one hundred Moroccan public school students graduate from university." This oft-quoted statistic was used in the last decade as political leverage by pundits, civil society activists, politicians, and media professionals to berate the abysmal state of the Moroccan educational system and to argue various platforms for reform. In these debates, literacy statistics served as entextualizations—framing devices that foregrounded specific understandings and erased others. Official Moroccan statistics collected in 2014 claimed 45 percent of the populations over age 25 had no education. Only 21 percent of that same age group made it through primary school, 12 percent through middle school, 10 percent through high school, and 8 percent to university (Haut-commissariat au Plan 2018, 38). That meant the state viewed half of the adult population as undereducated if not illiterate. In terms of families, that averaged at least one adult family member as illiterate in the state's eyes. Of those adults who did make it through some schooling, 99 percent read and wrote Arabic, 66 percent French, and 18 percent English (there was no mention of writing in Tifinagh, the Tamazight alphabet). Notice that literacy was again about reading and writing, not speaking or listening—even though most Moroccans I knew consumed news via television, radio, or Facebook video feeds.

International agencies lumped the various schooling levels together in reporting literacy statistics, though their numbers raised the question of methods and assumptions about schooling and skills (see Lavy, Spratt, and Leboucher 1995, 1). UNICEF's website in 2013 claimed 67.1 percent literacy in Morocco; at the same time the United Nations Development Program website claimed 52.3 percent from information they had collected in 2007. These numbers were up from the 1990s, when scholars claimed two-thirds of the population were illiterate (Ennaji 1991, 8), even using disease metaphors to explain the problem ("endemic illiteracy," Youssi 1995, 30). Urban areas consistently had higher literacy than rural areas, men better than women, youth cohorts better than their parents. In all cases, literacy appeared as a national and international concern, since mass literacy was assumed to be central to modern public participation and personal empowerment.

Ideologies linking literacy to public reasoning participation could be found in ethnographic studies of Moroccan educational contexts. Daniel Wagner (1993) led and reported on an oft-cited illiteracy research project in Morocco during the 1980s and early 1990s to determine cultural conceptions of literacy and how they might be used to better integrate Moroccans into state literacy projects. Wagner conducted the research because of the high illiteracy reported for Morocco despite twenty years of mandated schooling. His team asked what kinds of literacy were evaluated in national statistics and found that they did not include functional workplace, religious, household task–related, and social interaction literacy skills (Spratt, Seckinger, and Wagner 1991, 182). Those labeled by the state as illiterate still read a medication label, sold artisanal goods to foreign tourists, prayed, and navigated paperwork processes at the municipality offices. They did so by engaging the literacy skills of brokers: literacy specialists such as a local religious scholar (لفقيه [*lfqīh*]), family members, or informal ways of acquisition.

> In modern Morocco, where literacy counts in dealing with the structures of power in the wider society, children have partially reversed the old pattern of parent-child authority in the family. It is the younger literate or biliterate (Arabic and French) generation that now provides access to new sources of information, through literacy skills that interpret and mediate the outside society for their low-literate, nonliterate, or monoliterate (Arabic, Quranic Arabic or French) parents. (Wagner 1993, 56)

Thus, literacies were not linked strictly to formal public education (standard Arabic and French reading and writing skills), but rather utilized as resources in a much broader communicative framework involving local literacy practices beyond reading and writing (Street 1984). Building on Wagner's work, Boyle (2004) explored the role of Qur'anic schools in preparing students for state education in a small Moroccan town. Qur'anic schools, known as المسيد (*almsīd*), were a primary means of education prior to the French colonial educational system and involved aural memorization and oral recitation of the Qur'an. Those who did well might have the opportunity to continue their studies under the direction of Muslim scholars at لرزاوية (*zāwīya* [Sufi brotherhood shrine-centers]) or madrasas linked to university centers such as Qarawiyyin in Fez (Eickelman 1985, 50–56; Segalla 2009, 3–4).

The foregrounding of listening as central to Moroccan education predated nineteenth-century European colonial contact. Eickelman, in his study of twentieth-century rural religious education (1985, 56), cited Ibn Khaldun, born in Tunis in the fourteenth century, who recognized that the embodied experience of literacy was different in Morocco than other parts of the Muslim world, as it emphasized memorization and oral recitation of key texts as the basis for literacy. A key mnemonic device of this recitation was embodied collective recitation: sitting on the ground in rows, listening to a religious scholar or student recite a section, collectively repeating back the patterns of lengthened back vowels and nasalized consonant endings (Sells 1999), torso moving back and forth in rhythm with the sound symbolism of the Qur'anic verses.[8] The French altered these centuries-old educational-religious institutions. Instead of a community-sponsored and locally managed Qur'anic school, they promoted state-funded, centrally monitored, reading-focused colonial schools, which the postcolonial Moroccan state adopted as the foundation for public education (Segalla 2009). Qur'anic schools became optional private education for parents who wished their preschool-aged children to better learn Qur'anic recitation (Boyle 2004, 9–10). Drawing on the communities of practice literature (Eckert and McConnell-Ginet 1992; Wenger 1999), Boyle suggested that the preparatory classes of the optional *almsīd* socialized children into more formal registers, religious beliefs, and embodied values associated with Arabic and Moroccan nationalism. This tracked them for the language of public school instruction, *fuṣḥā*, while those who attended French preschool programs had more difficulty. In this view, public schools were not the only places to acquire literacy and its attendant societal values, historically or contemporarily.

Even in public schools, ethnographic studies provided key insights into the role of language ideologies and debates about public participation and relationality. Boutieri conducted classroom ethnography in urban Moroccan secondary schools, focusing on the linguistic mediums of instruction and metapragmatic statements about the political, economic, social, and moral significance of French and Arabic (Boutieri 2012, 2013, 2016). She noted that language learning, classroom discussions, and ideologies mirrored and enacted larger Moroccan societal tensions between technological advancement, employability, and political progress in reflexive ways. For many of her interlocutors, the static language pedagogy of Arabic as well as the subjects of study indexed Arabic's lack of progress and innovation for students, leading to their political, economic, and social disenfranchisement. García-Sánchez studied second-generation Moroccan immigrant primary-school-aged children in Spain to understand the ways educational contexts became sites for exclusion and minority socialization. She analyzed the interactional differences between the Spanish public school and local mosque Qur'anic schools, both of which taught immigrant students *fuṣḥā*, but for different educational purposes. In the Spanish public school, the teacher was sent from Morocco to help immigrant populations preserve their culture and language. Immigrant students would meet once a week to learn *fuṣḥā* and Moroccan culture while other school children attended Catholic religion classes. The local mosque held Qur'anic Arabic classes three times a week in the evenings after school and on weekends. Both taught a form of *fuṣḥā*, though the content varied. García-Sánchez observed how similar pedagogies of Modern Standard/Classical Arabic (guided repetition, memorization, and recitation) instantiated different discourses on what Arabic indexed: a secular route to modern cultural identity or a means to revive Islamic values. Thus, aural pedagogies of listening-reciting *fuṣḥā* could become a resource for different sociopolitical values (García-Sánchez 2014, 183–220). As all these studies noted, literacy instruction was more than learning to read and write—it was learning to listen and think and was deeply entangled in discussions of progress, civic and personal identity, state authority, and religion. But what kind of listening and thinking?

While I did not conduct fieldwork in recognized educational contexts, discourses about education permeated my fieldwork notes. Everyone from public school children to Moroccan university academics recounted to me the problems of the educational system: poor or nonexistent infrastructure, transportation and security woes, overcrowded classrooms, absent teachers who doubled their income by tutoring in private schools, lack of libraries and laboratories, poor but pricey textbooks, nonsupportive or undereducated parents, demoralizing disciplinary practices, required subjects that don't prepare students for contemporary job markets, rampant cheating and corruption. Of course, language was a key critique as well. Some colleagues I interviewed noted the difficulties students faced when they encountered *fuṣḥā* as the language of instruction in public schools instead of their natively spoken versions of Arabic or Tamazight—an ideology reaffirmed by Ennaji (2005), García-Sánchez (2014), and Boutieri (2016). In addition, I often heard that despite the multilingual legacies of French and Spanish colonial education, as well as decades of migratory exchange, Moroccans now knew less French and Spanish (and what they did know was street talk) than their parents' (or grandparents') generation. Yet in a seeming paradox, Moroccans adopted multilingual satellite television earlier than any other Arabic-speaking country, with satellite dishes proliferating from the early 1990s. Even before that time, French, *fuṣḥā*, and *darījā* programming appeared on national television from the mid-1970s, accessed via antennas in cities and battery-powered televisions in remote locations.

Given the high rate of student attrition, troubled educational contexts, and poor literacy rates, it would seem that Moroccans were ill-prepared, language- and cognition-wise, to make sense of Moroccan and transnational news broadcasts in *fuṣḥā* and French—the most commonly viewed broadcasts among people I visited. This was the claim made by the Open Society report I quoted at the beginning of this chapter:

> The most sensitive issues in terms of social and cultural diversity concern language, ethnicity, and gender. . . . Moroccans speak Darija, a dialect of Arabic, in everyday life. Darija is an oral language, not used in writing. The official languages are modern standard Arabic and French. However, both public service television stations and all printed media (with the exception of one magazine and a couple of newspapers) use formal Arabic, which is only understood by an estimated 40 percent of Moroccans, and formal French, which only 10 percent of Moroccans understand. French in particular is the language of the elite. The choice of language restricts access to public television for a large portion of society. For illiterate people, for whom TV remains the main source of information and entertainment, TV programming is not fully accessible. (Zaid and Ibrahine 2011, 51)

This report cited Zaid's year-long 2007 content study of, among other things, languages used on the two national television stations, Rabat (القناة الأولى [*alqanāt al'ūlā*, "the first station"]) and 2M (Zaid 2013, 13–14). The sample analyzed all locally produced and educational, social, political, economic, and cultural shows broadcast on the public television stations from 7 P.M. to midnight to quantify the languages used in relation to the supposed public who would access or participate in these programs. Most purchased foreign programs were in solely in French or *fuṣḥā*, but 35 percent of speakers on national programming used a mix of Moroccan Arabic and *fuṣḥā*, with French or *fuṣḥā* use at 33.3 percent. They compared these statistics with 2004 literacy numbers from the Moroccan Census Bureau to argue the following:

> The study concluded that the choice of language restricts access to and participation in public television for a large portion of Moroccan society. The choice of language allows access and participation for only the wealthy and highly educated classes. Half the literate population, 30.3 percent of the population aged 10 and above, knows how to read Arabic and French. About 17.3 percent or one-third of the literate population knows how to read and write Arabic alone. (Zaid and Ibrahine 2011, 53)

This report, and assertions by other scholars I encountered, relied on the language ideologies I have mentioned to make their claims: that individual literacy, glossed as reading and writing language skills, was central to interpreting aural television programming. These kinds of reports and analyses assumed that understanding news, talk shows, documentaries, and public service programming—often delivered in oral *fuṣḥā* or French—required an individual's set of analytical and cognitive skills, acquired primarily through formal school literacy in Morocco. Even as Zaid and Ibrahine explicitly articulated reading and writing—visual and graphic semiotic literacy ideologies—as central to reasoning and public participation, they presupposed individual literate listening skills as well.

Literacy and Awareness

الحلقة٢: قاري وماشي واعي

Episode 2: Educated but Unaware

I was invited by some friends late one summer night to eat grilled meat in what passes as a truck stop just outside of Fez on the national road (shorthand for slow route) toward Meknes. As we waited for the beef and liver kebabs to arrive, they asked me about my work. I shared with them an article I was writing about a phrase I had heard a number of times in Fez: قاري وماشي واعي (qārī wa māšī wa'ī, *"educated but unconscious/unaware"*). *It was an inversion of the phrase common among the educated about the problems of illiteracy:* ماقاريين وماواعيين (māqārīīn wa māwa'īīn, *"uneducated and unaware"*). *One of the women present, Loubna, said she figured out that formal education was not sufficient for literacy when she was seventeen. She was, at the time of our discussion, twenty-five and working at a French telecommunications call center, having studied economics in French for two years at the university but not completing her degree. Loubna explained that she always had poor Islamic education teachers in high school. One year, when she had to learn the inheritance laws in Islam (unanimously touted as complicated by students), her teacher talked a lot but did not know how to teach. She asked her mom about the inheritance laws. Her mother had never been to school, yet she explained them in such a way that my friend passed the exam in Islamic studies better than any previous year. That's when Loubna learned that awareness was just as valuable as education. She continued by saying that people who are uneducated can hear something and internalize it better because of their life experience than others who read books and don't get anything beneficial from it.*

At this point she inserted that her uncle (mother's older brother) disagreed with her. He was educated through middle school (a French brevet diploma) in Taounate, a rural region of the Rif Mountains north of Fez, before joining the military and ending up with a government position in Casablanca. According to several of my interlocutors, the brevet diploma used to mean a lot more than it does currently. Many individuals with brevet diplomas were recruited for government jobs after Moroccan independence because the need for teachers and administrators was so great. Loubna's uncle argued that formal education was key to awareness, but she disagreed with him. When I asked her why people of her uncle's generation thought differently, she thought it was the result of the French undermining the Islamic educational system in order to justify colonial rule. She said,

> *You know, our religion is expansive, and before the French, people used to have a vocation and study at a Qur'anic school or mosque at the same time. Even if they couldn't read, they would listen to lectures, and they had better interactions and style of life than currently. They were aware (*لواعيين [lwa'īīn]*), but the French did not value Islamic ways of knowing—in fact thought they were dangerous—and imposed the French educational system, inculcating a new generation of students with their ideas and values. Because they had been defeated politically, Muslims began questioning their system, and this allowed colonialism to create a division in communities through education.*

Loubna saw undermining Moroccan moral reasoning and behavior as a main goal of French colonialism and felt that French-educated Moroccan elites continued these trends in a form of cultural neocolonialism. For her, the contemporary educational system reflected this ideology.

*A few weeks later Ayah's mother (from Episodes 1 and 3) walked me home after I had spent the afternoon visiting the family. She talked about raising all her children by herself after her husband died, and how she sent them to government schools despite the difficulties. These days, she said, anyone could get an education, and parents encouraged their children, unlike during her youth, when parents didn't think it was useful to send kids to school. As we were walking through the streets, she kept talking about how many kids are educated (*لقاريين [lqārīīn]*) but not aware (*لواعيين [lwā'īīn]*). They studied, but they didn't have good influences when they left the classroom—they hung out with people who smoked and drank—so their education needed to involve morality if it was to be true education. She also mentioned that the teachers had not even been teaching that year; they had been striking for better pay several days a week, so the* *students were in danger of not advancing and lacking true awareness because of the educational system's failures.*

♣

As described in the previous section, studies of Moroccan literacy practices and educational contexts reveal some useful nuances in the idea of literacy. Several scholars argued that "traditional" Moroccans utilized formal and informal literacy mediators (Qur'anic scholars, public writers, literate neighbors, and children) to handle literacy needs, both prior to mass public education and at the time of their research among those without formal schooling (Wagner 1993; Erguig 2005). Wagner claimed that state modernizing projects influenced Moroccan understandings of literacy as an individual right and skill:

> Today literacy is often perceived as an individual's personal need and right, whereas it once was something a person as a member of a group or neighborhood might accomplish indirectly through mediators. . . . Now, however, the ideology of personal literacy has made a remarkably strong mark on public consciousness at all levels of Moroccan society. (Wagner 1993, 36)

Wagner identified changes in literacy ideologies and practices that pointed to a more individuated notion of literacy. Even as Moroccans began to recognize literacy as an individual skill, their ideas about what to include in literacy skills seems to have varied. As with most ideologies, they tended to be multiple and sometimes overlapped (Kroskrity 2010). Erguig surveyed and interviewed over 500 Moroccans from Rabat and surrounding rural areas between the ages of fifteen and forty to discover their understandings of literacy. He did so twice: in the 1960s and 1990s to see what changes they included in their understanding of literacy. Sixty percent perceived literacy in the 1960s to mean the ability to read and write, 50 percent viewed literacy as access to formal schooling, while 15 percent connected literacy to memorizing the Qur'an (even if that person could not read or write). In the 1990s, the numbers associated with these views diversified and increased: the ability to read and understand the Qur'an was linked to literacy by 64 percent of respondents, while 44 percent included the ability to memorize and orally recite the Qur'an without comprehension. In addition, bilingualism, competence with a computer, and well-manneredness (41 percent, 29 percent, and 54 percent, respectively) were included by Moroccans in the 1990s conceptions of literacy (Erguig 2005, 140–43). Moroccans in this survey defined literacy as inclusive of more skills than reading and writing, expanding it to a range of abilities not associated with reading and writing by scholars, such as knowledge of the world and access to information regardless of one's formal schooling. Literacy as understood by Moroccans in Rabat diversified over time to include reading, writing, listening, speaking, public schooling, bilingualism, Qur'anic recitation training, text-based skills, and electronic and moral competencies.

As evidenced in Episodes 1 and 2, literacy beyond reading and writing appeared in my observations and conversations with Fassis as well. They made a marked distinction between being educated, as in formally schooled, and literate, in the broader senses described by the Moroccans Erguig surveyed. Several critiqued the public "modern" education system for teaching subjects and skills irrelevant to the lived experience of Moroccan life and economic exigencies. As in Loubna's account in Episode 2, the most important forms of knowing involved interaction beyond the classroom. لقاري (*lqārī*), was the *darīja* word for "educated," and could refer to a number of different meanings beyond written literacy, including ability to recite the Qur'an, be multilingual on a spoken but not written level, and be knowledgeable through oral interaction with others. Loubna and others associated this idea with the phrase قاريين وما وايينش (*qārīīn wamāwā'īīnsh*, "learned but unconscious/unaware"): schooling was insufficient to make one literate. Those who deployed this notion, even if they didn't use the phrase, argued that graduates of Moroccan private and public educational institutions were not made aware of those things that were most important, such as appropriate social interaction skills, the true meanings of religious belief and practice, and practical training in new information technologies and business languages rather than how to read a Shakespearian poem. When I asked Toufiq for an example of someone "aware" and yet unschooled, he mentioned a colleague who worked as a carpet vendor in the medina. He had memorized most of the Qur'an and had enough functional fluency in French and Spanish to converse easily with most tourists on most any topic, yet he could not read anything written in a Roman-based alphabet beyond recognizing the difference between Arabic and "French" orthographic scripts.

Many of the university students I interacted with at the beginning of my fieldwork were concerned about finding meaningful employment after finishing their degrees, claiming that the curriculum did not educate them for the types of opportunities available. They learned to read and write English, French, and Arabic well enough to write a forty- to sixty-page research monograph in one of those languages. Yet these same students went unemployed for several years because they did not have the skills and the right connections to help them secure a job (Boutieri 2016). They ended up working with high-school drop-outs in the garment factories (Cairoli 1998); as an errand runner in a municipal government office; selling carpets in a tourist bazaar; or volunteering to teach English in an after-school program just to "get experience" in the hope that a private school might hire them later. Each position was unpaid (or underpaid at quarter the regular salary) and involved long training periods (from six months up to two years), with the understanding that they came to the position without the proper education. All this led to a perception that the state had failed in its welfare contract to provide employment to those who completed their education. Many claimed that more than 50 percent of high school students didn't graduate each year because the state did not want to be responsible for providing them jobs. For these Fassis, corruption, self-interest, and imported modernization theories drove government education policies, not لوعي (*lwaʿī*, true consciousness of the way things really were and should be). In a number of conversations there was a strong idea that Arabic grammar could not be truly understood without memorizing and internalizing the Qur'an, an action and skill not included in state definitions of literacy but clearly connected to listening and true understanding for some Fassis. The linking of the educational system's failures to unemployment woes engaged language ideologies about awareness and abilities.

In these accounts, formal schooling was not the only indicator of knowledge and language access capabilities. One of the conceptual terms Mohammed's family used to explain knowledge transmission in Morocco was لاحتكاك (*liḥtikāk*), literally rubbing against something but glossed as learning through close contact with others. This idea, that knowledge was acquired through friction, reflexively indexed "aware" educational processes as relational and social but not necessarily without conflict. Interactions could be loud, animated, and heated as well as quiet, observational, and respectful of authority, depending on the context. Real reasoning skills came through interaction with the ideas and perspectives and skills of others. Families I worked with mentioned how youth gathered and exchanged ideas about what they had watched or caught each other up on what they missed—the interaction being the way to make sense of news. One unschooled mother living in the Fez medina related that if she missed the news she would ask the neighborhood shopkeepers (who keep radios and televisions in their businesses), and they would recount the events for the last several days.

Distributed Literacy: Affective and Effective Reasoning

الحلقة ٣:الاخبار

Episode 3: The News

Ismail just bought a digital satellite receiver for the family,[9] *so when I came over for lunch they were watching Melody Hits, an Arab music video station created by Egyptian media businessman Gamal Ashraf Marwan. Their father died when the youngest, Ayah, was three years old, and the mother supplemented their meager pension by working in a garment factory to support the family. All three sons (two with university degrees in engineering) and eventually their sister Ayah (with a university degree in English) began working in the same garment factory: one as a machinist, another as a driver, another as an engineer, and Ayah as a dispensary clerk. Since all worked at the factory, they were rarely home, though this was a Sunday afternoon when most of them had the day off. We sat on the couches lining the salon of their modest two-bedroom apartment, located in a neighborhood built for public employees in 1970s Fez. These densely populated quarters had brick-based cement and mortar apartments, stacked two or three stories high and three or four buildings deep on each side of the alleys. Through the open windows we could hear the regular rhythms of Moroccan urban soundscapes—the wafting sounds of kids playing in the streets, neighboring families' televisions, pans clanging in their kitchens, and people greeting each other as they passed on the street that spring afternoon.*

After the younger brother, Ismail, left for work, the elder brother, Ahmed, came in and changed the channel to an old Egyptian movie. When lunch arrived, he changed it to al-Jazeera sports, which we watched through most of lunch, even after he left. Then Ayah's mother requested we change the channel to a news station—al-Arabiyya. Ayah teased her mother that the only thing she watched was news channels—al-Jazeera and al-Arabiyya—now that they had digital satellite television. Her mother had never been to school and would have been included in state statistics as illiterate. Despite her supposed illiteracy, she knew more about events displayed on that newscast than her daughter or me, though both of us could follow the fuṣḥā *narrative. I observed the daughter glossing the commentary for her mother a couple of times, giving the details in an abbreviated way, sometimes adding information that she felt important for the meaning but not included in the news narrative. The main gist of the news broadcast her mother could understand from her acquired* fuṣḥā *newspeak register—having learned important key terms and an ability to link images interdiscursively to those key terms. She explained that oft-repeated phrases and images were "types" of recurring events, scripts that became part of her comprehension. The verbal content was about upcoming elections in Iraq and whether or not the violence would hinder them, but the visual content was of American soldiers, roadside explosions, and market bombings. Her main reaction to what she saw was* مسكين, maskīn, *"poor people," or a shake of her head. She later said the American soldiers were victims in this conflict as much as the Iraqis, pawns in a game played by others.*

♣

Ayah's single-parent family was multi-income, multilingual, multiliterate, and diverse in their media interests. If based in analytical tropes of Arab patriarchal family decision-making practices, one might argue that the males dominated programming choices. In terms of meaning-making, one might posit interpretive authority with elders, the mother in this case, who followed and commented most on the news programming during the afternoon. Yet another may claim that the formal university education of the daughter made her a "literacy mediator" for family household needs (Wagner, Messick, and Spratt 1986; see also Garcia-Sanchez 2014), affording her a precedence and degree of authority. Yet that was not how this family understood their actions. They pooled their financial, affective, and linguistic resources not only to understand the news but to reason about its significance and effects (see Schulthies 2013).

Accounts of media reception and literacy levels in Morocco have described school-educated youth serving as media and information translators for their parents, via radio transmission, television programs, and newspaper readings (Davis and Davis 1995, 590–91, for a rural Moroccan context; Kapchan 1996, 215, for urban; Mernissi 1994, 86–91, for a historical Fez account; and Abu-Lughod 2005, 118, for an Egyptian example). Compare with Lerner's media and development theory of the mid-twentieth century, in which formal literacy and media consumption patterns correlated into "modern" political and cultural attitudes:

> The new literates constitute the corps of restless Transitionals that may remake Egypt and the Middle East in the next decades. Literacy is their tool, mobility their method, and the participant life their goal. For while literacy as a tool equips people only to consume print, in the deeper sense acquisition of literacy transforms a person. He acquires some of that capacity to move from particular to general, from concrete to abstract, which is standard in modern communications. Mastery of the logical conventions of grammar and syntax, which print imposes upon routinely acquired speech, is a long step in this direction. Thus, the illiterate Lebanese villager who found even "listening to things read" on the radio difficult, and preferred "being told" in the colloquial narrative of the oral tradition. An illiterate Egyptian villager explained why he learns less even from radio and movies than those who can read: "They see something I do not see, know about many things I do not know. [*What things?*] More about the world." (Lerner 1958, 253)

Notice the ways in which Lerner linked individual acquisition of reading grammar with ways of thinking, seeing, hearing. Yet he glossed literacy explicitly as learning to read print, with perception as a secondary and more significant outcome. Even then the analysis was that schooling made the difference in media attention practices—schooling that taught how to hear specific kinds of Arabic and French.

The Fassis I encountered had some of these same viewing patterns, yet their explanations differed. Instead of rapt individual attention increasing during television viewing based on the greater number of educated family members, cross-conversation while watching television was very common. Sometimes it would depend on the program genre, but often it depended on the participant framework: who was present, what interactional role they were assuming, and how they came to enter the room. In other words, education levels did not seem to affect whether or not people would talk to each other about television programming while watching together. Even though more family members were going to school, they regularly argued that the education was poorer than in the past. Increasing educational access did not mean increased literacy. Rather, it meant that literacy skills varied from person to person in each family, even among those who had attended the same schools. They relied on the strengths, skills, and interests of different family members to make sense of what they watched.

الحلقة ٤: يتصنطو ويناقشو

Episode 4: Listening and Debating

Mohammed and his wife, Meriam, were relaxing after eating lunch and casually watching the lunchtime news report on national television. Two of their daughters were cleaning up in the kitchen, while their son and I sat on the couches opposite them. Even though the husband and wife were the only ones who spoke in this interaction, the conversation was directed to all present—even the television. The news broadcaster was talking about the Foundation of Mohammed VI for Moroccans and its role in organizing and welcoming "Moroccans of the world"[10]*: the official term for Moroccans living abroad. In everyday speech, these Moroccans were called* vacanciin, *a hybrid French-Arabic word for vacationers,*[11] *those who come during the summer break. The conversation became an evaluation and critique of Moroccan institutions.*

At the beginning of her report, the news broadcaster described a new Auto-Route rest area the Mohammed VI Foundation opened in Tangier specifically to welcome Moroccans driving from Europe on visits home.

Mohammed:	Everything's named Mohammed VI (LAUGH) as if nothing existed before. (LAUGH)	*kulšī smmāwh mhamad issādis (LAUGH) (.) tā ḥājā mā kānat. (LAUGH)*	كلشي سمّاوه محمد السادس (يضحك) (.) تا حاجا ما كانت. (يضحك)	محمد:
Meriam:	Well, he left . . .	*īwāā smītū khalāā*	إوا! سميتو خلاا!!	مريم:
Mohammed:	The foundation of Mohammed VI, school of Mohammed VI.	*lmū'sisa dmhamad issādīs, lmadrasa dmhamad issādīs*	المؤسسة دمحمد السادس، المدرسة دمحمد السادس.	محمد:
Meriam:	His father worked on international relations [	*bāh kān khdām 'alā al'alāqāt dyālu 'alā barrā*	باه كان خدام على العلاقات ديالو على برّا]	مريم:
Mohammed:	[hmm]	*[mmm]*	[ممم]	محمد:
Meriam:	]and left the interior relations to him, so he worked on that.	*]wakhalā lū huwa ldākhil mā ykhdam huwa.*	]وخلا لو هو لداخل ما يخدم هو.	مريم:
Mohammed:	(It's all) a mess.	*mrawn.*	مروّن.	محمد:

The news broadcaster shifted to recounting the print newspaper headlines for the day. The editors cut to a visual of a newspaper, foregrounding a section in an article on poverty in the country, which the broadcaster read in fuṣḥā. *Ahmed preemptively read part of it out loud before the broadcaster did, but in* darīja, *even though the article and the broadcast reading of it are in* fuṣḥā.

Mohammed:	twelve dirhams (.) just two million!	*ṭnāš ldirham (.) ghīr jūj dlmilyūn!*	طناش لدرهم (.) غير جوج دلمليون!	محمد:
Meriam:	what's that?	*šnū huwa?*	شنو هو؟	مريم:
Mohammed:	two million Moroccans are living on twelve dirhams a day (.) two of (.) the rural regions (.) uh, a quarter of them are in the hinterland (.) mooooore!	*jūj dlmilyūn dlmaghāriba kī'ayīšū bitnāš ldirham finnhār (.) jūj dāū (.) alminātiq annā'īya (.) āā rub'a fī lmināṭiq annā'īya (.) ktāāār!*	جوج دلمليون دلمغاربة كيعيشو بطناش لدرهم فالنهار (.) جوج داا (.) المناطق النائية (.) آآ ربعة في المناطق النائية (.) كتاااار!	محمد:
Toufiq:	Let us listen.	*khalīnā nism'aū.*	خلينا نسمعو.	توفيق:

This interaction would probably qualify for illiterate viewing by government standards. Mohammed, the fifty-year-old father, did not complete middle school, though he had worked in the tourism industry throughout his life and knew how to socialize and sell in French, English, Arabic, Spanish, and German. His wife, Meriam, had never attended school, though she had been memorizing the Qur'an at a local adult literacy program at the mosque. Toufiq had dropped out of university to work in tourism as his father had. One of the daughters had not passed the high school graduation exam but had recently started working at a French telecom call center as technical support. The other was still in high school. Then there was me, college educated, but unable to speak *fuṣḥā* sustainably. I could read and follow *fuṣḥā* conversations depending on the topic, having acquired *fuṣḥā* in college courses, but my conversational Arabic was very much *darīja*. This family setting involved a wide range of literacy skills.

Notice that the reasoning work in this interaction occurred between the two "least literate" by state standards: husband and wife. Mohammed began with a critique: why did everything have to be in the name of the king? His comment was a dig at the cult of personality mobilized by many Arab leaders: naming institutions after the ruler was one way to exert political power through symbolic presence (Wedeen 1999). However, his wife countered this logic with an alternative view. Meriam shifted the focus away from symbolic power to historical analysis: the current king was encouraged by his father to focus on internal affairs. Thus the institutions with the king's name on them all pointed toward his concern for Moroccan citizens. While Mohammed did not fully accept Meriam's argument, he did not reject it. Instead, he reframed it: مروّن (*mrawn*): it was all a mess. In this way, he incorporated her historical analysis into his critique of Moroccan politics—one reiterated by most people even if they supported the current political leaders. Despite everyone's efforts, or perhaps because of corrupt ones, Moroccan institutions failed the people.

This evaluation continued into the next news topic: poverty statistics in Morocco. While the news broadcaster introduced her report, Mohammed leaned toward the television and read the cut-out of the newspaper article focusing on the number of Moroccans living on 12 dirhams a day (about $1.31 by 2020 currency exchange rates). The article was in *fuṣḥā*, as was the news broadcast, but Ahmed's quote of the newspaper article was initially in Moroccan phonology and syntax: !طناش لدرهم (.) غير جوج دلمليون (*ṭnāš ldirham (.) ghīr jūj dlmilyūn*): "12 dirhams (.) only 2 million!" He did so partly because it was common to discuss news in family settings that way, but also to focus affectively on the most striking part for him: there were Moroccans living on 12 dirhams a day! When Meriam asked for clarification, he elaborated: 2 million Moroccans live on 12 dirhams a day, with one-quarter of those living in rural areas. He had to self-repair once ("two of . . . a quarter of") because the details were being spoken at the same time as his restatement of the topic and ended with a critique using a very long vowel: كتاااار (*ktāāār*, "moooore")! His distrust of Moroccan institutions included their statistics: more than 2 million Moroccans were living in poverty. His son chided his outburst with a quick reminder that the details were being lost as he spoke: خلينا نسمعو (*khalīnā nismʿaū*, "Let us listen"). The whole group then listened in silence for two minutes until the broadcast moved on to the next topic: a report on Morocco's lack of religious sectarian conflict. No one commented further about the poverty report.

Building on the distributed cognition literature (Curtis 2008; Hutchins 1995; Mendoza-Denton 2007), I call the practices of Episodes 4 and 5 distributed literacy, the mobilizing of diverse linguistic and logic repertoires in a familial interactional context to unpack, frame, and evaluate news collectively. Each family member contributed his or her linguistic and cognitive skills to a negotiated, emergent, intergenerational construction of meaning. Even those without formal schooling followed the news and participated in critical analysis of events, their causes, and meanings. Formally acquired literacy (the ability to read, write, and listen in Arabic, French, and English) was one resource among many that Fassi families used to collaboratively interpret news events, take positions in relation to those events, and deploy those stances in relation to their perceptions of Moroccanness projects.

Lavy, Spratt, and Leboucher suggested that in Morocco, functional literacy, or the skills to accomplish tasks, should be described more accurately as socially distributed than individually located: "The development of methods to characterize literacy skills at the household level has been advocated as an efficient and potentially more valid way to evaluate the functional distribution of literacy in societies in which the family unit, rather than the individual, is the principal functional unit, wherein the skills and resources of each member are pooled and available to all members" (1995, 20). These scholars recognized that literacy practices in household settings involved more than individual reading and writing skills as a result of uneven educational trajectories. Rather than thinking of this as a deficit, a "functional literacy" practice that served as a Band-Aid bridging state educational failures, some Fassis viewed distributed literacy as flowing out of an older epistemological practice of distributed knowing, the generative friction of interaction (*liḥtikāk*).

Literate Listening Moroccanness Projects

What allowed the same set of interpretive practices, watching news in mixed-literacy-level homes, to develop divergent Moroccanness perspectives on the necessity of schooling to understand news media? Was formal education in French or *fuṣḥā* necessary to critically engage news accounts and participate in public debates? Could an educated individual with appropriate language skills lack the necessary awareness and knowledge to engage in effective reasoning that an uneducated individual brought to understanding news? Could an illiterate engage in critique, understood as reading (or listening-learning) in order to address public others (see Warner 2004, 24)? Was critique a modern liberal secular set of individual practices (see Brown 2009) that excluded distributed religiously trained ways of reasoning? I hope by this point I've demonstrated that literacy as an individual reasoning skill was a "listening subject" ideology, one that relied on the erasure of assumptions about listening, reasoning, awareness, and collaborative practices to work.

In the previous episodes, the Fassis among whom I worked rarely encountered news in a solitary context or manner. Whether at home, in cafes, at work, in taxis, or on public transportation, collaborative consuming and analysis was far more common. Newspapers would be passed around the train compartment and news topics discussed. Radio announcements in shared taxis would precipitate extended critiques of government policies and parties. While there were certainly programs, locations (such as cafes, Graiouid 2007)[12] and times of the day when individuals alone or peers together could and did watch television, homes formed a key component to collaborative watching, interpreting, and evaluating of television. In these episodes, comprehension was interactive, involving many family members (extended and even neighborhood fictive kin) with varying literacy levels, language registers, motivations, and interests—all of which shaped the meaning-making of viewing events. This recurring mundane collaborative work also precipitated political nonmovements, counterpublics laboring against restricting literacy ideologies.

For some of my interlocutors, formal literacy obtained through state-sponsored education did not determine reasoning ability in Moroccan family contexts because it was one resource among many and part of a collaborative process. For others, especially those who self-identified as educated, formal literacy was necessary for appropriate news consumption. The ability to comprehend spoken French or *fuṣḥā* was embedded in their idea of literacy and cognitive "awareness." The problem lay in the linguistic mediums of public education.

In all the debates, oral-aural aspects of practices and ideologies emerged as central to literacy, cognitive development, and political and economic participation. Literate listening, though differently understood, was a medium for mobilizing Moroccanness political projects. Both those who viewed aural comprehension of *fuṣḥā* as the impediment to awareness and those who saw distributed knowing (*liḥtikāk*) beyond the classroom as the key to awareness argued for linguistic and thus cognitive reform of the Moroccan educational system. The former belied the distributed and collective nature of linguistic resource use (people pooled their literacy skills in various genres and domains to accomplish all kinds of cognitive, administrative, political, and economic tasks) in order to advocate their Moroccanness via formal literacy projects. The latter downplayed the significance of institutional resources and formal pedagogies (in Qur'anic schools, public schools, vocational trainings, French and

English language centers, mosque adult literacy programs) in order to argue for *liḥtikāk*, their Moroccanness-via-interaction projects.[13]

Conclusion

In his insightful review of anthropological challenges to scholarship on literacy and modernity, Keith Walters suggested that sometimes our own literacy ideologies and practices preclude our abilities to propose literacy projects that fit the practices of target populations.

> Surveying much of the public and academic debate about literacy, I am forced to conclude that there is too little of seeing . . . the hyperliteracy that we so privilege, that so defines the core of our being, as a literacy among literacies. As a consequence of our failures, many suffer, not merely those whose language, logic and literate practices we dismiss, but also, as Geertz eloquently and rightly notes, we ourselves, who spring so quickly to defend our practices on the grounds of largeness of mind, objectivity, and tolerance. We have much to learn from those whose worlds and experiences are exceedingly different from our own. Confronting those worlds and those experiences should force us to face and examine our own assumptions, as individuals and as members of this culture, about the relationship of language and logic to literacy. Doing so will no doubt help us as we seek to understand what a right to literacy means, to whom it is to be offered, and on what conditions." (Walters 1990, 184)

I suspect he learned this from personal experience. Walters served as a Peace Corp volunteer in Tunisia during the 1970s and returned later to conduct sociolinguistic research of sound change in Arabic (1994, 1999). His interest in literacy, linguistic asymmetries, and social valuations of linguistic resources led him to think critically about ways to look past our own scholarly assumptions.

My Moroccan colleagues held some shared assumptions about literacy. They also differed. I found that implicit and explicit language-literacy ideologies were central to interpretive practices after analyzing with Fassi families' their news-viewing events and what they thought others were doing—or failing to do. While many Fassis who viewed themselves as literate and educated repeatedly bemoaned the misunderstandings of poorly literate Moroccans, others in Fez challenged a core "modern" ideology of writing/reading literacy as an individual skill, acquired only in schools, necessary for critical reasoning and, by extension, for news comprehension. I saw these as two public collectivities (among others) mobilized politically around literate listening and media ideologies. These were not the only groups, nor were these fixed categories. A self-identified educated family member that engaged in illiteracy critiques might evoke a different perspective when discussing the same topic with a group of college friends in a café. This particular phatic labor of relationality had a patterned quality, but not a fixity. Those two laments about awareness became disputed ground for fighting over what it meant to be literate, Moroccan, and connected in Fez.

As mentioned previously though, both included a listening ideology as central to literacy: a hybrid listening-reasoning ability acquired either through schooling or street interactions. Fassis aligning with either group used language as a medium to challenge or reproduce widely circulated scholarly narratives of objectivity, morality, and reason. On the one hand, to be literate meant to hear and understand spoken *fuṣḥā* or French, languages whose school-based acquisition would impart the ability to reason like a modern citizen should. To reason was to critique the arguments of others using the knowledge one had acquired through school interactions and content. On the other hand, to be literate meant to develop an awareness of the world based on everyday interactions. To reason did not mean to coolly and dispassionately analyze arguments, but rather to affectively debate and passionately defend them with others (Schulthies 2013). My Fassi interlocutors, who self-identified as products of the failed Moroccan educational system, lived not as individual interpreters in their media consumption practices. Instead, they demonstrated distributed literacy in practice, pooling resources gained through formal and information interactions. The ideology of distributed literacy built on Fassi notions of لاحتكاك (*liḥtikāk* [mingling/friction]) and واعي (*wa'i* [critical awareness]). Distributed literacy evidenced their adaptation of a precolonial Moroccan literacy ideology about embodied listening to the phatic labor of reasoning as they discursively shaped Moroccanness. I saw how these Moroccans oriented to the friction of interactional critique and not-always-consensual engagements among those with a range of literacies and linguistic skills in everyday Fassi homes and lived as though these domestic communicative practices powered public political discourse. In other words, everyday talk about news and how to understand it engaged larger debates about communicability and relationality (phaticity) underlying Moroccan collectivities. The notion that critique was a Moroccan democratic tool of all literacy levels recurred regardless of my interlocutor, though the critics didn't always assign that idea to others. These insights should help media scholars reexamine the key mediating role of local language-literacy ideologies in shaping understanding and participation.

3 Reregistering Media and Remediating a Register

Moroccan Morality Tales

Long ago, long ago	هدا شحال، هدا شحال
in the times before man learned to record/register with a pen	فيام زمان قّبل ما يتعلم الأنسان يزمم بالقلام
wise people were thinking wisely	كانو العقّال يخمو تخمام
and they created stories and illusions from imagination	ينزلو من لخيال حكيات و وهام
they organized it in speech and the understanding ones memorized them	نضموها فكلام وحفضوها الفهّام
and left them as heritage from generation to generation	و خلوها ورت من جيال لجيال
lucky is the one who drinks deeply and understands the words of the ancients	سعدات اللي روا و فهم كلام لقدام

(Opening title sequence, spoken in *darīja*, for 2M television series رمانة وبرطال *roumāna wabourṭāl*)

When I interviewed media producers at the 2M and Rabat television stations, they all squarely situated media as a tool for modernizing Moroccans. News, public service, and educational programs filled at least half of any given daily broadcast schedule. Even entertainment producers saw their efforts as an effort to teach Moroccans modern ways to relate to each other through civic virtues. Their civic reform efforts targeted an imagined Moroccan viewer with retrograde ideologies about Moroccan sociality and progress. Thus media was a tool for socializing modern Moroccans. One of the mediums for doing so that emerged in the last decade involved an "old" oral storytelling register revamped for television. In this chapter I explore what happened to state media's efforts to create a shared Moroccanness around gender equity messaging through a "revitalized" speech style, or socially significant register known as هدرة الميزان (*hadra lmizān*): rhymed prose associated with storytelling of generations past. How did Fassis understand moral literacy and sociality of *hadra lmizān* through the shift in mediums, from face-to-face storytelling circles to mass-mediatized state storytelling of civic education via television?

Both Fassis and state media producers calibrated the medium or channel shift of oral storytelling rhymed prose as doing the same Moroccanness work: preserving or revitalizing a "traditional" speech form that connected Moroccans morally. For my Fassi friends and media producers, *hadra lmizān* was associated with wisdom, heritage, street performance, a nostalgic past, and real-time audience response. Yet the register served different Moroccanness ends depending on the medium or channel they associated with it. For state producers, the rhymed prose register allowed them to convey "modern" civic values, such as gender equity, in a well-loved medium. They were renewing a Moroccan sociality form and imbuing it with modernity. For some of my Fassi viewers, rhymed prose validated a morality of the elders that had been lost in impersonal "modern" interactions: they missed the gender equity content entirely. What both producers and some of my viewers erased were the implicit and explicit media ideologies about how to relate to registers in specific mediums that shaped the messaging process. When adapted to televised entertainment serials seeking to shift Moroccan perceptions of women, the disabled, and magic, the unspoken practices of domestic television watching affected the messaging of *hadra lmizān* far more than the nostalgic appeal of the form itself. As I will argue throughout this chapter and into the next, these understanding gaps were particularly important for analyzing the meanings and politics of communicative failure and different efforts at renewal in Fez.[1]

When I began visiting Fez in the early 2000s, my friends and host families recommended I try to improve my Arabic by watching a daily adult literacy program, ألف لام (*'alif lām*), on Moroccan television. The program utilized well-known Moroccan actress Naima Lmcharki in the role of adult female storyteller; she would recount a brief morality tale in *darīja* (Moroccan Arabic), followed by a ten-minute reenactment of the story; finally, a panel of three participants would talk/write about the tale using a specific grammatical feature or class of lexical items in *fuṣḥā* (standard Arabic). As mentioned in Chapter 2, *fuṣḥā* was the language of formal schooled literacy in Morocco, despite its lack of everyday use. Folk and academic theories separated Arabic in two: spoken *darīja*, "dialect," and *fuṣḥā*, "the standard" used for literate written and official discourse, a language ideology known as diglossia (Ferguson 1959; Brustad 2017), though in everyday practice a much more difficult distinction to maintain (as I will explore in Chapter 4). The state assumed everyone needed to learn *fuṣḥā* to participate as citizens in national life, as *fuṣḥā* was the default assumption in claiming Arabic as the official state language. The *'alif lām* literacy learners were a pre-teen boy, a grandfather figure, and a middle-aged woman, I assume selected to represent the program producers' perceptions of targeted learners, but also to model intergenerational educational learning. The scenic backdrops for the stories were homes and village settings, the costumes reflecting the historical/mythical Moroccan past, and the *darīja* stories employing a rhymed storytelling prose Toufiq called هدرة الميزان (*hadra lmizān*), weighed or measured speech. Toufiq had previously encountered this *darīja* rhymed prose form when an "adopted" uncle used to recount mythical tales to his extended family on the rooftop of their home in the medina. But he had also heard it in settings that commodified entertainment and moral instruction: market storytelling circles that used to spontaneously gather in the open square outside Bab Boujloud when he was a child. Although Marrakesh's famed Jamaa el Fna Square boasted many well-known storytellers, Fez used to have a public storytelling tradition in Boujouloud Square, as well, though Toufiq claimed the state quashed it after the 1990 riots.

As part of *'alif lām*'s educational process, the *darīja* rhymed prose language style and storytelling settings indexed domestic space and sought to legitimate adult literacy by naturalizing the links between moral teaching and the home as a "modern" learning locale for "formalized" schooling. This fit within media executives' literacy ideologies, as listening subjects, that Moroccans did not know standard Arabic well enough to participate in significant media programming like news and political talk shows and documentaries. Hence the need to teach *fuṣḥā* (the formal language of the state and education) using *darīja* (the language of everyday use)—many viewers needed the training, and Moroccan storytelling was a well-loved channel for doing so among the adult target population. It also reflected the literate listening ideologies explored in Chapter 2: languages learned in school, such as French and *fuṣḥā*, were central for civic participation and thus Moroccanness. The program, which ran from 1999 to 2004, was touted by the Arabic press in Morocco and more broadly as a highly successful way to situate literacy within "traditional" instructional frames and produced over 200 episodes in its five-year run.[2] Lamcharki commented in an interview with a Moroccan cinema association that the state had a direct role in identifying storytelling as a lost yet revered domain among Moroccans, one in which the illiteracy fight could best be approached.[3] The interviewer praised the program for returning television viewers to their authentic and true identity through *darīja* while teaching the key educational and economic skills of *fuṣḥā*. I had no way of knowing how they assessed the effectiveness of this literacy program, but the Fassis among whom I lived felt that Arabic could be learned through this program. At the same time, they wanted me to learn about Morocco through the *darīja* storytelling. Over the last decade, I became increasingly interested in other state television programs that employed *hadra lmizān*'s rhymed prose to do Moroccanness work of connecting through "modern civic values" such as gender equity.

In Chapter 2, I analyzed the ways literacy-language ideologies shaped perceptions of news reception and what it meant to be a critical, informed, reasoning Moroccan. In this chapter, I explore how Moroccan program producers and Fassi audience members calibrated the Moroccanness feel and personhood messages of a morality register they lamented as "being lost" even as it was "revitalized" through a shift in mediums. As glossed to me by several viewers and a producer of a state-sponsored dramatic serial, *hadra lmizan* indexed the storytelling styles of an older generation in which "deep meanings" were attached to rhymed talk. State-sponsored producers recontextualized this rhymed prose from oral face-to-face contexts to mass-mediated multimodal venues, drawing on previous positive associations while attempting to accelerate new understandings of modern Moroccan civic personhood: how citizens should relate to each other and the state (Urban 2001; Goodman 2005). They employed elements and associations from previous usage, such as the morality indexed in proverb sound parallelisms, but altered the content and contexts to shape new citizen values, such as respect for diversity, the ineffectiveness of dark magic, and how to use cleverness to succeed by merit in a world marked by status and patriarchy. These contextualization processes involved remediation gaps (Gershon 2010a, 92), assumptions about what qualities of specific media can or should persist when a form moves mediums, as well as multiple ideologies of television participation frameworks. Both the remediation gaps and channel participation practices influenced Fassi responses and uptake of moral Moroccan personhood and sociality messages linked with *hadra lmizān*. Despite the producer expectations that rhymed prose would lend authority to the "modernizing" content, the Fassi viewers I encountered expressed nostalgic appreciation that their heritage was being preserved rather than a demonstrable adoption of the state's media and modernization values.

In her ethnography of U.S. youth media ideologies, Gershon argued that media were always understood in relation to other mediums, a process called remediation. The college students compared the different qualities and affordances of texts or Facebook or face-to-face breakups to make sense of others' unexpressed intentions (Gershon 2010a, 105). Similarly, discussions about the recontextualizing of *hadra lmizān* involved remediation, comparisons made between the various media in which people had experienced the speech form. However, instead of using remediation talk to understand state television's unexpressed intentions, as Gershon's youth had done, my interlocutors—Fassi viewers and television producers—employed remediation as a way to understand modalities of moral instruction. This chapter illustrates the role of remediation gaps and participant viewing ideologies to understand differing models of moral instruction mobilized to connect and make Moroccans. I present several examples of *hadra lmizān* reregistering by Moroccan state media and program uptake by Fassi viewers: one in which program producers explicitly revalorized the idea of the clever Moroccan female trickster and another that attempted to expand women's contributions to vocations, such as mechanics, deemed men's work.

Moral Rhythms of Storytelling: Market Circles and Domestic Spaces

الحلقة ١ : ارّيتَم والميزان ديال ناس لقدام

Episode 1: The Moral Rhythm of Elder's Talk

It was tea time, and Ayah's mother had laden the small table with pastries, bread, olives, boiled eggs split in half and sprinkled with salt and cumin. As she poured tea and coffee for us all, the television in the corner, tuned to one of the Moroccan national channels, 2M, contributed an additional voice to the multiple conversations that ebbed and flowed, sometimes demanding the attention of the whole group, at other moments a soundtrack backgrounding our crosstalk. As a promotional commercial for a Turkish dramatic serial began, Ayah asserted to me that everyone watches Turkish soap operas in Morocco these days (now dubbed with Moroccan voices and dialogues). When I asked her about dramatic serials based on Morocco's fabled past, like رمانة وبرطال (roumāna wabourṭāl) *or* حديدّان (hadīdān), *she admitted she didn't watch them; she worked too much at the garment factory and did not have time. She quickly followed her admission by asserting that Moroccans both young and old liked the serials, though, because they brought to life that which people no longer experienced: Moroccan life in the past, the way they used to talk in proverbs and stories to teach wisdom and morality. She felt that the new generation no longer understood these proverbs without a surrounding context to give them clues. Even though she had framed our discussion by revealing she did not watch these Moroccan historical dramas, she assertively stated that the thing she liked the most about them was the way they talked in rhymed prose:* رتم والوزن (ritm wa wazn). *She then made the following lament about the value of that way of speaking:*

The old folks were more clever than us because their speech was with wisdom and melody.	*nās lqdām dkīyyīn ʿalaynā linū hadra dyālhum kān bilḥikma walaḥn.*	ناس لقدام دكيين علينا لإنو لهدرة ديالهم كانت بالحكمة واللحن .

For Ayah, rhymed prose, the linguistic form in which Moroccans of an older era conveyed proverbs, stories, and other wisdom literature, indexed the superior communicative skills of those who used them. Since she set this within a discussion about the use of rhymed prose in a new wave of Moroccan television serials, she connected a nostalgic valence from one communicative medium (face-to-face interaction) to another (television). She did so using both an emblematic register name (اريتم والوزن [*ritm walwazn*, rhymed prose]), a chronotopic envelope indexing speakers associated with this way of speaking (ناس القدام [*nas lqdām*, the old folks]), and a positive evaluative stance toward the register (بالحكمة واللحن [*bilḥikma walaḥn*], with wisdom and melody) and its speakers (دكيين علينا [*dkīyyīn ʻalaynā*], more clever than us). Notice that she did so after explicitly stating she had not watched episodes of the television program herself but relied on chains of circulating talk about it. She may also have caught promotional ads displayed in these moments of interaction when the television served as backdrop to social visits, meal routines, and family life, but she did not state this explicitly. Ayah demonstrated an implicit ideology about what media is and does: one can know and connect with this way of speaking and the values it conveys without actually attending to the messaging content in a televisual medium. The "deep" morality of witty rhymed speaking performed previously in public market and domestic storytelling contexts had carried over into the mass-mediated venue.

Among the speech styles Moroccans associate with storytelling was *hadra lmizān*, "weighed speech."[4] It was a type of زجل (*zajal*), or oral vernacular poetry both written and spoken (Elinson 2017), historically linked with the lyrics of a "traditional" musical genre called لملحون (*lmalḥoun*) (Ennahid 2007); public market لحلقة (*lḥalqa*), "circle" performance by entertainers seeking to earn a living from commodifying their storytelling skills (Kapchan 1996); and grandmothers in domestic contexts relating morality tales (Mernissi 1994). *Hadra lmizān*, a more free verse rhyme than the *zajal* of popular poets, was also the base for proverbs circulated in everyday interactions. As glossed to me by Moroccan friends and colleagues, *hadra lmizān* entailed more than rhymed prose, weighted intonation, or a weighing of words—it included a register laden with wisdom and moral instruction, a linguistic repertoire associated with culturally salient social practices and their practitioners (Agha 2004). The performance of *hadra lmizān* by these groups (grandmothers, musicians, and street performers) had been in decline since the colonial period. Public performance entertainment spaces were circumscribed through the constraints of rapid urbanization and state security concerns, but there was also a shift in notions of taste and what it meant to be modern (Bourdieu 1986). Fassis I interviewed attributed the following factors to the register's contraction: changing kinship patterns (the shift from extended family dwellings to nuclear family apartments), the introduction of state-owned radio and television in the home, and the middle class movement away from street markets (souqs) toward European style shops with fixed prices (see also Kapchan 1996, 31; Newcomb 2017). Many Fassis referred to *hadra lmizān* as the speech of ناس القدام (*nās lqdām*, "the old folks"), a chronotopic reference to the register's generational retreat.

In 2003 UNESCO recognized the loss of public storytelling in Marrakech's famous Jamaa el Fna by deeming it an "intangible cultural heritage of humanity,"[5] though efforts for its reclamation had begun earlier by European culture makers,[6] as well as by Moroccan state-sponsored filmmakers and cultural associations. The initial state redeployment of public storytelling came in the 1970s via plays made for television, known as مسرحية البساط (*msraḥīyat lbsāṭ*, "theater of the simple"). These plays recreated Moroccan home and public square *lḥalqa* contexts. Moroccan playwright Tayyib Sadiqi made a malhoun song, الحرّاز (*lḥaraz*, "The Guardian"), into a television play starring musician al-Arabi Batma (he would later help create the populist Moroccan band Nass El Ghiwane). Television was not the only electronic media to adapt public market storytelling. Dramatist and author Mohammed Hassan al-Jundi created the popular afternoon radio theater الازلية (*alazaliya*, "The Eternal Tale"), to extend the reach of the storytelling circles he had attended growing up in Marrakesh. His "eternal tale" referred both to mythical tales and to the infinite possibilities of storytelling and used *hadra lmizān* to animate Moroccan versions of evocative tales from Arab oral heritage: the magic of rural life; the wise wanderer enchanting the sultan's court; the moral merchant's travails and triumphs; and the mortal female trickster.[7] Many Moroccans I spoke to remember fondly the imaginative flights woven by al-Jundi's oral theatrics.

The shift from face-to-face performances to electronic mediums involved assumptions about participant framework interactions (the roles and responsibilities of those engaged in and engaging the story) as well as shifts in *hadra lmizān*'s associations. In anthropology, enregisterment is a process by which distinct language styles or registers become associated with specific speaker traits and notions of personhood (Agha 2005). We link a register, or speech style, with iconic persons who use it in relation to their interactional practices. For example, we often think of youth and informal street interactions when the label "slang" appears. For many of my interlocutors, both program producers and viewers, *hadra lmizān* use evoked images of Moroccan ancestors in a "traditional" past proffering moral instruction. Of course, it helped that they bundled rhymed prose with specific dress (jallabas or kaftans), spatial configurations (storytelling circles), and temporal framings (premodern past). When Moroccan television producers made choices about what speech style to use in an interactional scene, how to "animate" a register, they indicated their position or evaluation of that register's social meanings. At the same time the process of remediation included gaps, ways in which the movement from one medium to another either made more visible or backgrounded links to those channels (Eisenlohr 2011).

The move from face-to-face tellings to other mediums involved chains of recontextualization moments. The redeploying of these storytelling techniques in new contexts linked traces of previous associations to current settings at the same time that it refashioned them as they accrued new time-space (chronotopic) alignments (Webber 1991). In a related example, Kapchan provided a detailed analysis of female herbalists' oratory strategies in the historically male-dominated marketplace of rural Beni Mellel Morocco, in which she observed the women's appropriations of male-associated genres and registers to signal authority and vulnerability. Other forms of women's public performance in the marketplace, such as female performers known as لشيخات (*ššīkhāt*), who sang in mixed-gender settings, carried associations with low culture, transgressions, and the breaking of sexual mores (Kapchan 1996, 39). The female herbalists were linked to these women because they drew attention to themselves in the public market instead of performing the quiet reserve of appropriate female behavior. Yet, the herbalist women were forced through difficult economic circumstances to sell herbs. They needed to retain their associations with morality and engage in public performance of oratory in mixed-gender settings to attract buyers and make a living. Though many of these women were formally unschooled, they performed a measure of authority associated with literacy as they used *hadra lmizān*, strategically embedding Qur'anic verses, formulaic religious aphorisms, wisdom literature, proverbs, and directives to position themselves as authoritative, respectable, and trustworthy in a social domain marked by bent truths and trickery (Kapchan 1996, 87–90).

Khalid Amine studied the ways in which North African playwrights Tayyib Sadiqqi, Ahmed Taieb el Alj, Zober Benbouchta, and Abdelkader Alloula revalorized the *lḥalqa* storytelling performance style as counterpoint to Western stage theater, creating a hybrid performance between the *lḥalqa* and staged theater (Amine 2001; Amine and Carlson 2008). In a novelistic autobiography, Moroccan sociologist Fatima Mernissi (1994) fictively recounted the domestic storytelling contexts of her childhood in the colonial past. She used the oral tradition of rhymed storytelling moments as a vehicle for discussing women's place and space, employing a reflexive, recreated childhood perplexity (through fictive dialogues) over learning gender norms for speaking and acting to explore feminist critiques of Moroccan society.

Since the rhymed prose register was linked with a specific speech genre conveyed by skilled artisans in multiple modes (sung or poetic oral storytelling), even in the past most people could not produce *hadra lmizān* themselves in a sustained way—but they valued it as part of their moral heritage. In the last decade, Moroccan state television producers have been using *hadra lmizān* and Moroccan fantasy tales to convey ideas about pluralism, gender equality, and political participation. In 2010, one of these state-sponsored storytelling serial episodes, حديدان (*ḥadīdān*), bested a televised European club football match between Barsa (Barcelona) and Real Madrid in viewership (5.5 million Moroccans were watching *ḥadīdān* instead of the football game). The program producer used this statistic to gauge the success of the storytelling genre's transfer to television and by extension the success of "modern" civic values.

الحلقة ٢: لحلقة لعصرية

Episode 2: Modernizing halqas

The end of May–beginning of June usually found the Fez medina full of tourists who had come to attend the Fez Festival of Sacred Music, a two-week showcase of spiritual performances by Moroccan and international musicians, as well as an annual conference for musical scholars. I had attended an afternoon concert at Dar Batha, an eighteenth-century summer palace–cum crafts museum in the medina, and had purchased several books at a table display. Most of the books were Moroccan novels and poetry in French, though I was excited to find two books of Moroccan folktales written in Moroccan Arabic rhymed prose by Ahmed Taieb el Alj. El Alj was born in the Fez medina and apprenticed as a carpenter before discovering the world of reading as an adult. He became one of Morocco's most beloved playwrights and media personalities. Among Moroccans he was most beloved for the lyrics he composed for famous Moroccan songs performed by Naima Samih, Latifa Raefat, and Abdelwahab Dukkali, though he also produced television plays and serialized radio dramas he personally narrated in the 1980s and '90s. The books of el Alj I purchased were a rare find: Moroccan folktales written in rhymed Arabic-script darīja *with a French poetic translation on the opposite page.*

When I brought the books to Toufiq's home, everyone loved them. Loubna asked me why I would buy such a book, and I started to explain my interest in hadra lmizān *folklore programs to them. Fatiha, Meriam's oldest daughter, said she enjoyed oral storytelling better than televised storytelling because it allowed her imagination to create a world of her own rather than that imagined by the producer. Toufiq began to ask his father, Mohammed, about the stories their uncle Titiou used to tell them years ago when they lived together in the medina, before building their house in the* ville nouvelle *neighborhood. The uncle worked as a public* hammam *(bath) manager, making a meager living, but regaling the family regularly with stories that could take several nights to finish. Mohammed said their uncle used to get his stories from* ألف ليلة وليلة ('alf layla wlayla, A Thousand and One Nights), *a collection of fantastical tales from the tenth-century Abbasid Era, and from traveling around and hearing folktales and serialized histories in the public storytelling circles of Marrakesh, Fez, and Meknes. Uncle Titiou's mother was from Marrakesh, so he traveled there occasionally. He had also memorized chapters of the Qur'an and would recount stories of Joseph and his favorite prophet, Moses. Toufiq was surprised to know that his uncle was educated, as he never observed his uncle demonstrating literacy skills while he lived with them. Everyone in the family waxed nostalgic in telling their favorite memories of the storytelling uncle. Toufiq shared a vivid memory of his uncle, who rarely watched television, setting aside time each* عيد لكبير ('īd lkbīr), *the annual Feast of the Sacrifice, to watch rebroadcasts of famous Moroccan television theater plays, among which was el Alj's play* المعلم عزوز (mu'alim azzūz).

A few weeks later I returned to their home after an interview with Moroccan television folklore serial producer Fatima Ali Boubekdi. The family asked how the interview went, and I shared with them some of what I had learned. The mother was disappointed that I didn't get a picture with her—she wanted to see what Boubekdi looked like. The discussion about her more famous programs, like رمانة وبرطال (roumāna wabourṭāl), *led to family members reminiscing about the radio plays that animated Moroccan folktales Uncle Titiou had performed for them as children.*

♣

For this family, *hadra lmizān* had explicitly fond associations with morality tales related by their uncle. They were pleased by the emergence of *hadra lmizān* in radio programs, books, and television dramatic serials and articulated the value of this way of speaking through their previous face-to-face medium. But even that form had links to other linguistic technologies: their uncle had learned some of his stories by watching Ramadan dramas and reading books. They valued the rhymed prose storytelling register for the kinds of stories they encountered: fantastical tales designed to teach the rewards of moral social relations and consequences of failing to connect appropriately. Toufiq's family held the positive associations of *hadra lmizān* that state media producers sought to mobilize for modernizing ends.

State Storytelling, Public Television, and Civic Education

Moroccan television had always been a state-sponsored venture. The first national station began broadcasting in 1962, not long after Moroccan independence from France in 1956. It began with and continues to adhere to a media-as-modernization ideology (Lerner 1958; Zaid 2010). I heard this orientation in my interviews and observations of several Moroccan media producers and viewers. In a "media as modernization" view, television's primary purpose was to socialize a modern citizenry through programs that taught literacy, civic participation, and modern values. Initially, Moroccan television did not have enough funding to produce local programs, so they purchased and broadcast international programming, primarily in French. As mentioned in Chapter 2, national television shifted to more locally produced programming, primarily in *fuṣḥā* and *darīja*, during the mid-'80s (Davis and Davis 1995; Zaid 2010). A private-public partnership created the second television station in 1989, 2M. With the advent of satellite television in the '90s, an explosion of private and national stations began to compete with Moroccan state television. In response to this, Moroccan television expanded to include a bouquet of special-interest stations, which by 2017 included the primary station Rabat, an educational/cultural channel, a religious channel, a channel for Moroccans living abroad, a sports channel, a Tamazight language channel, a channel for films, and a channel specifically for southern Morocco. There were also the quasi-private 2M in Casablanca and Medi1, a pan-Maghrib news station broadcast out of Tangier.

In 2005, the king, Mohammed VI, confirmed that television was a key element in the government's development goals. Thus television began as and continued to be public service television that some argued promoted the values of urban elites (Zaid 2009, 27–29). The idea of television as educational tool was one of the several media ideologies expressed by many Moroccans when I asked them what they thought Moroccan television's purposes should be. Thus a version of media and modernization ideology was shared by producers and consumers.

Programs were designed to elevate a presumably undereducated public. I have already described *'alif lām*, the adult literacy program that employed rhymed prose to teach *fuṣḥā* from 1999 to 2004. But that wasn't the only state program to mobilize *hadra lmizān* to teach Moroccans approved civic values. A human-interest program, أجي تشوف (*'ājī tšūf*, "come see"), appeared on the main state television channel in 2009 and highlighted the professional lives of everyday Moroccans engaged in "modern" occupations as well as "traditional" arts. I describe and analyze this in more detail later in the chapter.

In addition, independent media producer Fatima Ali Boubekdi began writing and producing several Moroccan folk heritage films and mini-series (التراث الشعبي [*turāth šša'bi*]) for television, using rhymed prose: تيغالين (*tighālīn*) (2002), عايشة دويبة (*'āīša dūwība*) (2004), أمودو (*'amūdū*) (2004), سوق النساء (*sūq nnisā'*) (2005), رمانة وبرطال (*roumāna wabourṭāl*) (2007), حديدان (*ḥadīdān*) (2010), and a spinoff series of *ḥadīdān* called نسولو حديدان (*nsūlū ḥadīdān*) (2011). During my interview with her in 2011, she said she felt like a grandmother to Moroccans, preserving the fading Moroccan Amazigh folk wisdom, fables, and expressive forms through her historical fantasy productions.[8] When I asked her why she chose an old speech style to convey contemporary ideas, she said:

> Measured speech, its rhyme, the melody that exists, it catches a child. Even if he doesn't understand the meaning, he can tell you that it's good speech. He feels it because the measurement is like a song, even if you don't understand the words, the melody takes you, the alliterative words give a rhyme, the dialogue catches people, even if they don't understand the meanings.

Boubekdi articulated a similar ideology to Ayah in the opening vignette: they both felt that people could feel the quality of the talk, even if they did not understand the content. She explicitly viewed her work as revalorizing the register, bringing it back to public space, but in this case a mass-mediated imagined public, and with stories to impart contemporary civic values. In particular, her chosen characters modeled fabled women and men in very difficult circumstances (orphaned, left to fend for themselves, born into poverty and low social rank) who used their cleverness, intelligence, and folk wisdom to achieve ascendancy in their social/spiritual worlds, as well as teach their neighbors through humorous verbal tricks.

الحلقة ٣: هدرة ومتال

Episode 3: Mediatized Proverb Talk

*For many Fassis, the best programs aired during Ramadan, the Muslim month of fasting, though they didn't always watch Moroccan series. As Chafiq's family waited patiently for the sundown call to prayer (*الأذان [al'dhān]*) that would announce to everyone to break the fast, they passed the time by watching television. A big tureen of* لحريرة (lḥarīra), *a tomato and chickpea soup, sat on the table next to multiple serving dishes of dates, flatbreads, juice, milk, and* لسلّو (ssillū), *a toasted flour, nuts, and seeds mixture made especially to boost energy* *during Ramadan. Even though Chafiq lamented the poor quality of Moroccan Ramadan programs, his family always had the television tuned to Rabat or 2M when the sundown prayer approached and while they broke the fast.*

One of the programs that aired after al'dhān *was Boubekdi's,* nsūlū ḥadīdān, *a series of ten-minute episodes contextualizing a Moroccan proverb with a story set in the mythical Moroccan past and ending with a riddle. In mediatized multimodal fashion, the riddle's answer could then be texted via phone to win 1,000 MAD (about $125). It aired just as people would have finished breaking their fast and before heading to the mosque for prayer. Every episode was titled with the proverb being explained, but each proverb was a slight variation on other versions, adapted for what she imaged were more contemporary sensibilities. That evening the episode illustrated the principle "buyer beware," or that people should not buy something simply to demonstrate their financial prowess, and was titled using a Moroccan proverb. Boubekdi took the title from a longer proverb:*

Don't buy until you've tried, or don't buy until you've searched.	*mātšrī ḥtā tjarrab, āw mātšrī ḥtā tqalab.*	ما تشري حتى تجرب او ما تشري حتى تقلب.

Chafiq later recounted the proverb to me as something like this:

Don't punch until you get close, don't plant until you fence, and don't make friends until you test them.	*mā ḍrrab ḥtā tqarrab wamā tzra' ḥtā tzarab wamā tṣaḥḥab ḥtā tjarrab.*	ما ضرب حتى تقرب وما تزعر حتى تُزَرَب ما تصحب حتى تجرب

The televisual story began with Hadidan, the main Joha-like character,[9] *dressed in "traditional" Amazigh clothing, sitting on the ground under an awning, sharing tea with some friends in a rural retrojection of a contemporary cafe setting. Set in a mythical rural past, Hadidan was relating to his friends what an amazing sheep he had to slaughter during the coming Eid al-Adha, the feast of sacrifice.*[10] *His poetic description had them all encouraging him to sell it, each besting the other in the amount they would pay for his amazing ram. A Jewish neighbor sitting in another corner of the awning "café" overheard them talking and offered to buy it for more than all the others. The assumption in the story was that Jews were typed as hagglers and would plan to sell it for an even higher price. He wanted to see it first, but Hadidan convinced him to buy it sight-unseen. After paying the agreed-upon price, Issac the Jew was angered to find out he had been tricked into buying a tiny sheep through Hadidan's clever words. Isaac took him to the local judge for redress. While the story didn't show the arbitration, it did include a post-mediation dialogue in which Hadidan had clearly won the case and began moralizing. After revealing Isaac's foolishness, Hadidan taught him and the audience by relating this modified version of the proverb:*

Don't trust until you try, don't punch until you get close, and don't buy until you check it out.	*mā tiqš ḥtā tjarrab wamā ḍrrab ḥtā tqarrab mā tšrī ḥtā tqallab.*	ما تيق حتى تجرب و ما ضرب حتى تقرب ما تشري حتى تقلب

Everyone in Chafiq's family was relaxing around the table after breaking the fast, except his father, who had slipped into the other room to pray. It was still an hour before he would go to تراويح (tarāwīḥ), *the extended ritual prayers observed at the mosque during Ramadan. Chafiq's mother was joking with her five-year-old granddaughter, and Chafiq was only half-listening to* nsūlū ḥadīdān. *When he heard the final proverb, he laughed out loud, noting how many Fassis are taken in by clever words. His mother looked up briefly and started recounting a story about someone selling diluted honey in the market, and how often Moroccans buy before they test it out. The moralizing tale resonated with Chafiq's family, even though they didn't participate in the riddle contest or note at the time the way they and Boubekdi reworked the proverb from agrarian social relations to contemporary consumer cash-based interactions. They were so embedded in the latter context and so ideologically attuned to proverbs as fixed genres that the modern consumer capitalist reworking seemed unremarkable.*

♣

As Bauman has noted, proverbs are a genre we often describe as fixed in nature (2004). However, the moments in which they are deployed, by whom, for which purpose, and in which linguistic form can tell us a great deal about the work involved in understanding and creating texts-in-context—as well as the kinds of persons such texts seek to connect. Proverbs are an interactional accomplishment that require an audience to perceive of similarities between instances of proverb usage while recognizing how it fits with the new context, or how the new contexts relate to previous usages. In Episode 3, Chafiq's family connected with the Hadidan proverb in rhymed prose by relating to the moral cautionary message: don't be a hasty consumer. But they initially missed the ways the proverb had been modified both in linguistic form ("plant" became "buy") and social application (agrarian sociality vs. impersonal cash consumer). By making the rhymed prose interpretation into a monetized riddle contest one needed a phone to participate in, Boubekdi was foregrounding a particular way of Moroccan relatedness even as she sought to revalorize the wisdom of the ancients. Those with mobile phones and the money to connect via texting were foregrounded in this sociality moment, even as she sought to instruct Moroccans about wise consumer practices. This metacultural work

(Urban 2001) of making equivalence judgments about contexts of proverb usage also involves background interactional histories that vary. Intertextual gaps (Briggs and Bauman 1992) are created when associations differ between viewers' and producers' knowledge of spoken genre forms (proverbs), their previous meanings, and the meaning of changes introduced through alterations to proverb content. While this was a simple example of an intertextual gap arising in mass-mediated interactions, it provides a framework for thinking about the connection problems in other moments between genres, forms, mass-mediated modalities, and audience reception contexts.

Rhymed prose was not only saved for proverbs or storytelling during this period: I observed it in mobile phone advertising campaigns, by a Radio Aswat call-in music dedication host, in human interest television programs, and in a television political talk show where host Mustafa al-Alawi recounted politician Nabil Ben Abdullah's career highlights. Though I found the use of rhymed prose interesting in these different genres, I never heard or observed Moroccans talking about these as examples of *hadra lmizān*, associating them with wisdom talk or a nostalgic past. As I spoke about *ḥadīdān* programs with Fassis, I found that many audience members who lamented to me on previous occasions that Moroccan life used to be better, more pure, and moral expressed positive associations of the poetic *hadra lmizān* form in mythic storytelling. They connected rhymed prose with a mythical and moral past because media producers like Boubedki bundled it with "traditional" clothes (many of which continue to be worn by Fassis), rural settings, and proverbs familiar enough to be recognized by at least some family members.

Storytelling Speech: Gender Equity Tales

Public street storytelling, as an interactional genre and vehicle for moral and cultural transmission in Morocco, had entailed multiple channels: visual, oral, and aural. It also involved multiple modes of use within each channel (the oral channel could be used to sing, chant, or speak linguistic features, the visual channel could be used to write, mime, enact, emote story elements), as well as a variety of linguistic codes (*darīja*, unmarked French-Arabic *darīja*, Tashelhit/Tarafit/Tamazight). Like most other identified registers, speakers who used rhymed storytelling prose coordinated sign systems into a multimodal and multimedia communicative array (Agha 2004, 31): they used vocal quality, gesture, dress, bodily comportment, and gaze to create character and morality distinctions. *Darīja* included noun and verb number and gender word endings that made naturally occurring rhymes frequent even in everyday conversation.

As described in ethnographic and biographical accounts, the public street storytelling genre employed the rhymed prose register in creative weaving with other speech styles (such as proverbs, wisdom literature, Quranic quotation, petitionary prayers known as الدوع (*ddu'a*), musical jingos, and spontaneous dance performances), to draw participants into an interactive space لحلقة (*lḥalqa*) in which the audience was expected to engage, encourage, respond, and act in relation to the tale and performer (Amine 2001; Amine and Carlson 2008; Kapchan 1996; Mernissi 1994). Street performers, and even domestic storytellers to some extent, might attract an audience through long extensions of a formulaic introduction, brief musical preludes, bawdy humor, event declarations, and directive calls to passersby. A formulaic introduction may have signaled the shift to performance through *hadra lmizān* and eventually moved into a freeform speaking that occasionally called on the features of rhymed prose to create associations with deep meanings without having to sustain the format throughout the program. As with English fairy tales, there was usually an element of chronotopic reference, creating temporal-spatial links between story-time and present tellings ("once upon a time" frames). Backchannel comments by the audience were interwoven by the storyteller to create morality moments in the tale, and the ending usually involved a collaborative moral evaluation.

I recorded an example of *hadra lmizān* in an introductory frame from a storytelling festival in Rabat in 2010, in which the storyteller interwove a formulaic rhyme scheme and stock phrases with the names of countries represented at the festival.[11]

There was, O gentlemen, even a time	*'īwā kān yā sīyādī ḥatā kān*	وا كان يا سيادي حتى كان !
even as God was in every place	*ḥatā kān allah fkul mkān*	حتى كان الله فكُل مْكان
there was even basil and iris	*ḥatā kān lḥabq wlsūsān*	حتى كان الحبق والسوسان
in the lap of the chosen and beloved prophet	*fḥajr nnabī lmuṣṭafā l'adnān*	فحجر النبي المصطفى العَدْنَانْ
when waters flowed in the garden of Salwan	*ḥatā kānit mīyāh dāfqā fjnān lsalwān*	حتى كانت مْيَاه دافقا فجنان السَلْوان
and birds trilled blissfully the tunes	*waṭīyūr rāyqā tirtil lḥān*	وطْيور رايقا ترتل ألحان
the blissful melodies well-made and measured	*bnaghām rāyqā mḥakūma lwazān*	بنغام رايقا محكومْةْ لوزان
there was, O gentlemen, even a festival	*ḥatā kān yā sīyādī wāḥd lmahrajān*	حتى كان يا سيادي واحد المهرجان
gathering five countries, Morocco, Algeria, Tunisia, Libya and Mauritania	*jma' khamsā dbuldān, lmaghrib, ljzā'ir, tūnis, lībyā wamūrīṭān*	جمع خمسا دلبلدان، المغرب، الجزائر، تونس، ليبا، وموريطان

This folktale performance began with a Moroccan discourse marker: إوا (*'īwā*), "so" spoken with rising-falling-rising intonation pattern, and signaled initiation of the speaker's turn. When followed by reduplicated past tense forms, كان حتى كان (*kān ḥata kān*), "there was even there was" and vocative يا (*ya*), "O," it became a story initiation cue. This could also be surmised by the surrounding participant context: a female narrator in Moroccan kaftan sitting in a large throne-like chair, audience opposite in rows of folding chairs, with lights and cameras trained on the stage. The narrator held a large book in her hands, acting as though she was reading the story from it rather than reciting from memory. Yet the phrases were so well-known as folktale formula that she stared at the audience as she spoke, turning her head to engage all. She invoked the Prophet Muhammad and nature as temporally placed witnesses to the events of the story. Each phrase ended with a rhyming—*ān* sound: *wlsusān, lsalwān, lwazān, lmahrajān*. The narrator adapted the last two lines to fit the rhyme, but included words with distinctively modern indexes: festivals organized by the state (see Boum 2012) and the name of North African postcolonial states—Tunis, Libya, Algeria, Morocco, and Mauritania (slightly modified to fit the *-ān* rhyming pattern). This last move contextualized the storytelling formula to that audience and storytelling festival. The audience responded with shouts and laughter, encouraging the narrator to continue. These kinds of cues illustrated the ways storyteller and audiences understood their participant roles, with the audience response an essential part of the narrated flow.

I turn now to the ways in which state storytellers sought to draw in a mass-mediated crowd in order to rework notions about gender equity. There have been a number of Moroccan films since the 1980s whose explicit aim was to raise the image and status of women in the country through positive female characters set in the mythical past. In *roumāna wabourṭāl*, produced and directed by Boubekdi for Moroccan national television's Ramadan programming in 2007, the focus was on a Moroccan female trickster, Roumana, and her simple cousin, Bertal. The setting was a southern Moroccan village often indexical of Tashelhit speakers, yet all the characters spoke *darīja*, reflecting the media assumptions of the 2M producers related in the introduction: the language with the widest mass media reach in Morocco was *darīja*. The heroine was born into poverty and low social rank, but used her cleverness, intelligence, and folk wisdom to succeed in her social and spiritual world (she even tricked Moroccan ghouls). Boubekdi conveyed to me that she reversed the moral hierarchies in this tale in order to challenge viewers: she revealed the ghoul to have goodness, and the girl avoided socially stigmatizing scrapes and ended up marrying the local judge in a Moroccan version of Cinderella.

Her television storytelling performance used Ramadan series advertising clips to draw an audience, relying on musical jingos/lyrics and visual storytelling to engage a non-present audience. While we may think of mass-mediated television as engaging multiple modalities to greater effect, Boubekdi explained that the televisual channel privileged sight but also constrained the storytelling modalities to the producer's own imagination (echoing Fatiha's observation in Episode 2). This contributed to the re-registering process in that the program writer chose to link new messages about Moroccan civic personhood (gender equity, etc.) to the positive associations of moral instruction in *hadra lmizān* forms. Since these forms often included difficult phrases and archaic words, television producers could utilize visual explanatory props and camera angles to animate the register in ways that face-to-face storytellers could not. As all good storytellers, they could also rework the storylines to convey particular meanings. Boubekdi recounted making a handicapped boy the vehicle for keen, insightful, witty commentary in one of her mythical series in order to invert a widely circulated perception that physical disabilities equate to mental deficiencies.

Although the interactions in these serials included non-rhymed phrases, Boubekdi explicitly sought to weave rhymed proverbs, oral wisdom phrases, and rhymed prose dialogues throughout scenes, explicitly evoking *hadra lmizān* in boundary moments, such as introduction and closing scenes, and key scene climax moments. In the introduction played at the beginning of every episode, a man's disembodied voice backed by a single string instrument signaled the street performance oral mode. The content itself referenced a time before recorded speech and explicitly associated social order with mythical morality tales related by elders. In other words, a new generation needed to learn from the proverbs, wisdom, speech styles, and stories not recorded in formal literacy registers, but through talk (Boubekdi's version of *liḥtikāk*). The introductory metaphors drew on what Flagg Miller called scriptive aesthetics, evoking writing through speech (W. F. Miller 2007, 53), and chronotopic space-time envelopes situated how an interlocutor was to understand the utterance in relation to the present moment. In this case, morality time was constructed with writing references backgrounded: "Long ago, before men registered knowing through pens" (*fayām zmām qabl mîyta'lam linsān yzamam blqlām*), wisdom was not preserved through wooden slates (*lûwhā*, index of Moroccan literacy practices in the precolonial past), but with speech forms made explicit as genres. By referencing a time before recorded speech, the introduction explicitly associated the social order with morality tales of elders and those who memorized their rhymed prose stories. Yet the irony was that this storytelling event was written as a scenario script and involved participants (producer, director, actors, camera and lighting technicians, film editors, promotional technicians) whose skills emerged through a series of written and oral literacy practices and events—all of which was backgrounded in the storytelling product.

Measured speech: Long ago, long ago	*hadra lmizān: hadā šḥāl hadā šḥāl*	هدرة الميزان: هدا شحال، هدا شحال
(visual image of main female character in a wheat field, contemplatively gazing off into the distance)		
in the times before man learned to record/register with a pen	*fīyām zmām qabl mīyta'lam l'insān yizamam bilqlām*	فيام زمان قبل ما يتعلم الأنسان يزمم بالقلام
(scene of two mythical jinn[a] talking together, followed by the young heroine sitting behind a masculine-like ghoul telling a story)		
wise people were thinking wisely	*kānū l'aqāl yikhamū takhmām*	كانو العقّال يخمو تخمام
(men of high social standing sitting in a circle counseling together in a well-decorated adobe home).		
And they created stories and illusions from imagination	*yinzlū min lkhyāl ḥikayāt wawhām*	ينزلو من لخيال حكيات و وهام
(female storyteller in a wealthy home with all the female household members gathered around).		
They organized it in speech and the understanding ones memorized them	*naḍmūhā fiklām waḥafḍūhā lfhām*	نضموها فكلام وحفضوها الفهام
(young heroine lying on the ground with a sheer green veil over her face, which she slowly removed)		
And left them as heritage from generation to generation	*wakhalūhā wirt min jiyāl ljiyāl*	وخلوها ورت من جيال لجيال
(young heroine in a cave recounting a tale to the ghoul).		
Follow with me, every night we narrate threads of a tale and beautiful story	*ṭib'ū m'āyā kūlā laylā nsardū khīyūṭ ḥikāyā waqiṣa jamīla*	تبعو معايا كولا ليلا نسردو خيوط حكايا و قصة جميلة
(single close-up shot of masculine ghoul turning back to heroine, followed by scene of veiled heroine speaking to an audience).		
Lucky is the one who drinks deeply and understands the words of the ancients	*s'adāt īllī rūwā wafhum klām lqdām*	سعدات اللي روا و فهم كلام لقدام
(Scene of woman stepping out of house guarded by two male servants to overlook terraced mountain fields, followed by scene of heroine and three young girls surrounding a fire in a dugout house. The introduction moved into a folk song with iconic links to folk singing group Nas al-Ghiwane tunes, and as the music picked up, the scene showed two men talking with the village fields in the background.)		
Song: Roumana and Bertal, Roumana and Bertal	*roumāna wabourṭāl roumāna wabourṭāl*	الأغنية: رمانا وبرطال، رمانا وبرطال
(montage of Pomegranate and Sparrow, names of female heroine and her simple-minded male cousin)		
Story and speech (Berber performance marker) and a lot (old term) of talk. Story and speech (Berber performance marker) and a lot (old term) of talk.	*qiṣā waḥadīt waḥadīt '* *āwāwā wašlā klām qiṣā* *waḥadīt waḥadīt 'āwāwā* *wašlā klām*	قصا و حديت و حديت أواوا و شلا كلام قصا و حديت و حديت أواوا و شلا كلام
(Close-up montage of individual characters speaking and/or contemplating others speech.)		
Wisdom and proverb, wisdom and proverb	*ḥikma wamitāl, ḥikma wamitāl,*	حكمة و متال، حكمة و متال
(montage of group interactional settings, primarily of storytelling settings)		
that are not preserved on slates or registered	*mā mā maḥfūḍa fluwāḥ mā zummhā zmām.*	ما ما محفوضة فلوحا ما زممها زمام
(montage of group interactional settings, mostly storytelling settings)		

[a]Jinn are mentioned in the Qur'an as beings of fire created before humans, some of whom felt slighted that God gave stewardship of the earth to beings of clay and dirt (humans) rather than the jinn (beings of fire). In some Moroccan traditions, jinn are malevolent or at least very temperamental creatures that afflict humans, possessing humans to satisfy their desires, and creating trouble for them (Mateo-Dieste 2013, 240–60; Rausch 2000).

In her efforts to make *hadra lmizān* accessible to a supposedly unfamiliar audience, Boubekdi utilized repetition of metered lines both for lyrical structure and as a mnemonic aid. But she also evoked repetition iconically to demonstrate the practices of storytelling, in which tales are told repeatedly. In addition, she relied on Arabic cognate accusatives (grammatical structures that employ a verb followed by an object noun derived from that same verb) for both poetic effect and to aid understanding of archaic terms in which the noun form may have been more known in contemporary usage than the verb form: زممها زمام (*zumumhā zmām*), "registered on slates." Despite the overall frame of an idealized past, Boubekdi wrote the introduction script employing habitual aspect verbs (يزمم، يخمو، ينزلو [*yizamam, yikhamū, yinzilū*]) in which the action was ongoing and incomplete, constructing a timelessness to these practices and their relevance. In other words, she was trying to connect contemporary Moroccans to a way of speaking and relating she assumed they might not fully understand.

After the program introduction, the interactions switched to conversational dialogue, but retained some of the rhythmic qualities of rhymed prose. The intervisual and chronotopic program precursor to *hadra lmizān* mentioned previously, the adult literacy program *'alif lām* narrated by Naima Lmcharki, provided a format for switching between storytelling rhythmed introductions and poetic conversational enactments. As part of the enregisterment process, *'alif lām*'s language style and scene settings offered indexical frames for a nostalgic mythical past, domestic space, and storytelling as moral genre. Boubekdi's opening montage created a new transmission link for these "oral" tales through intervisuality, drawing visual and discursive associations together. The key was educating a new generation, no longer as widely socialized to this register, through the fusing of television/cinema's visual storytelling as cue to *hadra lmizān* meanings. She illustrated the lyrical meter with a montage from series episodes (a woman relating a story to jinn and ghouls or to other household members, montages of conversational moments). The "deep meanings" of the genre were made explicit through the introduction in both the rhymed form and the content: new generations need to learn from the proverbs, speech styles, and stories recorded not in face-to-face registers or wooden slates, but through talk produced by someone who could not hear them, but imagined their responses in scripting the story. State television would help them connect in better ways to each other and modern values. *Hadra lmizān* linked with mythic stories was a way to do so, even as the messaging content socialized them into modern citizen values.

Another Moroccan television program to adapt *hadra lmizān* forms for moral ends was the civic education series أجي تشوف (*'ā jī tšūf*), "come see." It aired on Rabat, "the first" Moroccan state station, usually in the late afternoon and early evening, during prime Moroccan visiting hours, when Fassi women often visited each others' homes for tea. The program typically began with a short two-minute narration in *hadra lmizān*, in which a disembodied female voice introduced the profession or person through a rhymed prose riddle, extolling the advantages and struggles of the individual in navigating social, familial, and/or economic expectations. The format then switched registers to a non-narrated day-in-the-life—style reporting: the camera wordlessly following the Moroccan in her/his interactions and activities while each provided her/his own meta-narrative and reflexive accounts of interactions. There were continuous camera shots, instead of the edited shifting vantages of dramatic serials, and little outside narrative after the initial *hadra lmizān* framing. These episodes were brief (no more than twenty minutes) and ranged from following a Marrakeshi participant/organizer of a volunteer, all-male religious musical street performances[12] or a day in the life of a female mechanic to the motivations and strategies of a young, veiled, female chess champion.

In the following example, a female mechanic was praised not only for improving herself by entering a domain of men but for seeking in collaboration with those men to advance the field. Instead of the formulaic storytelling introduction of dramatic serials, this piece began with an educational proverb with chronotopic associations of a generic moral past (اللي تزادت فالراس كيتنفع [*īllī tzādat frrās kitnaf'a*], "whatever is added to the mind benefits"). The proverb was then explicitly restated in contemporary straightforward imagery (واللي تعلمها الإنسان ضروري يلكاها [*waīllī ta'alimhā l'īnsān ḍarūrī yilkāhā*], "whatever a human learns he will definitely use") and linked to "modern life" (العصرية گدّات الكفات الحياة الوقت [*lwaqt walḥayāt l'aṣrīya kadāt lkfāt*], "time and modern life equalize the scales") while retaining the *hadra lmizān* rhythm—all in an attempt to break down gendered profession norms. In this civic instructional moment, the producers used *hadra lmizān* and a known proverb, both adapted to "modern" values, in order to argue that learning of any kind, in this case, manual skills training in mechanics, is available for both boys and girls.

1	Whatever is added to the mind will benefit (proverb)	*īllī tzādat frrās kitnaf'a*	اللي تزادت فالراس كيتنفع
2	whatever a human learns he will definitely use	*waīllī ta'alimhā l'īnsān ḍarūrī yilkāhā*	واللي تعلمها الإنسان ضروري يلكاها
3	if he doesn't benefit himself, others will, and all will benefit	*īlā manf'a bihā rāsū yanf'a bihā ghīrū wakulshî kitnaf'a*	إلا منفع بها راسو ينفع بها غيرو و كلشي كيتنفع
4	time and modern life equalized the scales	*lwaqt walḥayāt l'aṣrīya kadāt lkfāt*	الوقت و الحياة العصرية كدات الكفات

5	it became for the girls as for the boys	*wlā kīf lwalād kīf lbanāt*	ولا كيف لولاد كيف لبنات
6	they are all the same if they study, learn, and have skills and capabilities	*kulhum bḥāl bḥāl mdām qrāūw wat'almū wa'andhum mūwāhīb watqāt*	كلهم بحال بحال مدام قراو وتعلمو و عندهم مواهيب و طقات
7	and it's not strange or difficult for girls to become specialists	*ūw māšī gharīb wamāšī ṣ'aīb 'ālbanāt ykūnū ḥarīfāt*	او ماشي غريب و ماشي صعيب عالبنات يكونو حريفيات
8	even in mechanics, which is purely a man's job, they show capabilities	*wafalmīkānīk īllī ḥirf rajālīya ymatiyāz yibīnū fīhā 'īmkāniyāt*	و فالميكانيك اللي حرفة رجالية بمتياز، يبينو فيها إمكانيات
9	they gain the trust of clients and improve their skills	*yiksabū tiqā lkliyān wayaṭawarū lmahārāt*	يكسبو تقة الكلِيان و يطورو المهارات
10	Mechanics is a sector with its own basics and rules	*lmakānīk qṭā'a 'andū 'āṣūlū waqawānīnū*	المكانيك قطاع عندو اصولو و قوانينو
11	and mechanic Khadija not only entered the job, studied, learned and kept quiet	*wakhadīja lmakānīkiya māšī ghīr dakhlāt lḥirfa qarāt ta'lamāt wsktāt*	و خديجة المكانيكية ماشي غير دخلات الحرفة، قرات و تعلمات و سكتات
12	she entered its world among the men and with them she began thinking about the rules and tools to organize it	*lakn dakhlāt l'ilmhā wabayn rjālhā bdāt m'ahum fatafkīr fšurṭ tanẓīm lqṭā'a wlāliyāt*	لكن دخلات لعلمها و بين رجالها و بدات معهم فالتفكير فشروط تنظيم القطاع والآليات
13	so, come and see	*'īwā 'ājī tšūf.*	إوا أجي تشوف

In this introduction to the program, the writer employed a rhyming *-āt* pattern, though not consistently. There were a few lines in which the speech did not rhyme, potentially signaling that content was more important than poetics. Just as the rhymed prose of the festival cited earlier in the chapter, the *'īwā* discourse marker was an initiation to turn-taking, but in this case it was used at the end of the rhymed prose segment to signal a genre change out of the female-narrator rhymed prose into everyday talk. Linked with a second-person command form, the last phrase invited the viewer to enter the visually narrated story that was to follow. In contrast to the folktale series of Boubekdi, this program emphasized real-time talk in order to foreground its civic message: come see how women are working in any domain. The didactic nature of the program reflected formal educational models, in which a specialist (teacher) imparted information and the viewer (student) internalized it. This contrasted against the interactional pedagogy of *liḥtikāk* discussed in Chapter 2, in which one learned through dialogue and debate with members of one's community. Come and see modern civic equality, but only at a distance.

Evaluating Speech of the Past: كلام الزمان (*Klām Azzamān*)

الحلقة ٣: لفيلم ولعائلة

Episode 3: Film and Family

On a different day, I sat visiting in a cafe with a Moroccan university professor and colleague. We ordered ice cream and caught up on our academic projects and family lives. I asked about these Moroccan historical-folklore series, and she confirmed that her own eight-year-old son watched them with his aunt and grandmother, who served as his caretakers when she was teaching. She did not watch the programs herself partly because of time constraints, but she appreciated a Moroccan-produced program that ended positively, without tragedy. Most Moroccan productions were French-inspired products of the realism that had been a hallmark of so many Moroccan filmmakers and discouraged many Moroccans from enjoying their own film markets (Dwyer 2004).

My colleague remarked that she noticed her two-year-old son seemed more interested in following the Moroccan series than adults or teenagers. Her observation was that perhaps he was attracted to the darīja, *or the bright colors of the sets. But she said what she noticed most was how many people were following the Turkish and Mexican series. Her mother-in-law followed the Turkish ones every day, and she cared for both boys sometimes, so they were following them as well. She was concerned, as her older son would ask her questions spurred by the Turkish dramas, such as can your younger sister get pregnant without being married? Then he would say that on such and such series the young Muslim girl had a baby and she wasn't married. She said she was constantly having to explain that this was not in accordance with Muslim religious law (*غير شرعي *[*ghīr šar'ī*]). On a different occasion, when my colleague's father died, her eight-year-old son asked why she and the other women didn't go to the burial, since women in the Turkish series did. She had to explain again that in Islam, women don't go to the burial. She then told him that perhaps because they have lots of Christians in Turkey they had been influenced by other customs and didn't know proper Islamic practice. She herself didn't know that but needed to come up with an explanation.*

*My colleague lamented that her unmarried aunt did nothing but follow the dramatic series. She gently mused that she didn't know if Moroccan women did that because they were seeking to escape from their unfulfilled lives, since they seemed to "live" (*عايش *[*'āyīsh*]) in the film, or if they were just bored. Perhaps they followed these soap operas because many of the Mexican and Turkish serials were now dubbed into Moroccan Arabic (C. Miller 2012), though they followed the Lebanese-dubbed Turkish films on MBC and then again when 2M* *rebroadcast them. She then added that maybe the reason they followed the Turkish and Mexican films more than Moroccan dramatic series was because the former had more episodes (around 30) and ran for longer during the year, whereas the Moroccan folklore series were shorter (four episodes) and showed primarily during Ramadan. She seemed to think the Mexican and Turkish series were not a good influence on children, because there were inappropriate relations and discussions in the series that modeled bad behavior and talk, and without parental supervision and explanation about what was immoral about that, kids could become confused. She felt it was more dangerous in* darīja, *because kids understood more and might pick up bad words or behaviors more easily.*

A friend told my colleague she shouldn't judge the dramatic series without watching them, so she tried to follow a series for a few days but could not finish because the material was hard for her to watch morally. She went on to claim that the high number of foreign soap operas dubbed into Arabic was a political move by the government to distract people from the real issues of civic development. My colleague mentioned Fatima Ali Boubekdi's folklore productions and said she had succeeded in one thing: making positive Moroccan series and films—it was nice to see something positive, modeling how people could succeed with cleverness. She wasn't sure people actually followed the programs to know if the stories told in the film were the same ones related to them as children by their grandmothers. In mentioning this, she recognized that storytelling forms changed based on the participant framework. At this point in our conversation, her sister brought the children to the café. She asked her eight-year-old if he liked ḥadīdān *or the Turkish and Mexican series better. He was very shy and didn't want to respond at first, but then he said he liked the Turkish and Mexican series better. When pressed as to why, he said the story was better.*

♣

In these examples and analyses of state television–sponsored programs, producers employed Moroccan rhymed prose and rhythmic speech to convey a mix of nostalgia for the ways in which wisdom was imparted in the past and contemporary educated elite values about Moroccanness: how modern citizens should think and act in relation to each other. I actually began analyzing these examples of state storytelling speech because I noticed varied Fassi responses to these programs in my viewing of television programs with them. *ʿĀīša dūwība*, one of Boubekdi's first series, came out in 2004, during my first year of fieldwork. At the time, if a family or individual wanted to watch a program after it aired on national television or on one's own time, they had to purchase an informal economy product called a VCD, a lower-resolution video format compressed to fit on a 700MB CD and played on an inexpensive VCD player.[13] Most of the time VCDs were pirated versions of films or music clips snatched from production sites, television broadcasts, or cinemas arriving via migration and contraband routes. Toufiq's friend Mustafa purchased a VCD of *'āīša dūwība* in January 2005, and then shared it with Toufiq and other friends and families. He did so because, he declared, it was difficult to find clean, family-friendly, positive-ending Moroccan programs. I noticed later, after repeatedly encountering the media and modernization ideologies of Moroccan television producers and analyzing the content of these storytelling programs, that he made no mention of the female trickster or "modern" civic values of these series. He didn't see gender equality as a "modern" civic value, but rather calibrated Moroccanness as elevating women by preserving their cleverness for what they choose to apply it toward rather than what "liberals" tried to impose.

That pushed me to ask how a subset of the target Moroccan audiences (presumed masses who needed education in appropriate Moroccanness) responded to these efforts at state storytelling. Even though media producers presumed undereducated Moroccan viewers, the mass-disseminated medium of television allowed for any number of possible viewers (including foreigners like myself). Did mobilizing the particular visual and storytelling affordances of television increase absorption of the producers' intended values and beliefs? Did Moroccans identify these civic virtues when producers coupled an old linguistic form with state-of-the-art technologies?

Of course, television talk occurred not just in viewing moments, but both preceding and subsequent to program airings, in taxis, buses, service encounters, workplaces, and homes. It was part of the interactional norms for small talk in Morocco life. Sometimes I initiated commentary from my Moroccan interlocutors: elites, producers, educated and "undereducated" viewers. At other moments, these emerged in the flow of everyday exchanges. Part of what I observed was the way in which viewing practices reflected an implicit media ideology about television. Most of the families who graciously allowed me to observe and record their television engagements did not see viewing as an activity in and of itself. Television was the background to social interactions, a potential interlocutor in group discussion, but the focus was on being attentive to and orienting to one's present family members and friends. In fact, as I reviewed my fieldnotes of television talk from 2004 to 2017, I encountered a common critique of people who عايش ('āyīsh), "live" in programs. They were censured for becoming too involved in following a serialized program or film at the expense of their other interactions. One way this media ideology was articulated to me was that television served as one contributor in an ongoing, emergent, and dynamic interaction. Sometimes the program content, style, and language were foregrounded by family members and at other times backgrounded in the flow of everyday meals, homework, talk about the day, political debates, and gossip.

With that in mind, I turn to my ethnographic accounts of viewer response to *hadra lmizān* programming. I observed not a single family who watched these programs attentively all the way through. Individuals followed content more closely than others, but since every family I knew placed the television in the salon that doubled as a dining room and sometimes sleeping quarters, disruptions from meals and cross-conversations and activities that occurred at the same time as television programs were the norm. Even when the focus was on relaxing through watching television, whoever had the remote control rarely left the television on a single channel all the way through a scene, as other family members would ask them to find something more interesting or provide an evaluative comment that would spark a discussion.

الحلقة ٤: افريل ٢٠١١

Episode 4: April 2011

One evening I sat with a family watching television while sharing tea together: mint green tea with copious amounts of sugar, me drinking lemon verbena herbal tea, and everyone munching on homemade sponge-pancakes covered in olive oil and honey called بغرير (baghrir), *and bread with* Le vache qui rit *cheese. The father and one of the sons slipped into the other room to pray the* maghib *(sunset) prayer. The mother, Zahra, her two daughters, and forty-year-old younger sister, Amina, and I began discussing Moroccan television stations' interest in Turkish serials and their dubbing them into* darīja. *Everyone expressed dislike for the new trend, even needling one of the daughters for her previous interest in them—which she fervently decried. Zahra mentioned Mexican soap operas as also being immoral, pointing to one named Diablo as emblematic of the genre. One of the daughters had used the remote to change from Moroccan television to a popular Syrian historical dramatic serial,* bab al-hara,[14] *while we talked. Amina teased one of her nieces about devotedly following* bāb al-hāra. *The niece justified her interest by saying that Syria historical dramas were moral and historical, while Turkish serials were fictional and modeled too much like Mexican telenovelas.*

During a lull in our conversation, the fifteen-year-old daughter who was channel-surfing with the remote turned back to the Moroccan national station Rabat. After the 8 P.M. *news in* fuṣḥā, *there was a series of ads for upcoming public events: the Mawazine pop music festival in Rabat and a comedy festival in Marrakech (which featured French-Moroccan actor/comedian Jamal Debouze).*

No one paid much attention to these ads except to agree briefly that public intellectuals who protested these events had one valid point. The state shouldn't be investing millions of dirhams in festivals that bring in foreign talent when there were so many unemployed and poor Moroccans (see Boum 2012). While we could hear the sounds of the father and brother praying in the other room, Amina asked if the Moroccan series episode rerun that just came on was from roumāna wabourṭāl. *Zahra said yes, and the fifteen-year-old daughter said no, it was* ḥadīdān, *and then claimed she had never watched a single episode. The mother asked where the remote was, and then said, "Let's watch something better than this," and changed it to the transnational Saudi-funded religious station Iqra, which was broadcasting a religious lecture on proper ways to care for one's elderly parents. We watched in silence until the men returned from prayer.*

A week later I was with Zahra and her thirty-year-old son when we went to visit her brother and sister-in-law in another city one evening. As we sat around visiting, drinking tea, and talking politics and family news, the television was on in the other salon entertaining her brother's toddler children. Zahra's brother talked about the unemployment problem in Morocco, relying on statistics he explicitly stated he learned from watching a state television news magazine program. At one point the conversation shifted to a discussion about how much Moroccan crown prince Moulay Hassan followed ḥadīdān, *such that (as was reported in Moroccan television according to the uncle) he gave a much coveted lifetime taxi license to the main actor and had his picture taken with him. They all then began to discuss how much they liked the idea of* ḥadīdān *and similar serials, like* roumāna wabourṭāl *and* 'āīša dūwība, *coming up with the series names even though they all admitted they didn't watch them. Zahra's sister-in-law mentioned how much she appreciated the presentation of Moroccan heritage, which she further glossed as the Moroccan proverbs and folktales, in these programs. No one else was preserving their heritage like Boubekdi in her series.*

♣

From the majority of these encounters and conversations, I identified little recognition that television producers were altering proverb content and folktales to convey gender values the educated producers believed were necessary for an informed and enlightened citizenry, despite an increased number of regional radio programs devoted to explicating and discussing the meaning of Moroccan proverbs in 2012–14.[15] However, that did not mean that the intentions of producers utilizing *hadra lmizān* in their programming to convey "modernist" Moroccan values were entirely missing their mark. Their message resonated with those who shared the same Moroccanness vision. One evening as I sat eating dinner in the home of a successful Fassi businessman and his family, the discussion turned to *ḥadīdān* and how much this man, his mother-in-law, and ten-year-old son enjoyed the programming. This family self-aligned with a cosmopolitan, educated Islam. The wife was training to be a state-sponsored female religious guide (مرشيدة [*mūršīda*]). They collaboratively constructed a happy response that these programs discouraged folk magic at the same time as valorizing their traditional past. They didn't mention gender or disability equity in relation to the program at all.

Conclusion

My account of *hadra lmizān* sociality projects is partial, multiple, and positioned—just as the ideologies I analyzed. It was shaped by the urban Fassi Moroccans who allowed me to observe their viewing practices and elicit their media and language ideologies. Yet they hint at ways in which we might understand the phatic labor of Moroccanness on state television, both in regard to channel failures and the social relatedness productivity of *hadra lmizān*.

Media ideologies, observed both explicitly in television talk and implicitly in viewing practices, were key to understanding what meanings traveled with *hadra lmizān* when it moved from public street and domestic storytelling to state storytelling. For television producers, the use of televisual storytelling techniques with a Moroccan "intangible cultural heritage" register facilitated its "translatability" for younger generations the producers and many audience adults felt were no longer socialized to understand *hadra lmizān's* deep meanings. State television producers' appropriation of this genre was an attempt to legitimate modernization projects (reinforcing a media for development ideology, see Lerner 1958 and Zaid 2009) and demonstrated the state's moral authenticity, or to quote the late Moroccan philosopher Mohammed Abded al-Jabri, "to seek our modernity by rethinking our tradition" (Abed al-Jabri 1999, 1). For many audience members, the preservation of this communicative heritage (wisdom of the elders) was more significant than any message embedded in the actual content, which many did not attend to directly because of an implicit media ideology that emerged out of family viewing contexts: one shouldn't pay more attention to the television program than the interactions going on around them. Appropriate Moroccanness was tied to ways in which one was to engage with the interactional moment, not just the message content. The iconic valence of *hadra lmizān*'s "deep sounds" could be grasped without having to watch the whole program.

Just as alternate possibilities for entextualization came through print technologies, state-sponsored media capitalized on the enregisterment potential of television in the drive to modernize Moroccanness. Through the creation of chronotopic equivalences and visual storytelling, *hadra lmizān* producers revalorized the form to authenticate state television's media and development ideology. But the kind of Moroccanness development producers advocated wasn't always the messages about appropriate social connection the viewers received. The circulatory iterations of this form were not new (from homes to markets to cultural festivals and television), nor was the commoditized labor. State television producers sought "newness" in the content of "modern" Moroccan relationality, such as gender equity, but hoped the wisdom of the "old" form would pave the way.

As I listened to the talk surrounding *hadra lmizān*, the audience evaluations that captured my interest included the reinforcing lament that previous generations were more clever than the current generations because they spoke with wisdom through rhythm. Several people explicitly articulated their pleasure that new generations would know the multimodal performance of *hadra lmizān*, wisdom through rhyme, yet they did not express attachment to modernist morality conveyed by producers in the same form. For the Fassis among whom I moved, the moral of this tale might be that mediums are only part of the message. Mediums get understood through sonic aesthetics, multimodal bundles, and participant frameworks that allow for alternatives to understanding what state Moroccanness and civic connection should be.

4

Scripting Sounds and Sounding Scripts

Senses, Channels, and Their Discontents

Darija, Langue nationale: L'arabe marocain, notre parler de tous les jours, n'est pas pris au sérieux. Pourtant, c'est la seule langue qui nous unit.

Darija, national language: Moroccan Arabic, our everyday language, is not taken seriously. Yet it is the only language that unites us.

—*COVER OF MOROCCAN FRENCH-LANGUAGE WEEKLY NEWS MAGAZINE* TELQUEL, *JUNE 15, 2002*

النقاش الوطني المطروح حول ماهية اللغة، الصراع اللغوي حول إدماج الفصحى أو العامية في الحقل الإعلامي، الفكري والتربوي إلخ و أثر هذا النقاش في رسم معالم الهوية المغربية المعاصرة. كيف يتم تعبئة بعض النظم المفاهيمية (الأيديولوجيات) اللغوية كحجج سواء من يرفع شعار الفصحى و العامية ...

أبو زيد المقرئ، مناقشة دعاة الدارجة

The national debate around the nature of language, the linguistic fight over the integration of fuṣḥā *or dialect in the media, intellectual, educational, etc., fields, and the impact of this debate in drawing the parameters of contemporary Moroccan identity. How do we mobilize some of the linguistic conceptual systems (ideologies) as proofs in the fuṣḥā vs. dialect debate?*

—DEBATING THE CALL OF ARABIC, ABU ZAYD AL-MUQRIʿ, YOUTUBE LECTURE, DECEMBER 2013

As described in these opening statements, the debate over which language form accurately connected Moroccans was intimately linked with nationalist ideologies. Some activists lamented that the language that really connected Moroccans was *darīja*, the everyday language of interaction but not that of formal writing, reading, or public communication, as evidenced by the *Telquel* special issue cited in the beginning epigraph. Among those were advocates for a multiculturalism embodied in the equalizing of the Tamazight languages, French, and Jewish ways of speaking, as we saw in Episode 2 of the introduction. They felt alienated by the official language of the Moroccan state: *fuṣḥā*. The linguistic medium was not connecting them appropriately. Yet others sought to preserve the Arab-Islamic identity and heritage tied to *fuṣḥā*, which needed to be reinshrined as a nationalist unity project. Others argued that the debate over what linguistic forms should represent Moroccanness was itself infused with political ideologies that needed to be interrogated. The argument about written forms of language was itself a lament about failed mediums: the forms used in the past had failed to bring Moroccans into appropriate unity. Moroccan scholars and politicians viewed *fuṣḥā* writing as an ideological tool of national unity because of standardness, a historical fixedness that stripped writing of its sonic, everyday *darīja* heterogeneity. All through the 1990s and 2000s, Fassis participated in these public debates about linguistic form. In this chapter, I take up their actual everyday practices tied to Moroccanness as represented in writing and the ideologies that informed their graphic-sonic medium relationalities. Although they lamented a lack of linguistic channel to unify Moroccans—a very modernist communication ideology—in practice Fassis' representational politics of writing Moroccanness was more about their physical channel ideologies than linguistic form anxieties. For Fassis, writing has always entailed forms of speaking.

As described in Chapter 3, *hadra lmizān* had become an oral register enscripted through written scenarios designed for radio and television spoken performance of civic virtues that producers sought to instill in Moroccans as a modern collectivity. Other genres during this same period were being enregistered as writing designed to be spoken by media-savvy Moroccans, and certainly to be spoken about: public advertising campaigns, graffiti, mobile phone texts, and *darīja* news publications. Rather than drawing on a scriptive aesthetics of evoking writing through speech (W. F. Miller 2007, 53), these writings evoked a sonic aesthetics of speech that should connect Moroccans through writing. Instead of thinking about orality and literacy as distinguished by listening and visual sensory channels, in this chapter I examine the ways in which Fassis heard writing speak and trained a listening "eye" to "hear" orthographies (writing conventions). They blended sensory channels in order to shape Moroccanness projects tied to specific linguistic mediums and media platforms designed to foster social connection and political relationality. In this graphic-sonic linguascape, the state only censured *darīja* in newsprint mediums, regardless of the content. This allowed *darīja* discontent to flourish in other platforms and via a wide variety of forms.

Scholars have written about Arabic soundscapes, the acoustic environments, listening practices, and ritual sounding in which Arabic shapes public discourse and Muslim subjects (Hirschkind 2006; Eisenberg 2013). Others have focused on the emergence of Arabic dialect writing as expressions of political movements, local advertising campaigns, and youth-driven social change movements (Caubet 2017; Hachimi 2017; Elinson 2013, 2017; C. Miller 2012, 2017). Both the soundscape and *darīja* writing literatures hint at the multisensory channel practices and ideologies mobilized to make kinds of persons, and they include laments about channel failures that motivated writing changes in the last decade. In this chapter I want to bring these two approaches together, to unpack the analytical dichotomy separating speech channels from writing channels, the ear and the eye. I do so because Fassis often did. Despite a long history of normativity tied to Arabic *fuṣḥā* writing, when Fassis wrote, they often did not adhere to *fuṣḥā* rules. Thus the debates about the failure of Arabic to unify Moroccans did not take into consideration the very effective everyday practices of writing Arabic in heterogeneous ways. Reading subjects did not surveil public forms of writing in Fez unless it appeared in newsprint, as I will discuss later. In other words, the medium mattered whether writing was supposed to be unifying through standardness or through graphic-sonic recognition.

There are two questions I seek to explore: What were the overlapping, partial, and fractional language ideologies that permitted representational diversity in publicly circulated written forms of Moroccan language usage? What might graphic inscriptions of Moroccan Arabics tell us about these practitioners' locally specific writing/listening/speaking ideas connecting writing repertoires to certain kinds of activities, specific channels, and the types of people who do them? In this chapter I focus primarily on *darīja* writing-reading-listening, though there were other circulating forms. Keep in mind the Fassi soundscape description of Chapter 1, the everyday kinds of spoken language I encountered and that Fassis employed, classified, and decried. That will help in relating the scholarly debates about the social work of writing I describe in this chapter, as well as Fassi channel ideologies about *darīja*, whether spoken or written. I analyze why Fassis writing *darīja* seemed to allow quite a bit of representational diversity (what I'm calling graphic-sonic orthographic heterogeneity) and how that related to specific channels (spoken, written, street art, books, mobile phone texting, WhatsApp, newsprint), and the kinds of Moroccanness projects that emerged from them.

While I didn't realize it at first, I found myself wandering through the visual representations of Moroccan speech, stumbling over the orthographic aesthetics (ways of writing), vocalizing the phrases to capture the rhythm and sedimentations of sound that Fassis heard when reading *darīja* in public and personal spaces (Ingold 2007, 15). As a wayfarer through Moroccan writing, I followed a path marked by others in order to train my listening eye. I learned to hear the rhythms and concatenations of speaking in the lines, curves, duplications, fonts, colors, and graphics of writing *darīja*. Wayfaring through a textual topography with Fassis involved attuning my sensory channels to work in tandem rather than in isolation, not focused on a fixed knowledge destination, but rather a kind of knowing that happened as I moved through and engaged Fassi–enscribed-ensounded channels, spaces, and moments. I continue to be interested in channel ideologies in this chapter. Just as I attuned to the sonic labor of "literate" Arabic listening in Chapter 1, I focus on the kinds of Moroccanness Fassis debated and lamented as they listened to and connected or disconnected with nonstandard Arabic writing in signs, newsprint, books, phones, messaging, YouTube, and WhatsApp.

Why would I be interested in nonstandard forms of writing and reading Arabic in Fez? Moroccan writers and readers did connective or phatic work of creating collectivities through orthographic sensibilities and graphic representations of Moroccan ways of speaking in media (print and electronic). This concern about how to relate through writing/reading reflected the tensions among various standardization, unity, and change projects tied to Morocco as a national linguistic community identified via a standard language ideology (see Silverstein 1996). The "standard" or national language of Morocco was *fuṣḥā*, or formal Arabic, which was supposed to unify Moroccans after independence from France and Spain by creating a shared language of connection. Yet the process of unifying through standard Arabic has not been a simple process, as we saw in Chapter 1 with regard to listening. I saw, through my Fassi friends, graphic-sonic inscriptions of Moroccan communication as a mimetic model of the sociolinguistic complexity in Morocco during the last few decades. They illustrated the dynamic playing out between competing centralizing projects and everyday diversity of channel practices designed for connection. They also demonstrated an awareness about the relationality work of centralizing and diversifying practices of language, as well as a willingness to use written forms in specific media platforms (newsprint and books) as meta attacks to chip away at competing ideologies (Jacquemet 2000, 38). In this chapter, calibrations of Moroccanness involved coordinating multisensory channels in the phatic labor of relating. This was not just a simple question of Moroccan multilingualism and genre conventions (as in Chapter 2), but reflected a growing analytical trend to view language as a continuum of resources people used to accomplish all kinds of social and political alignment tasks (Blommaert 2010, 41–43). The contestation between unifying and diversifying writing/reading/listening of *darīja* cut across many domains and resources, including Morocco's linguistic diversity, colonial and personal interactional histories, differentiated educational opportunities, dynamic symbolic markets, and sometimes divergent political stances (Schulthies 2015). As Agha has argued, "Utterances and discourses are themselves material objects made through human activity—made in a physical sense, out of vibrating columns of air, ink on paper, pixels in electronic media—which exercise real effects upon our senses, minds, and modes of social organization" (Agha 2007, 3).

In the deep ocean of language debates in Morocco, Moha Ennaji (mentioned in Chapter 1) has argued that language has been a key element of contemporary cultural and political divides (2005, xi). Abu Zayd al-Muqri', Moroccan linguist, Muslim political activist, Arab intellectual, and member of parliament, agreed that language has been central to Moroccanness projects and identified language ideologies surrounding *fuṣḥā* and *darīja* as foundational to waves of public conflicts, as seen in the quote at the beginning of this chapter. Both cast themselves as listening and reading subjects but called out to different addressees through their channel choices. While Ennaji wrote books and articles in English to external audiences and his English-language students at the public university in Fez, Abu Zayd chose to disseminate his work in *fuṣḥā* via recorded lectures he and his followers posted on YouTube.[1] Though seeking different audiences and argument outcomes, they both saw language ideologies as key to Moroccanness. With these scholars, I want to explore the mediatized lives of social connectedness circulating in graphic-sonic representational scripts of various media.

Public and social media circulation of written texts can be a political act, but not just because the writer provides supportive or subversive content.[2] Often we may focus on a text's ideas and arguments in order to get at meaning, but the form of writing and its medium of circulation are a graphic inscription of contentious ideologies about authority, morality, and modernity (Messick 1993; Mitchell 1988; W. F. Miller 2007; Sebba 2012). People who write texts they intend to share publicly make choices about the script they will use to convey their ideas as well as the delivery medium. Those choices, in a decolonizing Moroccan world suffused with French, Arabic, Spanish, English, and Tifinagh (Amazigh script) representational options,[3] as well as book, newspaper, blog, Twitter, WhatsApp, YouTube, and Instagram venues, can be a choice to align with centralizing projects (often state institution–driven), aspects of those projects, or centrifugal social divisions, what Bakhtin called heteroglossia (Bakhtin 1981, 67). I draw from linguistic anthropology notions of power, in which "the creation of social realities through the deployment of linguistic structures in discourse is the process through which broader socio-historical relations are sustained and transformed through time" (Phillips 2000, 192). The types of power these writers deployed was interactional (and thus their meanings were not entirely within their control) and presented several uncoordinated challenges to institutional structuring of representational writing/reading economies (Elinson 2013; C. Miller 2012). Instead of focusing on the writing/reading forms themselves, I want to demonstrate the ways Fassis calibrated Moroccanness through their everyday movements, ideologies, and interactions related to graphic-sonic linguascapes. But to do so, I do need to analyze spoken and written forms of *darīja* in Fez as they appeared in media platforms or channels. The link between written *darīja* forms and media platforms channeled graphic-sonic sensibilities that became venues for relationality reform. I hope our understanding of writing sensibilities as mediums of communicative change can be enhanced by paying attention to the connection work of Fassi multisensory channel coordination and language ideologies, about what they feel writing does for public relationality. *Darīja* could be heard and read throughout Fez, and the distinctions were telling of what reading subjects accepted as appropriate connection.

الحلقة ١: الخطوط المغربية، الكتابة المغاربية

Episode 1: Moroccan Scripts, Scripting Maghribis

While the temperature outside was a mild 22° Celsius (70° Fahrenheit), we were all layered in sweaters and jackets in the small apartment-salon-turned-tutoring-hall.[4] *Lack of heating in the non-insulated brick and cement residences meant that the 10° C mornings left Fassi building interiors colder than the outdoors. I was tutoring five French- and Arabic-educated Morocco university students as they prepared for English proficiency TOEFL exams. We had just finished another session, this one on verb tense agreement, and the students were gathering up their photocopied worksheets, pens, and notebooks off the table around which we had been clustered. Zoubida invited us all to Friday lunch at her family's home, adding that we should just "beep" her when we arrived at the Atlas post office in the Fez* ville nouvelle. *She would then come direct us to her family's residence.*

In the early 2000s, mobile phones had become less expensive and more common than fixed home phones in Morocco, but people still had to purchase recharge minutes to talk or text. "Beeping" quickly became the way to communicate without calling, even acquiring its own darīja *verb form, a mix of French and Arabic:* بيبي عليا (bīpī 'alayā, "*beep me*").[5] *After "beeping," texting was the least expensive way to communicate, as a text was 1 Moroccan dirham (MAD) and a phone call a minimum of 2 MAD (about $.20 USD). Everyone I knew who texted did so in* darīja, *but in a Romanized (Latin-character based) French orthography script (Caubet 2017). Arabic script capabilities were not introduced into phone designs until 2005, but even after that point, most of my Fassi interlocutors continued to text and interact online in Romanized* darīja *(Schulthies 2014b). Even as beeping fell out of use in the coming years, the Romanized texting continued its phatic connective work.* La bas? Ca va? Rani jaya daba daba! Nkoune had Cinema Rex. Ok? Feen raki? *"How are you? You well? I'm on my way right now! I'll be next to Cinema Rex. Where are you?" Mixed Arabic, French, and English forms reflected casual speech patterns in urban Fez, though the design affordances of European-language–based phones meant that Arabic (which has no capitalization) written in Romanized alphabets was automatically altered to default capitals at the beginning of new sentences. Additionally, Fassis taught to write in* fuṣḥā *or formal French were creative in adapting Latin-based character possibilities to expressions of Fassi-marked* darīja. *They reflected pan-Arabic orthographic conventions (such as substituting Arabic numerals for* darīja *phonology:* ق *replaced by 3,* خ *with 5,* ح *with 7,* ش *with x or ch), and quite a bit of spelling heterogeneity (*ساعة *["hour/time"], written as saa and sa3a). Despite the plurilingual practices of everyday* darīja *soundscapes that mixed French, English, Tamazight, Spanish, Egyptian, Emirati, and Syrian words, phrases, gestures, intonation styles, and registers, writing persisted as a monoscriptic practice: either Arabic or Latin-based orthographies (Schulthies 2014b). In other words, written mobile phone texts, online chats, or social media* darīja *almost always occurred in one orthographic style—at least until 2015. This may have been because the European and American design features of phones and computers initially didn't allow rapid switching between scriptic options.*

Yet these scriptic practices also pointed to Moroccanness projects. The writing and speaking affordances of specific electronic and print media regularly led to laments about the loss of specific kinds of relationality. One Moroccan educator I met with called the use of Latin-based orthographies to write Arabic a form of European linguistic colonialism, and another bemoaned the corruption of Arabic writing in a world where it is already threatened by French and English economic and scientific dominance. Another colleague related how her husband couldn't understand the Arabic writing of a 2M television advertisement until he spoke it out loud and realized it wasn't fuṣḥā. *He went on to question the target audience of this advertisement, since those able to read the Arabic script were not the illiterate Moroccans targeted by those advocating* darīja *use because of the poor educational system. In 2009, several Arabic Moroccan media venues began a campaign pushing back against a proposal to change the state administrative language from* fuṣḥā *to* darīja, *French, or Tamazight.*[6] *The title of their campaign was* ما تقيش لغتي (mā tqīš lughtī), *"don't touch my language." This phrase and its background on a red hand of Fatima intertextually linked to a Moroccan anti-terrorism public awareness campaign that emerged after the 2003 Casablanca bombings:* ما تقيش بلادي (mā tqīš blādī), *"don't touch my country." The visual call to preserve* fuṣḥā *as the national language of Morocco paradoxically seemed to rely on* darīja *and anti-terrorism, but perhaps signaled the way some Moroccans viewed Arabic as a continuum rather than two separate languages (see Parkinson 2003 in relation to Egyptian Arabic). For some Fassis,* darīja *was the medium of family and social life, but not for writing, and certainly not in French-influenced script.*

This moral panic among self-identified intellectuals about problematic writing channels did not seem to register with most of my phone (and later social media) contacts, who happily communicated in a myriad of written forms. But that didn't mean they were not attuned to these laments about writing Arabic. Facebook, then WhatsApp, emerged, as my Fassi interlocutors preferred social media platforms. By 2014, I noticed a few of my Fassi friends writing almost exclusively in Arabic script, even when writing French words in darīja. *Toufiq was an early adopter of Romanized Arabic in the 2000s. In 2013, he told me explicitly he interacted on social media in* darīja *written with Arabic script to assert his Moroccanness and encourage others to do so. Another colleague, a professor of English, wrote primarily in Arabic script on WhatsApp as an index of religious commitment—even when the content was not religious. Others only used Arabic script when circulating religious quotes, memes, or seeking a laugh through the out-of-place formal register, and the rest of the exchange involved Romanized* darīja. *Despite explicit ideologies of* fuṣḥā *or standard French as the languages of writing (F. Laroui 2011, 68), Fassis and other Moroccans communicated public and interpersonal messages via a variety of written forms. This wasn't just a way of writing* darīja *in electronic mediums, it was also part of print practices linked to a range of Moroccanness sociality projects: shifting political opposition movements, grassroots literacy projects, projects to document and valorize oral folklore, marketing campaigns, youth-driven social media modernity, and anti-terrorism nationalism campaigns, as well as political apathy.*

The Sounds of Writing

In de Saussure's early twentieth-century European theorizing about the relationship between sound and its representations, the focus was on the sound-image, a psychological impress of sound on the mind (de Saussure 1959, 118–20). He did not think of sound as a material form, a sound wave with tangible effects; it was a channel for expressing a psychological sound-image, as was writing. Ong argued that the sight of the written word was necessary for the creation of de Saussure's sound image and the idea that words could objectify and reference things (Ong 1982, 17). Sounds were suspect for these language scholars, because "nonliterate" people focused on the sounds themselves instead of the content of meanings lying behind the sounds (a key European elite language ideology we saw in Chapter 2). For Ingold, the division between sound and its representations was a modern construct unknown to medieval and classical European authors. Writing in previous eras refused to be fixed; it "wriggle[d] around, refusing to be quelled by the objectifying duress of visual surveillance" (Ingold 2007, 27). Ingold argued that the environmental soundscapes, gestural coordination, and bodily comportment of writers could be heard from the page by readers before the twentieth century. The problem emerged when writing and speaking were linked to a single sensory channel (writing with vision, speaking with hearing), erasing the blending coordination of sensory channels and the materiality of vocal or manual bodily gesture.

> If writing speaks, and if people read it in their ears, then [the claim] that a familiarity with the written word necessarily leads people to listen to speech as though they were looking at it cannot be correct. . . . If writing speaks, then to read is to listen. . . . Who is to say, then, that as the medieval cleric traces the inscriptions written on the page, following them with his eyes and perhaps his fingers as well, and murmuring to himself as he does so, his mind is not just as much filled with voices as it would be if the words had been read out to him? (Ingold 2007, 14–15)

For the Fassis among whom I worked, hearing writing speak was not a lost language ideology or practice lost during modernity. Most of them had learned to read through recitation of memorized examples of Arabic or French grammar (known as dictation). Even as they practiced *fuṣḥā* writing composition, vocal recitation of memorized passages and dictation writing were standard pedagogy in Moroccan schools (Boutieri 2016, 75). Even learning to pray or read the Qur'an involved aural memorization, manual inscription, visual recognition, and oral recitation, blending multiple sensory channels as part of the reading process.

Image 1: Newspaper kiosk and bookstore

Image 2: School textbooks and stationery store

الحلقة ٢: الكتابات الفاسية

Episode 2: Fassi Texts

Despite its 1,200-year history as a religious and cultural capital of Morocco, Fez boasted very few bookstores. Novels in French and (less so) fuṣḥā *were sold at newspaper kiosks. Stationery stores sold school supplies and textbooks. There was a secondhand outdoor book market in Lido, where university students sifted through piles of paperbacks and bound photocopied texts for their courses. Religious texts, such as booklets of petitionary prayers and Islamic guides to interpreting dreams, might be sold by sidewalk informal vendors who spread a handful of books on a sheet or walked around the bus station. I found only three bookstores that sold social and cultural history books, and I visited them every year. I quickly learned to buy whatever I found interesting, because there were few copies, and I often never saw them again. There was no public library in Fez—only private libraries that required memberships, fees, or specific affiliations to access. The one book that was in almost everyone's home was a Qur'an—but beyond that, most Fassis did not have bookshelves or personal libraries. Beautifully bound books were often Islamic religious texts, and only a few homes had them—those of religious scholars or university professors. School textbooks were most common and often quickly resold after students used them.*

As mentioned previously, the Fez Festival of Sacred Music in May–June usually brought a contingent of cultural elites to the city. The festival also raised the visibility and price of cultural consumer products, such as novels, poetry collections, musical albums, and instruments. After attending an afternoon concert of the Fez Festival, I purchased several books of Moroccan folktales written by Ahmed Taieb el Alj in fully voweled Arabic script darīja *on the right side of the page and translated French on the left, reflecting the writing orientations of each script: French's left to right and Arabic's right to left. Most print materials in Arabic, excluding primary school grammar books and Qur'ans, do not include the vowel diacritics, and Arabic readers everywhere are taught to read without them. The inclusion of vowels pointed to the ways in which el Alj anticipated the readers need to hear the* darīja *words as they read them. When I brought home the books everyone in the family loved them, with two of the daughters reading them out loud. They struggled at points to read the Arabic, unaccustomed to reading* darīja *folktales or books in Arabic script, but laughed out loud at certain clever rhymes and expressions. The youngest daughter, just thirteen, was fascinated. In fact, after her older sisters finished reading the books, she sat in the corner of the room and read them aloud for more than half an hour by herself. It was the first time I saw her immersed in something that wasn't a school textbook or a mobile phone.*

Image 3: Ahmed Taieb el Alj folktale, "The donkey and the cow," written in Arabic script *darīja* with French translation

Platform Language Ideologies and Nonstandard Arabic

What might it mean to read and write in nonstandard linguistic forms and for whom? One of the most important ideologies of historically literate societies has been that writing is for reading, a set of physical and cognitive activities designed to identify the "meaning" of a text (Blommaert 2005, 114). In a folk theory of writing common in the United States, the connection between writing and reading is assumed to be direct and unmediated, simply a matter of visually apprehending what is graphically inscribed. However, as many scholars have noted, this view of writing as a decontextualized, transparent, one-to-one medium for understanding meaning neglects the ways in which different communities understand the process of reading a written text or view the ways to "read" various written genres based on the contexts or participants present (Boyarin 1993, 6). Some forms of writing are meant to intertextually evoke, through multimodal signals, ways of speaking tied to historically significant social distinctions and thus involve heterographic functions of writing that go beyond simple encoding and decoding dictionary meanings.

This can be seen in explicit discussions of writing language ideologies, as well as everyday writing and reading practices. In his highly influential article about the failure of Morocco's post-independence Arabization policy written in 1973, Moroccan intellectual Abdallah Laroui outlined some indexical (context-reflecting) connections between specific forms and Moroccan publics. Like Abu Zayd al-Muqri' and Moha Ennaji, Laroui advocated the idea that linguistic forms were tied to political ideology:

> The King was acting in a clearly defined and bound semantic field, the field of ancient classical Arabic, nearly mummified, paradoxically affecting both the illiterate masses and the old politico-religious elite. Political moderate ideology, with its technocratic tendency, was linked to the use of French, while socializing revolutionism grew out of the use of modernized Arabic. In all this, individual psychology mattered little; what counted was the social structure which expressed itself through the linguistic tool. (A. Laroui 1973, 35)

Notice how Laroui distinguished sociopolitical categories within a heterogeneous Moroccan society (monarchy, illiterate masses, politicoreligious elites, technocrats, revolutionary socialists), but viewed the "languages" as homogenous wholes: Classical Arabic, French, Modern Standard Arabic (no mention of various forms of *darīja* such as an urban unmarked French-Arabic register, regional registers such as Marrakeshi or Fassi *darīja*, polite talk or street *darīja*, etc., or even Tamazight, Tarafit, Tachalhit). In this statement, Laroui recognized the pragmatic force of language choice in which speakers reflected their sociopolitical projects through linguistic signs. However, he did not view these linguistic signs as *creating* the conditions for those social projects. Instead, he stated that those who pushed for Arabization were dissatisfied groups who often did so using French (A. Laroui 1973, 43). He seemed to be referring to the graphic forms of these "linguistic tools," as conveyed through his choice of specific sensorial and institutional framings: clearly defined, bound, semantic, mummified Classical Arabic; technocratic French; social revolutionary [educated] modernized Standard Arabic.[7]

This has been a common assumption about linguistic forms—that they merely reflect political and social ideologies. To write, then, would link a linguistic container (Arabic or Latin-based script) to a particular project (literacy, political transparency, secularism) as a proxy vehicle in furthering the cause. Within that view of language and meaning-making, two possible strategies to halt that cause would be to foster linguistic purity ("self-censorship" encouraged through *fuṣḥā* Arabization in mass education) or to shut down offending mediums. However, if we expand this perspective to allow linguistic forms to create rather than just reflect contexts for political projects—to be linguistic acts that potentially transform—then we would need to study the ways in which people in reading and writing moments construe, respond to, ignore, and add acceleration or allow inertia to slow its force in social life.

Bakhtin noted that all instances of observable language use simultaneously reflected centripetal and centrifugal forces, standardizing and diversifying ideologies and practices (Bakhtin 1981, 270–72). While he was interested specifically in novel writing forms, I observed these tensions in language spoken in cafes, posted on billboards, or texted on a cell phone. Speakers or writers might highlight or foreground the unity, consistency, and centralizing aspects of linguistic forms at certain moments (its standardness), while other contexts might privilege the heteroglossic characteristics of an utterance (its social or geographical "dialectness"). For Bakhtin, a certain unifying quality was necessary for each graphic inscription to be understandable, the centralizing pull of sharedness. At the same time, these forms were "entangled, shot through with shared thoughts, points of view, and alien value judgments and accents" because of differences in users' repertoire command, access, and social indexical values (Bakhtin 1981, 276).

In Morocco, the tension between the centripetal and centrifugal forces of reading subjects manifested itself in language ideologies that relegated specific written linguistic forms to particular mediums. *Fuṣḥā* and French were the standard forms for print mediums, *darīja* in Romanized scripts most often used in texting, instant messaging, smartphone apps, and mixed scripts for billboard advertising campaigns. And yet composers of written forms regularly mixed scripts and written forms of spoken varieties across mediums. A text message from a telecommunications company might employ Romanized *darīja* script and standard French in the same message to attract aspiring elites, employing an assumption about their language-and-medium platform ideologies and histories. An online newspaper might print most of its articles in a form of "educated *darīja*": Arabic script *fuṣḥā* with occasional *darīja* phrases. Fassis often considered those *darīja* publications because they were not entirely in *fuṣḥā* and were explicit about countering government policies through content and language choice (see the section on newsprint). For scripts to become explicit or subtle attacks against centralizing ideologies, they needed to draw upon well-known language-and-medium-platform ideologies and erase any practices or

Image 4: Méditel billboard in Fez with French loanword in *darīja* orthography

variations that did not fit those ideologies. Orthographic heterogeneity was one of those practices: the use of nonstandardized spellings, script-mixing, and writing practices for grammatically governed dialects and standards.

Orthographic Heterogeneity: Many Ways of Writing the "Same" Sounds

As mentioned previously, due to French colonialism and continued economic, political, and educational influence, many French words were part of an unmarked variety of urban *darīja* (C. Miller et. al. 2007). This was so much the case that Moroccan telecommunications firms in the late 2000s regularly wrote French words in Arabic scripts or Arabic words in Latin-based scripts. Méditel began a recharge campaign offering double minutes during certain times of the month: 100 minutes for 50 Moroccan dirhams (MAD). In 2011, they changed that to an advertisement that claimed they were offering double recharge from that time onward. They advertised this on Moroccan television, in magazines, and on billboards (Image 4). The basic campaign ad was in white Arabic script on a red background, suggesting the company logo and the Moroccan flag (which are also red). It read الضوبل بدا, *ḍḍūbl bidā*, "double begins" in white with بدا, *bidā*, scratched out and another Arabic word written in yellow superscript: ديما, *dīmā*, "always." The first word written in Arabic was a French term that had become part of everyday *darīja* by the late 1990s, even for those not formally educated in French. The company logo, Méditel, was written in white Latin script on the bottom right-hand corner, the Arabic version of the script smaller and in yellow just above in superscript to the left: الميديتل, *almīdītel*, suggesting that the Romanized French version of the logo was more significant.[8] Fassi spoken usage confirmed this, as they always called it Méditel without the Arabic definite article ال *al*. As observed in Image 7 included on page **125**, many telecomm advertising campaigns borrowed mobile-phone texting practices and would write *darīja* in Latin-based scripts. That advertisement was primarily in Arabic-scripted *darīja*, but one portion—the campaign slogan—was in Romanized Arabic: ع became a 3 and ح was represented with 7 in *sa3a 7orra* "free hour" (pay twenty dirhams and you can have an extra hour of talk "free"; thirty dirhams and you get two hours "free").

One of the key language ideologies operating in Morocco that allowed for orthographic heterogeneity (many ways of writing the same thing) was a view that the Arabic script, and hence writing in Arabic, were reserved for standard Arabic, whether the Qur'an or the more simplified *fuṣḥā* (Elinson 2013, 716–17). By extension, French written in publicly circulated venues and mediums should also be standard French. Many of the Fassis I interacted with did not expect nonstandard spoken forms of communication in Morocco to take written form in formal genres and spaces, and thus there was no push for standardizing the way one wrote "the dialects." Advertising was one such nonstandard domain. In fact, Moroccan producers (and consumers) expected visual recognition of *darīja* to require oral diacritics for phrases and sentences so readers could sound out the register. All other Arabic was written without the short vowels marked unless explicitly an elementary school reading/writing primer. For example, the folktale books published by Ahmed Taieb el Alj were voweled Arabic script *darīja* with a parallel translation in standard French. The Arabic was in a nonstandard orthographic style, and the *darīja* needed vowels to facilitate reading—which people often did out loud, since that was the way they encountered storytelling forms.

How might we make sense of this scriptic heterogeneity for billboards in the wake of the strong state ideologies that writing should be standardized? Because Fassis brought different histories and experiences to an interpretive moment, the meaning possibilities of specific linguistic resources and their ways of representing them varied. This was because they depended on both the larger social context (or co-text, genre, participant frameworks, nonlinguistic signs) in which the linguistic forms occurred, as well as their language ideologies and medium expectations (which were often not fully shared) to make sense of it all. In the previous illustration, the size of the Arabic script on the logo may have reflected the initial target and investment market of Méditel: urban, aspiring, French-educated Moroccans. The mixed French in *darīja* on the same billboard advertisement addressed a public school, Arabic-educated audience (a much larger percentage of the population than French-educated urban elites). While I was doing fieldwork in Morocco, none of my Moroccan interlocutors found the French-word-in-Arabic script (or vice versa) exceptional, but rather viewed the writing of *darīja* rather than *fuṣḥā* in public spaces as more noteworthy.

Image 5: Bayn advertisement

Telecommunications company Bayn (the brand itself an Arabic term in Romanized script meaning "clear") began an advertising campaign for reduced pricing on phone minute recharges in 2012. The ads used Arabic script with the unmarked French-Arabic code-mixed variety on a green background (an indexical nod toward Moroccan nationalism and Islam, both of which are regularly symbolically represented with green): الصُولد قْلِيل وْلاَ كْثِير، الُهم هُو تْحَكَّم فِيه, *aṣ-ṣold qlīl wlā ktīr, al-muhim huwa tḥakum fīh*, "Whether the sale is small or big, the key is to control it." While the Arabic word for "big" or "lots" was written in *fuṣḥā* with the ث, *tha*ʾ, most Moroccans pronounced ث, *tha*ʾ, with Moroccan phonology, as a dental stop instead of a dental fricative, ت, *ta*ʾ.[9] The French word *solde* was written in Arabic transliteration الصُولد, and most of the initial syllables were written with a *sukkun* (Arabic diacritic for no vowels) instead of the initial short vowels, indicating *darīja* phonology instead of *fuṣḥā*. Advertisers assumed Moroccans were not used to reading *darīja* in Arabic script, and thus the regular inclusion of diacritic marks. Fassis had been writing spoken Arabic forms in Romanized characters since the development of mobile phone and internet chat technologies (Caubet 2005; Schulthies 2014b; Warschauer, El Said, and Zohry 2002), thus reflecting the initial Latin-based affordances of these technologies as well as their own French educational training. The advertising companies that voweled Arabic script *darīja* were assuming a need to socialize Moroccans into reading *darīja* as well as reinforcing the sonic-graphic sensory blending required to understand the writing.

One of the central processes of Moroccan state-building after independence in 1956 was unifying the nation through designating an official language and educational language planning. This debate emerged from specific ideologies about what language was and should do: should Morocco capitalize on economic prospects that acquiring French would afford despite its colonial vestiges and at the expense of the Arab and Muslim identity upon which the independence movements built their platforms (A. Laroui 1973, 33–34)? The state decided initially to Arabize, though that proved difficult to implement immediately and controversial for various publics (Seckinger 1988, 68–90). Elites set up parallel educational systems that extended colonial policies, educating their children in private French schools, while mass public education was mostly Arabized (some subjects at the tertiary level, such as science, math, law, and engineering were taught in French). I recognize that my characterization of post-independence language questions is a simple dichotomy that does not reflect the full range of perspectives that contributed to the debate (see Boum 2008; Segalla 2009). However, the issue of national language choice involved centripetal linguistic forces, the process of standardizing language and providing a rationale for the privileging of certain forms of language in specific public domains (such as education, business, government transactions), whether it was Standard French or Standard Arabic. This was not just a question of places and genres where these standardized language forms should be used (like ministries and schools), but also an implicit decision about the ways in which they should be represented.

Moroccan official languages had spelling conventions and rules about how to write Arabic or French in different genres, such as a government form, school textbook, building placard, business letter, or street sign. Moroccan state language policy from the 1950s onward empowered the historical ideology that writing was reserved for standardized language forms, *fuṣḥā* or French, to facilitate literacy and national unity, generate a productive professional sector of society, and embody and disseminate a rational orientation (an ideology partially instilled from European language ideologies and partially refashioned from Arabic educational ideologies; see A. Laroui 1973, 45). Writing a news article, sign, law, public speech, or textbook for the widest possible viewership privileged *fuṣḥā*, since that was the language variety the state imbued with public authority, visibility, and identity. However, mass education in *fuṣḥā* was not realized until well into the 1980s, and even then quite variably. Thus the political sensibilities of *fuṣḥā* (associations with the Muslim-Arab identity and glorious past) were sometimes foregrounded over content meanings.

The act of writing Arabic in these publicly approved forms framed the writer as aligning (however loosely) with a standard language ideology and the meanings associated with it, despite the persistent presence of written genres, such as plays, pamphlets, proverb collections, amulets, internet chats, mobile phone texts, advertising signs, and short dialect dialogues within novels, in which

Moroccan writers employed a mix of local varieties (*fuṣḥā*, regional/social Arabics, and Tamazights) with a variety of orthographies (Aguadé 2006; Caubet 2005; Elinson 2017; Kapchan 1996). To write in Morocco was to graphically represent bundled associations of literacy, progress, rationality, public institutions, and the complicated tensions between European and Muslim identity aesthetics, not all of which neatly correlated with a specific language variety or scriptic choice (Caubet 2005, 241; F. Laroui 2011, 153–54; Segalla 2009, 258). For some, French was the preferred modernity medium, for others *fuṣḥā* (Elinson 2013, 715–30; C. Miller 2012, 419–40). Yet others thought of *darīja* or Tamazight as the vehicles for modernization, as illustrated in the debates surrounding languages of educational instruction I wrote about in Chapter 3 of this book. In a post-Arab uprisings drive for understanding, it might be tempting to map these language indexical orientations (French vs. Arabic, *fuṣḥā* vs. *darīja*, progress vs. identity) and chronotopes (those demonstrating a practical gaze toward an inevitable future and the latter a stubborn attachment to a glorious past) onto Moroccan reform political groups vying for political, economic, and educational change (secularists vs. Islamists). However, I believe such dichotomies miss the ways in which so-called Islamists warned of a future Euro-linguistic/economic/educational imperialism, or that so-called secularists called for political/linguistic pluralism in *fuṣḥā* because of Morocco's literary and cultural history. These chronotopic erasures and elisions hid the fact that many Moroccans of varying educational backgrounds could communicate across political (and linguistic) divides despite the public (and private) educational system's supposed epic failure. It also ignored the very important assumption that formal literacy in any language was a necessary condition for public political and economic futures. It also ignored the ways these chronotopes and linguistic resources could and were mobilized by many parties to accomplish a variety of situationally salient social acts (Schulthies 2014a).

Several scholars have argued that the public written visibility of Moroccan spoken varieties has changed in the past few decades (Caubet 2017; Elinson 2013; C. Miller 2012), allowing more place for *darīja* writing in Morocco. While this has certainly been the case in Fez, I want to think more about the ways soundscapes and written linguascapes continue to rely on multisensory channel blending to shape both centralizing and distinguishing Moroccanness projects in Fez.

Hearing Written *Darīja* in WhatsApp

What do Fassis hear when they see *darīja*? Social media writing was one of the key ways in which I recognized Fassi blending of sensory channels when engaging writing. In 2015, I analyzed eighty WhatsApp messages collected from fifteen Fassi colleagues between the ages of twenty and thirty-five. As mentioned, after 2014, WhatsApp was the preferred social media platform for my Fassi friends. The platform let them call each other using an internet connection, leave vocal recorded messages, and send images and texts to individuals and groups. Many of my Fassis had WhatsApp group chats for family members, siblings, college friends, coworkers, and co-hobbyists (those who followed *malhoun* or *andalusi* musical performances and groups in Fez). The multimodal affordances of Whatsapp and other social media platforms facilitated the kinds of sonic-graphic sensorial blending I observed throughout the past decade, even though it was a relatively new media platform.

The group chat analyzed in this chapter was between six Fassi friends who were finishing their last year of university studies, three young men (Mehdi, Oussama, Hamza) and three young women (Khadija, Nissrine, Salima), although Hamza does not respond in any of this interaction. As with all group chats, members could jump in or out at any point in the ongoing conversation, which took place between 10 P.M. and midnight a few weeks before their yearly comprehensive exams. At one point, there was a forty-minute gap between responses, but the bulk of the exchanges occurred over a period of fifteen minutes in pretty rapid-fire succession.

The only Arabic script that appeared in this group chat occurred in the first line and had a visible *fuṣḥā* marker, the indefinite accusative alif at the end of the word جميعا (*jamīʿan*), "all." Khaddijaaa evoked the ironic tone of this formal utterance by following it with a sonic marker, the Arabic laughter abbreviation هههه (*hhhh*). While I don't have the utterance that came before this one, the participants told me they were in the midst of discussing their upcoming exams. I assumed the *fuṣḥā* use was in relation to the classroom language style.

Mehdi responded in line 2 with a Romanized laughter abbreviation (Hhhh) that was automatically capitalized on the European-designed smartphone keyboard. He then expressed a desire that their teachers cancel the upcoming exam, again using the Romanized script to write *darīja*. Mehdi's sentence was incomplete, *mssab madirouch*, "wish they wouldn't," eliding the transitive verb and object "give us the exam," knowing his friends would hear the rest of it as they read. He finished with a mischievous emoticon so they would know the tone with which to hear his writing. Nissrine's response in line 3 was a *darīja* interjection of ironic exasperation, a visual representation of a widely used Fassi agreement form (*Wayeeh*). Even now I can hear the breathy, long, drawn-out quality of this utterance as I read it on the page. Khaddijaaa agreed with a French *Oui*, "yes," and the discussion paused for about forty minutes.

When it resumed, the rest of the group chat centered around a new topic, the announcement that afternoon about the American visa lottery results and the discussion about how to win that immigration opportunity. Migration was a regular topic in Fez throughout my fieldwork, as many families had at least one family member living abroad. Fassis debated the benefits and disadvantages, the conditions that pushed Moroccans to migrate, and the best ways to navigate various visa regulations. Much of this exchange focused on finding out if there were any tricks to winning a lottery visa and the lack of future these youth saw for themselves in Fez.

This group chat took place primarily in Romanized, French-based orthography *darīja* mixed with French and some English. The typing on the smartphone keyboard, along with the spoken feel of this *darīja* interactional writing style, precipitated significant spelling diversity, vowel and phrasal elisions, vowel duplications and unrepaired typing errors, capitalization of initial words (even though there is no capitalization in *darīja*), and letter substitutions for Arabic letters. Only occasionally did group members repair their typing errors, and mainly when the word was difficult to recognize without the correction (as in line 48, *sqhbfi*, which was repaired in line 49 to *sahbti*, "my friend"). In addition, all of the *darīja* written in Romanized script employed French spelling conventions, indexing the perduring influence of French on the educational system despite the growing influence of English in everyday Fassi soundscapes.

The biggest indicator of the blending of sensorial channels in this interaction was the utter absence of punctuation to indicate the tone of the writing—the friends in this group assumed their addressees would hear the intonation markers signaling statements or questions. Even in the *darīja* writing of print publications, punctuation was used to mark the end of a statement or question. In Fassi social media *darīja*, readers were expected to hear the tone as they saw the words. The punctuation was limited to an occasional exclamation or question mark for emphasis and Salima's intermittent use of period punctuation as a space marker between words (lines 21, 30, 32, 41, 47). Most of the questions were marked with question discourse cues (*wach*, *kifach*, *chnu*, *3lach*) or inferred pragmatically from the responses of the group members, as in lines 21–23. Another clue as to the blending of sensorial channels was the use of personal names to indicate responses for specific addressees, since this was an ongoing group chat, and sometimes it could be several posts by others before one could respond to a previous question (see lines 13, 23, 28, 68). In addition, there were representations of vocal interruption cues (line 24), expressions of ironic exasperation (line 3), and indignant surprise (line 61). Lastly, the interactions involved spoken discourse cues such as the *darīja* vocative marker /a/ attached to Salima's name in line 45 (*asaalima*, "hey Salima") and the ironic use of the backchannel cue *yeki*, "right" (though literally it means "O you" feminine) in line 58 (see the appendix for the entire transcript).

	Participant	Text	English Translation	Analysis Comments
1	Khadddijaaa	سؤالنا جميعا هههه	He asked all of us hhhh	*fuṣḥā* indefinite accusative marker, Arabic script, with Arabic laughter abbreviation (هههه) signaling ironic formality
2	Mehdi Allem	Hhhh mssab madirouch x)	Hhhh [I] wish they wouldn't [give us the exam] x)	*darīja* in Romanized French orthography, automatic capitalization of initial laughter abbreviation (Hhhh), circumfix negation of modal verb, transitive verb elided, hand-typed mischievous smiley emoticon
3	Nissrine	Wayeeeeh	wayeeeh	*darīja* interjection of ironic exasperation
4	Khadddijaaa	Oui	Yes	French
5	Oussama	Hamza ga rahom biiyno l9oor3a dlmirican had le3chiya	Hamza said they're going to show the American lottery this afternoon	*darīja* in Romanized French orthography, typing error *ga* should be *gal*, "said," number substitutions for ق، ع
6	Nissrine	Hhh feeen	Hhh where	*darīja*
7	Nissrine	Htaa na biit nmxhii	I too want to go	*darīja* elided *a* vowel in *ana* "I", doubling of letters to indicate long vowels (aa, ii), use of xh instead of ch for š (which others in this group chat used), probably from rapid typing on smartphone keyboard
8	Salima	site	Website?	French
9	Nissrine	:3		Cuteness smiley emoticon
10	Oussama	Ana majabch llah	God didn't bring it to me (I didn't get it)	*darīja* free-standing 1SG pronoun for emphasis, transitive gerund with circumfix negation, invoking the name of God as determiner of outcomes is common for Fassis
11	Salima	passe site	Send website	French
12	Oussama	Ook att	Ok, wait	English Ook, French abbreviation *att* for *attends*

The content of this group text was precipitated by Oussama when he mentioned the visa lottery, but most of the exchange occurred between Nissrine and Salima. From the interaction, it was clear that Salima saw no future for these Fassi youth. Significantly for this chapter, they all demonstrated the kind of multisensorial blending required for hearing written *darīja*, but also the ambivalence toward any kind of *darīja* orthographic standardization. Sometimes /š/ was written as /ch/ (line 15, *majabch*) or /x/ (line 54, *hadxi*), sometimes vowels elided as in line 18 (*mjbch*) instead of line 15 (*majabch*). This orthographic heterogeneity indicated a partial alignment, or at least a socialization toward, noncentralizing forces at work in Fez.

Written *Darīja* Linguascapes in Fez

Since I first visited Fez, public spaces were awash with scriptic diversity on signs, billboards, and wall graffiti. I began photographing scriptic heterogeneity and asking my Fassi interlocutors what they thought of these signs. The first place I lived was with a family in an older neighborhood of the French colonial *ville nouvelle* known as Atlas. The Altas roundabout served as a key bus stop and red taxi station, where one could catch a shared taxi to anywhere in the city the taxi driver was willing to take you, while just outside the nearby mosque was the place to catch shared white Mercedes taxis headed to surrounding towns and villages. A long side street was packed with bread and pastry shops, fruit and vegetable stands, dry good groceries, butcher shops (differentiated by beef/lamb and chicken/turkey offerings), and, closer to the main roundabout, male-dominated cafes that spilled onto the street and sandwich shops with the smell of rotisserie chickens beckoning. Many Fassis passed through this main artery connecting the *ville nouvelle* to outward radiating neighborhoods, and advertisers capitalized on this mobility hub.

One of the first bits of scriptic *darīja* I noted were the advertisements at the intersection to the roundabout (Images 6 and 7). Advertising professionals employed French-Arabic digraphia in their campaigns, using multiple writing systems (orthographies) to represent a single language in the same space (Dickinson 2015, 508). This French-Arabic digraphia register regularly appeared on billboards, flyers, newspapers/magazines, electronic devices, and clothing, sometimes playing with sonic homologies (things that sound similar) in scriptic form. One telecommunications company, Méditel (Mediterranean telecom), created a sonic-scriptic link between the "tel" of Méditel and the French feminine marker "elle" in their graphic representation of the company "Méditelle" to market phone products for aspiring Moroccan female professionals (Image 6). The Arabic and French orthographic representations

Image 6: Billboard advertising Meditél mobile phone services with French-Arabic digraphia

Image 7: Billboard advertising INWI mobile phone promotion with mixed Romanized Arabic and Arabic scripts

sounded exactly the same when spoken—the distinction occurred in the scriptic-sonic sensory blend and addressed a specific audience.

Advertisers also addressed targeted audiences by employing youth-inspired online scriptic sensibilities developed for texting and chatting, such as use of 3 for ع and 7 for ح in *saʒa 7orra*, into billboard, print, and television commercial mediums. In Image 7, mobile phone company INWI used a large billboard to advertise a minutes refill promotion, using Arabic script to write *darīja* (عبّر كبغيتي [“*express* as you wish”]) and French words that had been incorporated into *darīja* (الروشارج [“recharge”]), as well as Romanized and Arabic script *darīja* digraphia: ʕ*saʒa 7orra*, تقدروا تقاوموا الجديد ديال (“Can you resist the new free hour [offer]?”)

Just across the street from my apartment building entrance, graffiti appeared on an old French building that was demolished and replaced with new buildings a few years later (Image 8). Some basketball and hip-hop fans had used the abandoned building as canvas for their nighttime activities, writing in nonstandard English (ChicAgo BILLs, HIP Hop, 2PAC).

State public schools in Fez in the last decade changed from Arabic and French labels to Arabic and the Tifinagh script (chosen as the orthography for

Image 8: Street graffiti as index of youth politics

Image 9: Pluralingualism of public school sign in Arabic and Tifinagh

writing Tamazight, Tashelhit, and Tarafit; see Image 9). Ingold has argued that representations can carry chronotopic cues to their sociohistorical lives (Ingold 2007). For Fassis who did not identify as Amazigh, Tifinagh characters in the early 2000s Fez were signs of divisive political protest rather than national recognition. After 2003 and again in 2011, when the king officially recognized Amazigh languages as official languages, those same signs became state-sponsored displays of public services, especially schools. Even then, some of my Fassi colleagues were concerned that the state's already stretched finances were being used to promote Tifinagh in Arabic-majority–speaking areas. They explicitly linked graphic representations to tensions about graphic-sonic channels for Moroccanness in Fez.

As I moved through the city, I found other signs of speaking through writing. In the medina, herbal medicine shops seeking to draw in both local Moroccan customers and French tourists with Orientalist imaginaries advertised in both French and Arabic (Image 10). The handwritten sign in the center included fully voweled Arabic script alongside the French (عَشَابُ البُوعِنَانِيَة [HERBORISTERIE BOUINANIA]), unusual even for Arabic handwriting, as could be seen when compared with the all-Arabic sign on the right. It advertised the oldest and most well-known herbalist shop for Fassis, that of Ahmed Ben

Image 10: Pluralingualism of medina shop signs

Chaqroun, and continued to advertise only to Arabic readers. The *darīja* oral-visual blending of sensory channels was evidenced in the missing ا of احمد (*ʿaḥmad*) and ابن (*ʿibn*), pronounced in Moroccan phonology without the initial alif: العشاب حمد بن شقرون (*alʿašāb ḥmad bin šaqrūn*, "Herbalist Hmad Ben Chaqroun") and without vowel diacritics. In this way, the Arabic assumed Moroccan-specific speaking among a clientele who had received some formal literacy education.

Another sign, in a neighborhood adjacent to Atlas, foregrounded socio-educational histories and aspirational indexes. A high school tutoring business placed two signs above an apartment complex door advertising in both French and Arabic (Image 11). The business offered help with topics included in the baccalauréat, or high school completion exam (math, physics, economics, natural science, accounting), courses in language learning (including Arabe, Français, Anglais, Allemand, Espangnol), and computer skills training. The name of the business, INFO 6 SCHOOL, was borrowed from English, but the rest of the larger sign was in French. The smaller sign above the stairwell entrance transliterated the English name into Arabic script: إنفو 6 سكول (*ʿinfū 6 skūl*), while the rest of the Arabic translated, in abbreviated form, the topics on the French sign: study support, languages, computing. English was increas-

Image 11: Tutoring sign pluralingualism as aspiration index

ingly an index of educational prestige in Morocco, and this business mobilized the sonic resonances of English in opting for this Arabic transliteration instead of a translation. All these were examples of public signs that interpellated readers who could hear the writing speak. Without reference to spoken Fassi registers, these written *darīja* forms would not make sense. But street signs were not the only medium platform in which *darīja* writing circulated: Moroccans also wrote and read via linguistic technologies such as newsprint.

الحلقة ٣: قراة مشاركة

Episode 3: Distributed Reading Out Loud

Meria`m's sister Yaqout was in the process of negotiating a marriage proposal, and since their parents had passed away, their older brother, Mohammed had come to discuss these things with Yaqout's intended. He was staying at Meriam's house in Fez, as he resided in a different city. I sat eating breakfast with them the morning after the marriage discussions had concluded and they were about to return home. One of Meriam's daughters, Faiza, entered and started reading the newspaper her uncle had brought the day before. Newspapers were often circulated through multiple readers. Café owners would buy several newspapers in the morning for their customers to read. Papers would be left, *borrowed across tables, and read aloud among groups at tables (see Cody 2011 for a Tamil example). Newspapers would also be shared in train cabins, by workers in factory transport buses, and among family members. Television news reported on print headlines from newspapers aligned with a specific political party each day.*

Faiza read out loud a portion of an article in the women's section about the health benefits of saffron for relieving tension and preventing cancer. The newspaper was in fuṣḥā, *and Faiza read it as such out loud, including the complex vowel markings not written in the Arabic script but trained into her at school. Reading aloud was common courtesy in informal family gatherings and part of the distributed literacy work mentioned in Chapter 2. Most print publications were in* fuṣḥā, *standard Arabic. As she was reading, Toufiq commented in* darīja *that the best part of the newspaper was the section informing people about the benefits of certain foods, medicines, and products. Faiza agreed with her brother, while their mother, Meriam, added that the health benefits had to come from the threads of* بلدي, (beldī), *(local) saffron, indigenous Moroccan saffron rather than imported varieties. Zoubida went on to read out loud another part of that section on the health benefits of different herbs. Meriam mentioned that Beni Mellel and Marrakesh were Moroccan towns famous for* beldī *plants, and her older brother Mohammed agreed. Meriam's younger son nodded his agreement but added that people in those towns were involved in too much dark magic and backward thinking. His uncle Mohammed countered by saying that Beni Mellel people were hard working, and the city had grown a lot—it was not as it used to be. Meriam's son seemed to back down out of deference for his uncle, but I was not sure his ideas changed.*

♣

As seen in this ethnographic episode, even reading Arabic in the most iconic of media, newsprint, involved a listening eye acquired through oral dictation in formal school settings. As the next section demonstrates, newsprint was also the most contested of mediums for nonstandard Arabic forms. Writing *darīja* news on paper raised the ire of Arabic gatekeepers deeply concerned about proper relationality and its Moroccan political implications.

Newsprint Publics: The Politics of Writing *Darīja*

The press in Morocco had been split, even before independence, between Arabic and French standard orthographies, or formal graphic representational systems, and in the case of Arabic, specifically *fuṣḥā*. Each political party had its own press mouthpiece, such that specific newspapers and magazine were explicit about their political orientation and motives. Thus, the Moroccan printed and later internet-based press reflected a media ideology that newsprint was supposed to reflect the perspectives of the party funding and supporting it. Producers constructed and readers interpreted articles and layouts in light of that expectation and often "triangulated" meaning by reading, viewing, and discussing other news venue accounts, as described in the introduction.

Moroccan print newspapers written in *darīja* were very rare and short-lived, publishing between two to four years. Why would *darīja* print newspapers have such short lives? Moha Ennaji claimed that governments and the population of North Africa viewed dialectal Arabic as a corrupt/incorrect form of Arabic useless for public discourse and thus both self-censored and were discouraged from writing news in *darīja*. He identified one *darīja* paper in the 1980s, اخبار السوق (*akhbār as-sūq*), that the state shut because it "aroused people's interest in change" (Ennaji 1991, 12). He inferred that the content was problematic but embedded it in a section about attitudes toward written dialectal Arabic, implying that the form itself was part of instigating change. Elinson described the same paper as a French-inspired political satire project to document working-class lives through their language (2013, 718). In other words, the state "heard" contentious Moroccanness through the written *darīja*. According to Elinson's interview, the producers claimed that their paper folded because of poor financial moves, not government pressure, even though the political cartoons lampooned official policies regularly. Since much of the print publications were financed by political parties, it seems the writers of *akhbār as-sūq* did not manage to get political support for their mediatized ideology of raising everyday working-class forms of language to the political stage.

I observed this ideology, that certain representational forms (standard orthography) should be the visible face of specific mediums (newsprint) similarly in debates surrounding two Moroccan news weeklies published in the beginning of the twenty-first century: خبر بلادنا (*khabār blādnā*), and نيشان (*nīshān*). Each of these mobilized nonstandard Arabic for political projects: adult education and oppositional party politics. They also evoked aural reading (a graphic-sonic ideology) as part of their mobilization projects.

Elena Prentice was an American from a wealthy family of multi-generation diplomats and spent summers of her childhood in Tangier, Morocco, as well as Paris and New York. In 1989, she returned to direct the Tangier American Legation Museum and began to study Arabic. She felt that Moroccans undervalued *darīja* and that the differences between *darīja* and *fuṣḥā* complicated literacy education. Using a nonprofit she founded in the U.S., she began publishing 5,000 copies of a free weekly paper, خبار بلادنا (*khabār blādnā*), "Our

Country's News," from 2002 to 2006. The paper was eight pages and had sections for national news, folk stories, health news, recipes, songs, proverbs, phone numbers for public service agencies, jokes, and a crossword puzzle—all in Arabic script *darīja*. Prentice distributed the newspaper through a network of American adult language and literacy programs, similar to the one she had founded to teach women in the Tangier old city where the Legation was located. I first encountered this paper at the American Language Institute in Fez in 2002 while I was taking *darīja* courses. Since Prentice herself did not write Arabic, she mobilized several Moroccans to help her write content for the paper each week. Two of my Fassi *darīja* and *fuṣḥā* teachers helped write sections of the paper, contributing stories and jokes each week. Prentice claimed a much larger readership (20,000) than the number of copies printed, since she knew that Moroccans shared print materials on a regular basis. In addition to the newspaper, she published many adult literacy pamphlets: a *darīja* translation of the king's speech on changes to the Moroccan family law in 2003; a *darīja* booklet on modern health and cleanliness; an adult literacy booklet that taught the Arabic alphabet in *darīja*; and a grammar of *darīja* in *darīja*. Each of these employed *darīja* in a *fuṣḥā*-modified Arabic script with the explicit aim of challenging the centripetal force of *fuṣḥā* state language policies. Even though she regularly argued in interviews with other newspapers that Moroccan Arabic had a standardized grammar, she did not elaborate on regional writing or speaking differences or the common practice of orthographic heterogeneity (nonstandardized writing). In this way, she sought to further state literacy goals but in the contested form of written *darīja* in simplified and voweled Arabic script. Why voweled? Because the audience she explicitly targeted were undereducated Moroccans unfamiliar with engaging print without the sonic cues left off all Arabic books and newsprint.

Unfortunately, the project had limited visibility and distribution. Because her networks were tied to American language programs, the publication's distribution was urban, foreign, and elite based. Most of the undereducated populations she sought to reach never saw any of these publications. Even when they did, the Arabic voweling and content indexed childhood literacy, poverty, and women for most of the Fassis among whom I shared the publications. Some of my Fassi colleagues trained in European linguistic theories did appreciate that she was recognizing *darīja* as a valid language variety, but no one thought her literacy project was something under which they would raise their own children. It was very much iconic of disadvantaged Moroccans, a good project to help the poor.

Other newsprint publishers employed *darīja* in French-based orthography and Arabic-based orthography to challenge state policies, suggesting that *fuṣḥā* press was an elite mechanism for undermining civil society and democratization gains (in contradiction to Laroui's claim that French was the language of elites). French-language Moroccan weekly *TelQuel*'s Ahmed Benchemsi was one of these, publishing نيشان (*nīshān*), *darīja* for "Straight Up/Direct," an Arabic press weekly magazine from 2006 to 2010.[10] The Arabic weekly *nīshān* clothed a political ideology in an Arabic orthographic form with *darīja* context-creating indexes and iconic resonances. Despite repeated claims by the press and public intellectuals that *nīshān* was a *darīja* news magazine, most contributors wrote in *fuṣḥā* with occasional *darīja* words used for iconic effect. Perhaps that was because the contributing journalists had been trained in the standards of *fuṣḥā* publishing. On the surface, it would appear that Benchemsi and his colleagues mobilized *darīja* in *nīshān* to reflect their oppositional stance, choosing to express critique in a nonstandard language in order to tear down elite power. While that may be part of the story, a closer look at the magazines' uses of *darīja* helps us think about the semiotic processes by which the writers rallied the context-creating properties of *darīja* -as-opposition. In *nīshān*, the bulk of each article was written in *fuṣḥā*, even though *darīja*-sprinkled terms garnered the greatest discursive visibility because of their marked quality. Fassis did not expect to see *darīja* written in a news magazine, which potentially gave it prominence and weight in ways that tied it indexically to the historical moment when written newspaper *darīja* was outside the norm. Thus *darīja* took on a different iconic quality, one of resistance for the writers (and potentially readers), even as they reproduced the centripetal language practices and ideologies of writing substantive information in the conventions of *fuṣḥā*.

Nīshān explicitly stated a stance of political opposition to religious and political taboos. It printed religious jokes, for which the state fined it 80,000 MAD (about $8,500 USD) and banned the editor and writer from print journalism for two months. Court battles ensued the following year when the publisher was sentenced to three years' imprisonment for disrespecting the king. The paper was forced to cease publication for financial reasons, though Elinson argued that this was government power exercised through indirect means (2013, 719). For Elinson, Benchemsi's main publication, TelQel, managed to stay in print partially because its readership and advertising base were internationally situated rather than local.

Both Prentice and Benchemsi contributed to the contentious reform politics of the last two decades by clothing Moroccan ways of speaking with overt and indirect resistance pressure through the moral authority of newsprint script. They either espoused media ideologies promoting state projects such as adult literacy (*khabār blādnā*) but through a divisive language form (written *darīja*) or contested official behaviors and actions using *darīja*-marked *fuṣḥā* (*nīshān*). They paved the way for subsequent Moroccan online newspapers to incorporate Arabic-script *darīja* into their publications, such as گود (www.goud.ma) and Hespress (www.hespress.com), and regional websites, such as fesnews.net. Yet, the online uses of *darīja* press did not garner as much opposition as the print versions. My Fassi interlocutors suggested this was because the internet medium had already been colonized and commodified by *darīja* chats and social media.

Conclusion

Although official debates about what language medium should connect Moroccans revolved around the failures of Arabic/Tamazight/French multilingualism, or *darīja/fuṣḥā*, in practice scriptic choices in mobile phones, internet, and television during the period of my fieldwork were far more varied and heterogeneous than the newsprint just discussed. They evoked a graphic-sonic sensibility that Moroccans connected via nonstandard Arabic, even as they raised the specter of Arabic as a troublesome connective medium. There would have been no controversies about writing news in *darīja* if *fuṣḥā* were not seen by some media producers as a failed Moroccanness medium. Media ideologies about graphic inscriptions in publicly circulated mediums were in an expanding centrifugal phase partially due to a contemporary contention between semiotic orders: linguistic orthography ideologies whereby an Arab should write in Arabic (most often *fuṣḥā*); colonial and cosmopolitan economic ideologies whereby success can and was measured through command of multilingual resources; and genre conventions and media ideologies whereby written forms in specific genres such as WhatsApp chats, mobile phone texting, tweets, and YouTube comments reflected and created the social diversity, divisions, and linguistic technologies of Moroccan ways of speaking (Schulthies 2014a). The orthographic heterogeneity illustrated in the examples I described did not just reflect individual juxtapositions of two ways of writing the same thing in multilingual contexts (Angermeyer 2005). They were also different from previous ethnographies of writing studies discussing orthographic diversity such as grassroots literacy (Blommaert 2008), indigenous language revitalization projects (Faudree 2013), and artifacts of individual novelty (Androutsopoulos 2010). This graphic diversity reflected and produced a linguascape in which reading and listening were not tied to separate sensory channels, but rather entailed each other through a graphic-sonic sensorium. To read *darīja* was to hear the Moroccanness personas embedded in the orthographic heterogeneity of forms. This also reflected a media ideology that written forms of Moroccan and spoken varieties in advertising and social media were not domains covered by state standardization projects: scriptic heterogeneity and hybridity were accepted, expected, and a mark of cosmopolitan Moroccanness, even as advertisers targeted specific audiences through font sizes, colors, social indexes of politeness, slang, and choice of script. Newsprint publications, however, continued to face opposition to *darījization*.

Reading subjects with a vested interest in the unifying language ideology of standard Arabic promoted the centripetal work of gate-keeping and policing boundaries of linguistic technologies within their ascribed purview. Linguistic technologies such as spoken, handwritten, print, and electronic registers had within them genre distinctions that self-appointed centralizing gatekeepers, as reading authorities, did not feel the need to clarify as assigned to one domain or another. As mentioned, private or nonstate genres such as letters, plays, proverb collections, amulets, internet chats, mobile phone texts, advertising signs, and short dialect dialogues within novels were often allowed a flexibility in orthographic conventions that textbooks, newspapers, and parliamentary laws were not. All of the forms I share in this chapter were publicly circulating, leaking into the domains of standard gatekeepers. However, during the first two decades of the twenty-first century, Arabic language academies and state censors had not included orthographic policing of advertising or personal communication technologies, such as cell phones and social media, within their orbit of concern, leaving a wide range of graphic possibilities for hearing Moroccanness. That does not mean that individuals did not take up the centripetal mantel when the state failed to do so, but it did mean that heterogeneity of writing reflected that Fassis had an unmarked mixing of many different linguistic resources as a communicative norm, using bits of French, Arabic, English, Tamazight, and other ways of speaking and writing in their everyday lives as an ambivalent response, in some cases, to state centralizing projects.

These examples of social media circulation demonstrate the idea that Fassis can and did draw from a variety of scriptic and sonic resources. The purity of standardness was implicitly rejected in *darīja* multiscriptic sensibilities in most media platforms—except newsprint. Graphic utterances illustrated, in a multisensoral, striking way, the overlapping centripetal and centrifugal forces in the life of language Bakhtin identified so long ago. The language ideologies underlying orthographic heterogeneity of Moroccan Arabic representations illustrated the blending of sensory channels assumed in *darīja* writing, the sounding of script and scripting of sound. It also pointed to a range of social work performed in everyday life by different ways of writing/reading the same thing. To reiterate, to communicate in a specific written graphic form was to align oneself with a Moroccanness relationality project. At times these social connections involved ambivalence and disregard, agreeing with the principle but not the means of connecting, actively resisting centralizing connection projects through assigning political values to specific graphic forms, and viewing "lost" forms of language as social means to a commercial end.

5
Mediating Moroccan Muslims

So Moroccans—My Benefactor—have lived under the influence of a school that bears all of these characteristics. It has branded their collective identity with this mark, and has made of their understanding of the religion, of their devoutness to it and of their granting it authority over their daily affairs in their various manifestations a support and a porter toward this Sunni religious horizon, which—My Benefactor—both the common and distinguished people have started to realize its special distinction. They have also started to recognize because of it the Islam of beauty, tolerance, and fraternity that the Prophet of mercy—your grandfather—came with.

—*SHAYKH MUHAMMED AL-TA'WIL, RAMADAN LECTURE BROADCAST ON MOROCCO'S RELIGIOUS TELEVISION STATION,* ASSĀDISSA, *THE MOHAMMED VI CHANNEL*

They say Islam is a religion of ease, not a religion of hardship.	*gālak al'īslām dīn yusr, māšī dīn 'usar.*	گالك الإسلام دين يسر، ماشي دين عسر.

Moroccan paraphrase of hadith, a saying of the Prophet Muhammad

Arguably one of the most constant elements of the Fassi soundscape for centuries has been the echoing resonance of the call to prayer, الأذان (*al'ādhān*), broadcast five times a day from the hundreds of minarets scattered across the old walled city, the French *ville nouvelle*, and the rapidly expanding outlying neighborhoods. Despite a long tradition of precise time calculations in the Maliki school of Muslim religious legal interpretation, each call to prayer from every mosque never quite started at the same second, creating an echoing effect throughout the city. It was and continues to be one of the most beautiful aspects of the Fassi soundscape to me. Each call to prayer was uttered in Qur'anic Arabic, the main source for the standard Arabic *fuṣḥā* described in earlier chapters. Some mosques began each day before dawn with an additional petitionary prayer, or الدعاء (*du'ā'*), before the obligatory call to prayer. Some reciters would put more pause between phrases, which also contributed to the slight distinctions in each sounding. But the call, with its slight lengthening of specific long vowels, doesn't vary in pitch or octave as much as the forms used elsewhere in the Muslim world. There is an ever so slightly rising tone carried across the punctuated phrases: "God is Great, God is Great, witness there is no God but Allah, witness Muhammad is the Messenger of God, come to prayer, come to salvation." The national television station also broadcast the call to prayer, but according to the prayer time in the capital, Rabat, which was about seven minutes later than Fez.[1] The call to prayer regulated time in Fez, and not just religious time, such as when to pray or start or break a fast. Visiting and leisure times were often calculated as occurring after صلاة العصر (*ṣalāt al'aṣr*), the late afternoon prayer. Importantly, the call to prayer interpellated Fassis as Muslims, no matter whether they viewed themselves as committed, ambivalent, Sufi, Salafi, secular, well-versed in Islamic law and sciences or not (Spadola 2014). The call as a medium did not differentiate Muslims, but Muslims certainly did in regard to the kinds of connective channels they used, and with very real-world consequences. Fassis regularly lamented that Moroccans did not know how to be Muslim and critiqued the signs of each other's religiosity, precisely because of the specter of failed Muslim sociality embedded in ongoing conflicts over proper Islam.

As a temporal frame and historical fulcrum, May 16, 2003, was regularly evoked in accounts of Morocco's response to religious extremism.[2] In May of that year, "Islamists" coordinated attacks in Casablanca commercial venues (a tourist hotel, a popular café, a Jewish cemetery, community center, and restaurant), killing 37 Moroccans, including the extremists themselves, and 8 Europeans, and injuring nearly 100 others, the majority of whom were Muslims. The Moroccan king and state officials since that time have promoted the Moroccan model of Islamic practice (النموذج المغربي [*namūdhaj almaghribī*]) as the best deterrent to extremism based on the religious leadership of the Moroccan Alaoui monarchy, the Ash'ari theological doctrine, the Maliki school of jurisprudence, and al-Junayd Sufism (I'll explain these concepts later in the chapter). Print, television, radio, and internet mediums were all mobilized to educate local and transnational audiences on the core beliefs and practices of a historically tolerant Moroccan religious model, entextualized as continuing the tradition of religious coexistence from the Andalusian era.[3] In 2004, the ministry of religious affairs created the Mohammed 6th radio station for the Holy Qur'an,[4] and a television channel of the same name in 2005 (known as السادسة [*assādissa*], or the sixth station in the Moroccan satellite bouquet—nicely mirroring the king's name as the sixth Alaoui monarch named Mohammed).[5] They also began a campaign to distribute Qur'ans and Maliki religious law materials printed in Maghribi calligraphic form throughout Africa and Europe; proliferated pedagogical institutes for training imams and counselors (المرشيدات والمرشيدون [*almuršīdāt walmuršīdūn*, male and female religious guides]) from West Africa, North Africa, and Europe;[6] televised Moroccan religious talk shows, scholarly symposia, and lectures such as the Dar Hassaniya speech mentioned in the quote at the beginning of this chapter; broadcast instructional videos on proper ritual practices such as prayer in a mix of *darīja* and *fuṣḥā*; and broadcast visits of the king to Muslim communities across Africa, Europe, and the Middle East. This immense effort revolved around Muslims recognizing and maintaining relationships with other Muslims through specific kinds of mediums, ways of speaking religious discourses, and multimodal sign arrays in anxiety-heightened contexts of Muslim-on-Muslim violence. I call this process phatic labors of recognition, one that relied on a multimodal coordination of sign bundles via specific channels (linguistic, gestural, sartorial, and electronic).

In his insightful ethnography of Muslim mediation in Morocco, Emilio Spadola explored the competing calls of Islam in underclass, struggling, populist neighborhoods of Fez. In particular, he focused on the ways that media called Fassis as Muslims, exploring the repeated ritual processes and practical acts of communication that called Moroccans to kinds of communal belonging tied to elite or commoner Islam.[7] For Spadola, the communicative medium mattered insofar as the medium itself called Moroccans into forms of sociality (2014, 2). I too argue that the "call" of particular mediums, or channels, is significant. I also want to pay attention to the ways that Fassis lamented specific semiotic affordances, or qualities of language and media channels, as a means to calibrate Muslim connectedness. The contrast was not just between elite or commoner forms of Islam, but about whether there was a Moroccan model of Islam, whether or not Fassis agreed with other people's linguistic and clothing markers of that model, and whether the medium (clothing, speech, television, pedagogy) was effective in making Moroccans the right kind of Muslim. In particular, the issues surrounded whether a channel facilitated connections between Muslims and proper forms of Islam or carried dangerous affiliations (or parasites) with corrupted Islamic practices and Muslims. This chapter will begin with Fassi discussions about media and proper markers of Islam; move to the ways scholars and some Moroccans view channels as dangerous rather than mere vehicles for Islam; the way the state has used specific mediums for channeling a Moroccan model of Islam; and spend the latter half on Fassi responses to this mediated calibration of Muslim Moroccanness. Their responses may surprise you.

I hesitated to include a chapter on media and Islam. It seems so reproductive of Euro-American phatic anxieties about mediums that radicalize Islam. Even so, as this chapter suggests, Fassis regularly expressed concerns about the channels by which Muslims learned and shared Islam and the resulting kinds of Islam and Muslims that emerged from those contacts. Why focus on the communicative work of Muslim religious recognition and connection? First, the vast majority of Fassis self-identified as Muslim even though Jewish-Muslim religious coexistence was often touted as central to Moroccanness (Boum 2013). Fassis evaluated and critiqued each others' religious practices regularly, but also claimed that private and state-promoted Qur'anic schools were full of Fassis interested in improving their Qur'anic recitation knowledge. The city was home to dozens of Sufi shrines, where Fassis would gather to learn embodied practices and utterances that would draw them closer to God. Even state-sponsored adult literacy classes targeting women were taught in mosques and used the Qur'an, in both its oral recitation and written modes, as a key literacy medium. They debated the length and style of beards, clothing, and head coverings, as well as other embodied markers of religious alignment, such as the small mark on the forehead made when rubbed against the prayer rug regularly.[8] Fassis watched religious satellite television stations, discussed religious websites, circulated religious videos on computer disks or later via Facebook and WhatsApp throughout the decade of my fieldwork. Fassis also lamented regularly that Moroccans no longer knew real Islam, despite a half-century of state-mandated Islamic education in the schools.

The divisions between ways of connecting as Muslims were not just intellectual debates, but a phatic work of calibrating Moroccanness. On the one hand, the state felt that it needed to shape religious narratives and signs in order to derail acts of public violence against Muslims and non-Muslims. The fact that it did so also indexed its insecurities about past forms of recognition labor: it could not assume direction or control over Moroccan connections to Islam. On the other hand, Fassi discussions about the motivations and sociopolitical fallout of ستاش ماي ("May 16th 2003") were common in my first years of fieldwork and continued through the development of الداعش (*dāeʿš*, Daesh), the Islamic State movement. These discussions often occurred while families gathered together in their homes, with the television, an internet video, or social media post prompting (some discussion related to the lack of proper Islamic practice. In other words, discussions about religion, media, and the state permeated everyday life and involved semiotic and electronic channel ideologies. Several of the families and students I spent time with endlessly discussed what qualified as appropriate ways to signal religiosity. Some would support the state and its media stance toward religion, and others would critique it. Sometimes I heard a person support an aspect of state religious practices to me and critique it with others, depending on their interactional contexts and participant frameworks.

الحلقة ١: التعرّف على الإسلام في فاس

Episode 1: Recognizing Islam in Fez

It was a Friday, and I was invited to lunch—the most important meal of the week for many Fassi families. According to Muslim practice, men were enjoined to attend the Friday noon prayer at the mosque and listen to the sermon before the prayer. Women who wished to could also attend, but it wasn't as incumbent upon them. Families would then gather for a long lunch, often around the fabled Moroccan couscous. I had been invited to eat with the family of a retired military officer whose daughter, Belqis, was working on a master's degree in English at the university. I arrived just as the father was leaving for Friday prayer. He was dressed in لجلابة (jellāba, *Moroccan "traditional" clothing, a long, loose robe with hood and long sleeves), but he only did so for the Friday prayer and religious events. None of the females in this household wore headscarves or other markers of religious identity, but they all fasted and observed the religious holidays. Belqis, her mother, her fourteen-year-old brother, and I watched the twenty-four-hour broadcast of Lebanese-based music program Star Academy's contestant residence, and then an Egyptian dramatic serial, and finally the 2M news in* fuṣḥā.

When Belqis's father returned, he started to tell us all about the sermon that day. After May 2003, the ministry of religious affairs sent out the Friday sermon topics to all mosques to mitigate the spread of extremist ideas through official institutions. The state-written sermon was all about the tolerant social relations Muslims should have toward non-Muslims. This prompted from me a story about a recent encounter I had trying to get computer equipment fixed. A friend had taken me to a friend of a friend to repair my drive. The friend owned a shop that sold Islamic texts and pilgrimage preparation materials. When we walked in, I was a little surprised, because his friend had a long beard and wore لقميص والسروال (lqamīs wasūrwāl, *long shirt and pants), clothing I had associated with* الاخوان (īkhwān), *so-called "Islamist" supporters. I came to understand later that* īkhwān *in Fes was a blanket term for those who displayed outward signs of strict religious commitment but did not always align with any particular political or religious group. It was always used as an out-group identifier: no one ever called themselves* īkhwān, *but rather* اهل السنة (ahl assunna), *People of Sunnah, the same term others in Morocco used to signal their nonalignment with any particular Muslim group. I often heard* īkhwān, *or its Fassi synonym* بولحية (bū llaḥīya, *father of the beard*),[9] *used negatively by those who had suffered reproach from some of the more strident* īkhwān. *Other Fassis tried to be more tolerant of religious difference and called them* الملتزمين (almultazamīn), *the committed. While in the shop with my friend, I was further surprised when the man behind the desk spoke to me in the best British Received Pronunciation English I had heard in Morocco. When the computer technician arrived, he walked in wearing the same long beard and clothes as the shop owner, but with a new pair of Nike trainers—and spoke to me with Brooklyn-accented English. Belqis, her father, and I all laughed at how my American-media-informed assumptions had been ruptured by this encounter. Her father then said that Islam has always been about tolerance, and only a minority of Muslims were led astray into extremism.*

Later that evening I joined Ayah's family for tea. They talked about what it meant to be Muslim and how the state had its own interests in keeping people from real Islamic education. People, including producers of government media, threw out anything the īkhwān *said because their ideas were extreme, but* لحجاب (lhijāb, *(women wearing headscarves and dressing modestly)* *was Islamic and not something that should be discarded. They claimed that most Moroccans didn't know what Islam really was, they were simply Muslims by inheritance. They were very happy with the king's management of religious affairs, but wished that the leaders of the current government would teach real Islam instead of trying to secularize parts of Islam, like the inheritance laws of the Qur'an, that didn't fit outsiders' images of religious equality.*

A few days later I recorded another family collectively watching the 2M religious program الإسلام سلوك ومعاملات (islām sulūk wamuʿāmalāt, *"Islam, behaviors and comportment") The fifty-year-old father, Abderrahman, dominated the post-program discussion: "This program is eloquent. They aren't like* إقرا (īqrāʿ, *a Saudi businessman-owned religious station) or* المنار (almanār, *satellite television station for Lebanese Shi'a political party Hizbullah), they don't bring a guy in a* jellāba *(traditional Moroccan clothing), but a suit and tie. The guy types in a computer instead of a sheikh asking another sheikh a question, meaning we are modern. And how does he explain? In* darīja *of Morocco, meaning the easy dialect not like the difficult grammar, declensions, and expressions of formal Arabic. Those others are better than this one, in terms of eloquent Arabic language* (fuṣḥā), *but they say things in difficult discourse the common people can't understand. This one doesn't demand a high level. He doesn't say a word that would confuse you. I like it." This father related to the program presenter because the sign array (suit and tie,* darīja, *computer-relayed correspondence with lay Moroccans rather than scholarly experts) fit his notion of* خطاب الديني (khatāb addīnī, *the field of religious discourse*).

In each of these interactions, I was called to record perspectives on what real religious discourse connecting Muslims was or should be in Morocco. Each involved an analysis of religious sign bundles: clothing, speech, mannerisms, tools, mediums, channels. Not everyone agreed, though, about which sign arrays represented real Islam, but all had something to contribute to calibrations of Muslim connection and Moroccanness in Fez.

Channels: Electronic and Linguistic Intermediaries or Parasites

At some point, coiners of fixed "dictionary" reference terms in multiple languages determined that informational flows resembled constrained waterways and iconically linked the word for "canal" with that of "electronic channel": القناة (*alqanāt*, Arabic), "canal" (French), "channel" (English). According to one baptismal tale of iconic-indexical relationality, Latin (canna) and Arabic (*kanā*) words for "channel" were both related to Greek κάννα, *reed/cane*, which derived from a Sumerian term for a plant with a hollow stem readily converted to a container for the passage of other things. The reed constrained air to make melodious sounds, directed darts and air to a target, managed water to extend one's siphoning or irrigating abilities, channeled information to extend one's persuasive reach. Not much of the constraining affordances of channels were foregrounded in these usages; rather, the focus was on facilitating flow. Under the influence of Jakobson, communicative channels bore these indexical traces as factors that demonstrated the presence, efficacy, or ending of physical contact and psychosocial connectedness (Jakobson 1960, 355). In this model, channels served to connect and only brought attention to themselves when they didn't work as expected. Jakobson later developed the notion that elements of his communicative model could work as duplex signs (Jakobson 1990), meaning they could refer to something while saying something about the speaker's identity. Kockelman applied Jakobson's interest in duplex signs that merged code (linguistic conventions) and message (instances of use) to channels (2010, 414–17). For Kockelman, channels are mediums that connect signers and interpreters, whereas code connects signs and objects (although code in the sense of semiotic conventions can also be a channel as it mediates). Signs could be directed toward channels and close off other signer possibilities (channel-directed signer); they could be directed to interpreters who were then expected to become channels to other signers (signer-directed signer); they might enable mediation because of the indexical traces they left of the path they took (self-channeling channels); or determine an interpreter based on where the sign began (source-directed channel). In each of these duplex instances, signers, interpreters, and channels shaped each other rather than serving as empty transmitters for sociality.

As mentioned in the Introduction, Malinowski's critique of Enlightenment referentialist language ideologies proposed that one of the key functions of language was to recognize and maintain sociability, his phatic communion (1936 [1923]). Channels could serve as intermediaries, or facilitators opening a path between communicating entities, or be viewed as failing to do so for some reason and become a troublesome, interfering mediator (Kockelman 2010, 413). When Moroccans lamented the failures of channels, whether semiotic (as in collective recitation, style of dress) or electronic (as in television channel, internet website), they made visible the mediating possibilities of mediums (Eisenlohr 2011, 267). Building on work by Elyachar (2010) and Kockelman (2011), I view the phatic communion in Muslim majority Fez as labor, a fraught work of Muslim recognition and sociability tied to critiques of mediation channels. Rather than seeing phatic sociability as effortless and empty, I suggest that specific contexts of significant religious talk overlap phatic relationality, critical causal analysis, affective alignments, and collectivity-building in these examples of state-directed Islam mediations. I will also explore the duplex nature of channels, the perceptual materialities that select and screen Moroccan Muslim collectivity alignments. Electronically mediated Moroccan Islamic practices and their uptake in urban Fassi homes may help us better understand the multimodal sociality of Moroccan Islam, in which channels, codes, and religious collectivities are differentiated or made the same.

In media analysis of the Arabic-speaking Muslim world, I found that television, radio, and internet channels were undertheorized or overdetermined: electronic media were either the transparent and unencumbered facilitators of information flows and public participation (I'm thinking of Wael Ghanem's Revolution 2.0 in which Egypt's Arab Spring uprising worked via social media mobilizations) or hypodermic needles of radicalization and misinformation (the numerous analyses of Al Jazeera giving voice to Muslim extremism or the ways "jihadi" websites radicalized vulnerable youth). In other words, they were intermediaries (facilitating mediums) or mediators (interfering channels). These vacillations played out in Morocco regularly, most recently in a claim (made March 16, 2016) by Ilyas El Omari, leader of then–opposition political party *Parti Authenticité et Modernité* (PAM). In a national television interview, he accused *assādissa*, the Moroccan religious television station, of cultivating extremism in the deployment of terms and expressions and the selection of topics and speakers.[10] In response, the national news on the Rabat television station and other news outlets shared a report issued February 11, 2016, by American Media Abroad praising *assādissa* for "conveying a message of civility and tolerance through faith . . . promot[ing] Morocco's own religious heritage—such as its centuries-old legal and spiritual traditions and unique style of Qur'an recitation, all conveyed through the country's distinctive Arabic dialect."[11] The television channel here was cast as a mediating parasite and an electronic extension facilitating Moroccan Muslim connection that distorted or facilitated depending on one's perceptual field. It was not a neutral medium but carried traces of political alignments. The national television channels were seen as promoting a tolerant, moderate Islam through *darīja* and a unique style of collective Qur'anic recitation. For El Omari and others, they were making Muslim extremists through their selection of religious speakers, topics, and ways of speaking. In the case of the *assādissa* producers, these electronic channels were signer-directed mediums, duplex human-electronic channels directed toward interpreters who were expected to become channels to other signers (Kockelman 2010, 417). The Fassi interpreters were then to connect to other Moroccans as specifically tolerant kinds of Muslims. For El Omari, these were channel-directed mediums, closing off other ways of being Muslim in Morocco because they screened other kinds of Islamic representations: women without headscarves, those calling for the equalizing of inheritance, scholars who provided critical reform perspectives on Islam.

الحلقة ٢: لمسارية فالمجتمع الفاسي

Episode 2: Strolling through Fassi Relationality

It had been five months since the start of the 2011 Arab uprisings, and the normally contentious Moroccan multiparty political environment (Willis 2002, 2014) had added two layers: the 20 February protest coalition and supporters of the king's constitutional reforms. Two weeks remained before the constitutional referendum proposed by the king, in which the citizens would vote to disperse the monarch's powers among regional councils, an independent judiciary, and direct elections for the prime minister position. Moroccan celebrities made a music video encouraging everyone to vote. Talk shows endlessly debated referendum outcomes. Social media was awash with slogans and position statements. Back in Fez for summer fieldwork, I jumped into a shared taxi headed toward the Fez medina and encountered mid-conversation a discussion between a mid-forties woman and the taxi driver. The driver was narrating a tale about early Muslim leader Abu Bakr and drawing connections between his enlightened rule and King Mohammed VI. The woman affirmed that Islam was the best model for reform in Morocco, citing a religious program she had watched on television and comments her مرشيدة (murshīda, female religious guide) had explained to her women's study group at the mosque. The king had created the murshīdat[12] program in 2006 to train women as religious counselors and leaders of study groups based in Moroccan mosques and schools. As we threaded our way through the crowded noon traffic, the woman went on to explain what she had learned from the murshīda about proper ways to perform the pilgrimage to Mecca and avoid those who exploit Muslim travelers. As they commiserated over ills in the world, the taxi driver lamented that the difference between good and evil was the width of a thread, a Fassi proverb I had heard before. Weaving together television evidentials, murshīda instruction, and religious traditions, the taxi driver and his rider constructed an alignment with the king's reform project even as voices clamored dissent elsewhere.

When I arrived at the home I was headed toward, I found the family watching the national news, which included a report about some members of the 20 February movement who were calling for a boycott of the referendum vote. The twenty-year-old daughter, Chayma, stood up after watching for a few seconds and uttered كدابين، منافقين (kdābīn, munāfiqīn, "Liars, hypocrites"), as she left the room. I understood the lack of response by the family members who continued watching as confirming their assent with her statement. I had known this family for years and had observed them regularly challenging utterances they did not agree with from their television and face-to-face interlocutors. I also knew they had mixed perspectives on Moroccan politics: everyone lamented widespread government corruption, yet some members supported the king's reform efforts and others felt disillusioned by decades of what seemed like lack of development support for Fez. No one in this family supported the 20 February movement, which they had informed me consisted of secularists and salafis (those seeking a return to "original" practices of early Islam)—both extremists in their view. As Chayma left the room, Chafiq changed the channel to السادسة (assādissa), the Mohammed VI television station that was broadcasting a prerecorded recitation of the Qur'an set to nature images, and most everyone in the room turned to a discussion about the high price of fish in the markets.

A day later, I sat in a Fassi neighborhood beauty parlor getting my hair cut. It was a small shop just for female clients, only about seven feet tall and ten feet long with windows covering two-thirds of the small storefront. The exterior windows were covered in hairstyle images so no one could look in, allowing veiled women to relax, remove their headscarves, and enjoy the salon away from pry-

ing eyes. Despite the heat of the day, the bright lights in the styling mirror, and the cramped quarters, the door was closed, making it incredibly warm. I sat in one of two swivel chairs in front of a mirror, while the stylist clipped my limp hair and chatted with my friend Fatiha. She had removed her headscarf while we sat in the salon, and they began discussing trending haircuts. The stylist mentioned how much she like my companion's style—it reminded her of one of the contestants on the Moroccan serial game show لالة لعروسة (Lalla Larousa). *The prime-time weekly program on "Rabat," the first national television station, pitted newlywed couples against each other in a range of competitions to see which couple would survive eight weeks to win a free wedding celebration, new house, and a honeymoon trip.*

As she switched to the blow-dryer to style my newly layered locks, the stylist asked if Fatiha had been following the Lalla Larousa *series that year. Raising her voice slightly above the din, Fatiha said she didn't have time to follow it. Almost in rhythm with her blow-styling hands, the stylist quickly replied that now my friend could catch up on recent episodes online. She relayed something I had observed even from the U.S.—one could follow many Moroccan programs on YouTube, DailyMotion, or Vimeo those days, as people regularly posted Moroccan television programs for kin living abroad. That was also about the time that the Moroccan national television and radio company (SNRT) also began posting select recorded programs on their website, though live broadcasting would have to wait until 2014, would be removed in 2016, and would be returned in late 2017. As the stylist ran her fingers through my freshly coiffed hair, Fatiha capped the discussion with a polite but gently pointed critique: people spent more time following and chatting about television programs than they did prayer.*

Religious Discourse and the State's Moroccan Model of Islam

This section will get rather technical in describing the state's official elements of a Moroccan model of Islamic practice, so bear with me as we wade through the details. This will be important to understand the responses that come later. As I mentioned previously, since the 2003 Casablanca Moroccan bombings, the Moroccan government had been very keen to regulate الخطاب الديني (*al-khitāb addīnī*, religious discourse) (Bouasria 2012. While religious reform projects were not new (Spadola 2008), several scholars have noted the ways these reforms strengthened the power of the king (Bouasria 2012 El-Katiri 2013). In particular, this reform project has sought to specify which kinds of religious sociality relations would connect Moroccans as Muslims. The primary administrator of these projects was nominally the king, Mohammed VI, who directly managed the Ministry of Religious Endowments and Islamic Affairs

(MREIA), whereas all other ministry heads were distributed among and appointed by democratically elected political parties.[13] In this sense, the king, who claims descent from the Prophet Muhammad, managed religious life far more directly, explicitly, and visibly than other political institutions.[14] From 2003 until the writing of this book, MREIA managed religious training for both national and transnational Muslim religious leaders, *assādissa* media programming, Qur'anic and other print publications, and the issuing of *fatwas* (personalized rulings about specific practices; see Agrama 2010), Friday mosque lectures, education in rural Qur'anic schools (التربية العتيقة [*tarbīya al'atīqa*, "ancient education"]; these latter three domains previously somewhat independent of the state), and funds from religious endowments (purported to be the most flush of any ministry and used to finance the Moroccan model outreach).[15] More specifically, they promoted the Moroccan model of Islamic practice, النموذج المغربي (*namūdhaj almaghribī*).

The term "Moroccan Islam" has been around since the colonial period. French (and American) scholars and administrators used it to name (entextualize) a form of pious leader veneration organized around Sufi religious associations and Sunni descendants of the prophet Muhammad known as لشرفاء (*ššurufā'*) (Eickelman 1976).[16] Many scholars have described and analyzed this concept (Bouasria 2012 Burke 2014; Combs-Schilling 1989; Eickelman 1976; El Mansour 2004; Geertz 1971; Hammoudi 1997), so I will direct attention to a few elements that seemed salient for my analysis. Some scholars have assumed the Moroccan Sufi-Sunni-Sharifan connection was unique, since ancestor veneration was most often associated with Shi'a forms of Islam, and Morocco aligned as Sunni, meaning that they adhered to the Qur'an and Sunnah (a select set of sayings and recorded deeds of Muhammad) as doctrinal sources. Pious descendent veneration has been a key source of contention for Moroccans who claim this as an un-Islamic innovation (البدع [*albida'*]) along with other specifically Moroccan practices such as collective Qur'anic recitation and praying with one's hands down rather than crossed across one's chest. Several American-influenced scholars have argued that Moroccan Islam was promoted by the French as a means of social control (some have even argued it was created by the French through a screening and selection of specific rituals—see Burke 2014), and capitalized on by the Moroccan monarchy during the struggle for independence (Spadola 2014, 12–13).

Since 2003, Moroccan officials employed the term النمو جذ المغربي (namūdhaj almaghribī), "the Moroccan model" as an "immunizational tool" to various forms of extremist tendencies (notice they did not use the word "jihadist" or "Islamist," both terms regularly employed by foreigners to describe Muslims merging political and religious extremism).[17] This model was based on the religious leadership of the Moroccan king, called امير المؤمنين (*āmīr alm'ūminīn*, "leader of the believers"), a title previously given to a politicoreligious successor of the prophet Muhammad, such as Omar Bin Khatab. The larger phrase used on national radio and television broadcasts to introduce the king and his policies has been صاحب الجلال محمد السادس امير المومنين وحامي الملة والدين (*sāḥib aljilāla muḥamad assādissa āmīr alm'ūminīn wahāmī almila widdīn*, "His majesty Muhammad the sixth, leader of the faithful, protector of faith and religion [religious practices/spirituality])." In this way, he was not a signer or interpreter, but a screener and selector who foreclosed or enclosed the channels that connected Moroccan Muslims to God's knowledge. Use of this term by Moroccan leaders created a speech chain indexing their political and religious links to الراشدون. (*alrašīdūn*), "the rightly guided caliphs" who led Muslims in the first decades of the seventh century (first century in the Muslim calendar), after Muhammad's death.

Another core aspect of the Moroccan model was Ash'ari theological doctrine. This has been the most widely accepted Muslim epistemological framework (though there are others) that considers reason as complementary to revelation as long as one humbly recognizes the position of the reasoner in relation to the divine giver of the message (Alomary 2011; Hirschkind 2006, 150). One cannot understand God's logic for judgments and laws entirely, but since God is just, whatever he states as good is good and whatever he says to avoid should be avoided. In Jacobson's terms, Ash'ari doctrine explicitly defines reason and revelation as channels connecting an addresser to addressees, God with reasoning Muslims. The Qur'an and well-documented sayings of the prophet Muhammad (Sunnah) are the key sources of revelation and central to the ways Muslims reason under the Ash'ari doctrine. In circumstances where there is not a clear statement in the Qur'an and Sunnah, scholars trained in religious sciences can make analogy with similar situations in which there is a known position and rely on consensus of the scholarly community. Despite these time-honored traditions of Ash'ari reasoning, not all Fassis chose to recognize these processes, arguing with the somewhat haphazard or selective ways this emerged in everyday practices of Muslims in Morocco (see Bouasria 2012, 39).

Maliki jurisprudence is another cornerstone to this model. Those who follow this interpretive tradition distinguish it from other Islamic legal schools by its reliance on a wide range of legal sources, a flexibility of interpretation based on analogous reasoning, and its religious tolerance.[18] Maliki jurisprudence has not been the only source for Moroccan laws (legal codes have drawn from French law and other legal logics), but it has been a unifying element of Moroccan religious life (El-Katiri 2013, 55). More importantly, Maliki school as practiced in Morocco is manifest in a host of specific semiotic signs, such as ways of placing their arms straight while standing during prayer, forms of Qur'anic recitation such as group recitation, the *jellāba* (a long loose-fitting covering) as religious dress, the style of الأذان (*al'ādhān*, broadcast call to prayer), and an emphasis on oral transmission of key instructional texts (often in poetic form such as the الآرجومية [*alārjūmīya*]). These specific signs conatively call out to Moroccans as Maliki Muslims to connect with God and other Muslims, but also reflect those who answer that specific call.

The last piece of the model is Al-Junayd Sufism, officially understood as "sober Sufism," focused on devotional associations that organize religious practice through a wide range of paths tied to the historical significance of لزاوية (*zāwīya*), "meeting houses" in Moroccan political and social life (Hammoudi 1997; Spadola 2014). Previously the monarchy sought to curtail the political influence of *zāwīya* associations and religious scholars trained through Qarawiyyiin, but after 2003 the state promoted specific Sufi associations as key to "moderate" Islam. By designating Junayd Sufism as central to Islam in Morocco and appointing a prominent member of the Boutchichi Sufi order, Ahmed Taoufiq, as minister of Islamic Affairs, the state channeled previous Sufi-led reform movements into official policy (Bouasria 2012 46). In contrast, *īkhwān* (a notably variable term in Fez as described previously, though often translated as "Salafi" in the U.S. and Europe to denote extremists) were more literalist in their theology,[19] with reason a dangerous epistemology and Sufi orders/practices a corrupting innovation of Islam that had no place in worship.[20]

But it wasn't just the *īkhwān* or religiously strident who felt some Sufi practices were un-Islamic. There were many kinds of Sufi associations in Morocco, and not all Fassis viewed them as promoting appropriate forms of worship. I attended a circumcision celebration for a friend's son in which the family had employed عيساوة (*'īsāwa*, a musical group tied to an ecstatic Sufi order), to provide the entertainment. In early twentieth-century reform movements, *'īsāwa* were among the problematic Sufi groups the religious leaders and king curtailed because they mobilized Fassis in "non-modern" ways, communicating through "older communicative forces—the holiness [*baraka*] of saints, the intoxicating power of crowds and music . . . private jinn exorcisms and ecstatic trance" (Spadola 2008, 121–22). The friend, Ilham, who had brought this group to the family gathering, saw herself as an educated, urban Muslim, one who prayed, fasted, read the Qur'an, dressed modestly (including a headscarf), criticized the rigidness of *īkhwān*, decried government corruption, and enjoyed the Fassi tradition of religious praise music, such as *'īsāwa* songs performed in *darīja* that venerated God and the prophet Muhammad. She did not approve of the ecstatic trances tied to *jinn* exorcisms also linked with *ʿīsāwa*. One extended family member at the party began dancing ecstatically to a *ʿīsāwa* song, such that another family member had to hold her so she wouldn't fall or run into other people. Several of Ilham's family members commented later how backward that practice was and how it ruined the enjoyment of others who wanted to celebrate without channeling that parasitic aspect of *ʿīsāwa* practice. For these Fassis, Sufi praise music connected Moroccan Muslims in appropriate ways as long as it served as an intermediary and not a troubling mediator of problematic religious relations (*jinn* possession).

Moroccan officials regularly promoted a bundle of exemplar signs, both iconic and indexical, for their model. The minister of Religious Endowments and Islamic Affairs, Ahmed Toufiq, stated in 2015 that Moroccan mosques embodied the quality of Islam's central tenet, توحيد (*taūhīd*), "the oneness" of God through the single square minaret rather than the multiples that regularly appeared on Ottoman-inspired mosques of the Arab East. Even though it has long been unofficial policy for Moroccan ministers and government officials to wear the Moroccan hooded *jellāba*,[21] in 2014 the president of the Moroccan parliament banned the wearing of non-Moroccan Islamic clothing ("Afghani" dress) during parliament sessions. The *jellāba* as a Moroccan form of Islamic dress, often worn with the hood folded in a specific way over the head, was standard for all government officials during religious events and for scholars who appeared on the *assādissa* station programming. There were several forms of religious head-covering options for men: the off-white or yellow wrapped scarf known as الرزة, (*alrazza*), associated with rurality; the conical and iconic red Fez, worn by the king, government officials, and parliamentarians on official occasions with an off-white لسلهام (*sselhām*, a long lightweight cover) and *jellāba*;[22] and the طربوش الوطني (*tarbūš lwaṭanī*—named "the national hat" because of its association with the national independence movement of the 1940s and '50s), the wool cap with a slight elongated indentation at the top. The *tarbūš lwaṭanī* was worn regularly by Mohamed V, king during French colonial rule, and prior to that by العلماء (*ʿulamaʿ*), Maliki religious scholars trained at Qarawiyyiin. It was also worn by politicians such as ʿAllal al-Fasi (one of the leaders of Morocco's 1940s independence movement)[23] and later by Abderahman Yousfi (leftist opposition politician who became prime minister in the 1990s) and Muhammad al-Raissoui (key religious scholar associated with العادالة والتنمية [*alʿādala wattanmīya*], the Justice and Development Party, abbreviated PJD in French and known by opponents as the "Islamist" party, which has led the government since 2011). State-sanctioned Moroccan المفتي (*lmufti*, scholars awarded the ability to give *fatwa* by other *ʿulamaʿ*) who appeared on Rabat television in the '80s and '90s, such as Abdel

Karim Daoudi or Ghazi al Houssaini, also wore the *tarbūš lwaṭanī* with a *jellāba*, and several religious scholars on *assādissa*, such as Moustafa Ben Hamza, do as well. Another exemplar was the Moroccan calligraphy style الخط المغربي (*alkhaṭ almaghribī*), with its unique diacritics and stylistic forms (van den Boogert 1989), which indirectly indexed Qur'anic speech, as it was no longer used in print publications, except in Qur'ans distributed in West Africa and Europe by the king in his promotion of the Moroccan model. Maghribi calligraphy was also used in palace proclamations in a neo-calligraphic form, using contemporary scanning technologies and font innovations to iconically link handwriting to authentic religious authority (see Clarke 2010).

Two other iconic indexes of Moroccan Islam were the specific Qur'anic recitation style ورش عن النافع (*warš 'an annāf'a*), associated with North African Islam and those who carried it to West Africa and Europe,[24] as well as the practice of collective Qur'anic recitation, which indexed Moroccan Sufi *zāwīya* sociality and collective attunement to God (Eickelman 1985). While oral poetry has always been important for Arab literary tradition, Moroccan Islam took pride in preserving and cultivating the Andalusian instantiation of Maliki legal "texts,": مختصر ابن إسحاق (*mukhtasar ibn 'īshāq*), ألفية ابن مالك (*alfīya ibn mālik*), الآرجومية (*alarjūmīya*), التهفات الحكم (tuhufāt alhukkam), in collectively recited oral poetic form for mnemonic transmission. Moroccan religious students historically had to orally memorize and recite the entire Qur'an, the summary of Maliki jurisprudence for "illiterate" scholars in the *alarjūmīya* and *alfīya* poems, as well as *tuhufāt alhukkam* and *mukhtasar ibn 'īshāq* before they could then study the commentaries explaining what these texts meant and begin writing their own rulings (Eickelman 1985, 56). They did this collectively. This pre-universal education approach to literacy was different from Arab East models of religious education that emphasized reading and reciting of visual texts rather than mnemonic acquisition of oral texts (Eickelman 1985, 59). It was not important whether the Moroccan collective form of Qur'anic recitation gave rise to collective Sufi لدكر (*ddikhr*), performances (repeated collective repetition of the names of God as a form of transcendent worship) or the other way around. The key point was that in the early 2000s they indexed each other. In Kockelman's terms, collective recitation (whether of the Qur'an or the names of God) had become a self-channeling channel; it had left indexical traces of the habit that made possible other passages through that form. Not everyone approved of those channels, even among those who did not align with *ahl as-sunna* or more strident *īkhwān* positions (see Episode 3).

The preference for oral/aural channels in Morocco persisted even among those who did not subscribe to the Moroccan model of Islamic practice. All of the Fassis I met who self-identified as followers of religious discourse

(طالب الخطاب الديني [*ṭulāb alkhiṭāb addīnī*]) had received at least a middle-school public education, which meant that they could most likely comprehend the formal forms of Arabic used in religious texts. However, books (aside from the Qur'an) were rare or nonexistent in all their homes, and many preferred the knowledge gained through aural لاحتكاك (*liḥtikāk*), as described in Chapter 2. In fact, most of them listened or watched religious lectures, often sharing them with family, friends, colleagues, and those they felt needed guidance. When I began fieldwork in 2003, VCDs and MP3s of religious lectures were sold on street corners alongside pirated Hindi and American films. This was about the time that Mashreqi (Arab East) religious satellite stations exploded in the early 2000s and became prominent mediums for religious knowledge. As related to me by many Moroccan interlocutors, the VCDs extended the indexical traces of VHS and cassette lectures of the late '90s (Hirschkind 2006), which proliferated outside of state censors. Later, they began sharing lecture video clips through MSN Messenger chats, Facebook posts, and WhatsApp links. The Mohammed VI station for the Holy Qur'an, *assādissa*, was a Moroccan state effort to counter Saudi, Qatari, Emirati, Egyptian, Syrian, Palestinian, and Lebanese as well as Salafi and Islamic State religious ideas spread through these video lectures.

Not all Moroccan Muslims, however, aligned with the Moroccan model of Islamic practice, not even those categorized by the state as extremists. The debates over what constituted appropriate Islam were staples of everyday conversations. I regularly encountered debates between Fassi interlocutors over whether or not collective recitation was a dangerous innovation because (1) it was not done during the time of the Prophet; and (2) people might breathe in the wrong spot or give emphasis to the wrong syllable and corrupt the Qur'anic meaning.[25] In addition, a huge debate surrounded the proper form of embodying prayer—should one pray with arms down to one's side as the Maliki school encouraged, or folded across the chest as the Hanbali school argued the Prophet used to do. In addition, those who saw the state as needing to reform its relationship to Islam argued that Islam was more tolerant of practice than the state religious programs signaled and that religious practice should be private, as in other developed democracies. To them, beards, headscarves, *jellābas*, and collective recitation were all indexes of nonmodernity and illiteracy.

Part of the state, at least the MREIA, weighed in on these debates, using the mosques but more importantly electronic media to screen and select what constituted the Moroccan model. Religious programming was part of state television and especially radio from the 1960s, with a Friday mosque lecture broadcast every week; a scholarly conversation program, ركن المفتي, (*rukn almufti*), "the Mufti's corner" (in which a religious scholar would respond to questions about religious practice in a very staid and boring way, according to Moustafa); regular Qur'anic recitation in the *warš 'an annāf'a*, Maliki style, by well-known Moroccan reciter Abderrahman Ben Moussa (what another Fassi called the "sleeping" style of recitation because it was so slow); and the five-times-daily broadcast of the call to prayer in Rabat. Between 2007 and 2017, MREIA used *assādissa* as a key tool in the channeling of religious discourse, linking its programs to YouTube channels accessed through smartphones and computers, embedded the videos in the ministry's website, offered live-streaming via the national media website (snrt.ma, which didn't always work), and argued to have reclaimed 85 percent of the Moroccan viewing public from Mashreqi (Arab East) religious stations. In a revealing glimpse into the producers' perceptions about the religious education level of *assādissa* audiences, a short program on correct Maliki ablution and prayer practices was broadcast at every call to prayer time (five times a day), with instructions in a rhymed prose form of *darīja* and showcasing an individual dressed in modest European or traditional Moroccan attire. Collective recitation of a portion of the Qur'an or key Maliki texts written in a poetic style were broadcast multiple times every day, highlighting a different Moroccan mosque community. Individual recitation of the Qur'an in a more "lively" paced *warš 'an annāf'a* style was also broadcast daily, most often with nature photography in the background.[26] But not all forms of recitation practiced in Morocco were included. Those that involved more "unruly" or "unorthodox" vocal and bodily engagement/possession were specifically excluded (Spadola 2014, 2). Those who argued against collective recitation and Sufi practices were also not given voice on the station. Women scholars and Qur'anic reciters were regular presenters on *assādissa*-featured programs, and a program introduced in 2015 highlighted contributions of nineteenth- and twentieth-century Moroccan religious scholars in order to demonstrate the tolerance and deep historicity of the Moroccan model. Women rarely appeared without headscarves (in contrast to Moroccan streets and other Moroccan television stations in which women did); those who called for separating religion from public life, as well as those religious groups who opposed the monarchy, were absent from *assādissa*. Thus the screening and selecting led to claims by opposition groups on the left and the right that the state promoted extremism and/or corruption of Islam.

The channel *assādissa* for all perspectives was an electronic extension of Moroccan state speech, extralegal utterances that carry a legal force (Butler 2004, 80), one that distorted or facilitated the connecting of Muslims depending on one's perspective.[27] The alignment depended partly on the signer and interpreter's media ideologies and history of channel interactions. This was evident in the last account I included in Episode 1, where Abderrahman felt that

2M's religious program best represented Islam as modern through the choice of clothing (non-bearded suit and tie), knowledge system (computer), and interactional mode (*darīja*). Others aligned with the *assādissa* programs, displaying the semiotics of Moroccan Islam: *jellāba-* and *hijāb*-wearing scholars, collective recitation in *warš 'an annāf'a* style, with most lectures given in a mixed *fuṣḥā* with *darīja* interlingual glossing. Others decried *assādissa* because of the exclusions mentioned previously. Those who argued against collective recitation and Sufi practices as part of Islam were also not given voice on the station (the so-called *īkhwān-* and Salafi-leaning groups). As Kockelman has suggested, religious programming in Morocco was both a source-dependent channel, in which the channel origin depended on who and how it was received, and a self-channeling channel, a path leaving indexical traces that facilitated future relations/practices (Kockelman 2010, 415).

These kinds of duplex channel signs could be seen in interviews with two Moroccans producing الخطاب الديني (*khiṭāb addīnī*, "religious discourse"). One was with a religious scholar who held one of the state-appointed chairs of (religious) sciences (كرسي العلمية [*kursī al'ilmīya*]), the chair dedicated to explaining the scholarship of Imam Malik, upon whose work the Maliki school was founded. As the keeper of the chair of Imam Malik, he offered weekly study sessions and lectures on Friday evenings at a mosque in Rabat, focusing on a section of Imam Malik's *hadith* (sayings of the Prophet Muhammad) collection. None of these religious sciences chairs was a paid position, but each held high prestige and state support. These sessions, like each of the study sessions and lectures given by those holding a chair of religious science,[28] were broadcast on *assādissa*, embedded in the MREIA website, posted on YouTube, and disseminated via social media. The other interview was with a previously incarcerated "reformed Salafi" with an active Facebook presence. A self-declared داعي (*dā'ī*), caller to Islam, he also offered lectures and study sessions, but to private groups, and did not have an official position from which to disseminate his religious discourse. Neither viewed himself as a state representative, though both were deeply invested in contributing to *khiṭab addīnī*. They also had much to say about the state's channeling of religious talk and action.

الحلقة ٣: قنات الخطاب الديني

Episode 3: Channels of Religious Discourse

Moustafa saw himself as an informal student of khiṭāb addīnī *and encouraged my interest in Fassi attitudes toward religious programming. I had known his family for years and knew him to be a regular follower of religious lectures on*

YouTube and other video hosting websites. While his family members would often have discussions about religious topics, he was the one to cite Moroccan religious scholars and encourage his friends and family to learn more about them rather than relying on the satellite channel religious lectures from Egyptian, Saudi, or Emirati scholars. He felt I needed to better understand the perspectives of those who participated in khiṭab addīnī *and took it upon himself to arrange interviews with two Moroccans heavily involved in that field. He came up with this idea after attending a lecture by Said al Kamali about why Moroccans should study the science of* fiqh *(scholarly rulings about Islamic practice) with his mother at Qarawiyyiin's College of (Religious) Sciences in Fez. Professor al Kamali taught Islamic studies at the humanities and social sciences college of Mohammed V University in Rabat. He also held one of the thirteen Moroccan chairs of religious sciences, the one dedicated to explaining the scholarship of Imam Malik. Moustafa tried to meet Shaykh al Kamali after his lecture in Fez, but he had been surrounded by Fassis trying to ask questions and take selfies with him. A few weeks later, Moustafa read on Facebook that Shaykh al Kamali was giving a lecture in Sefrou, a small town about twenty minutes from Fez, that day. He called me and suggested we try to attend the lecture and see if we could get an interview with him. Unfortunately, we missed the lecture and found out that Professor al Kamali was headed back to Rabat, but Moustafa managed to procure his phone number. He called and asked if we could meet him to discuss the role of* assādissa *in shaping Moroccan religious discourse. Said al Kamali graciously invited us to his* kursī al'ilmīya *lecture that Friday and agreed to meet after giving his lecture and the evening prayer.*

We made the two-hour drive to Rabat after the afternoon prayer, ṣalāt al'aṣr, *arriving just before the sunset prayer. Since non-Muslims were not allowed into Moroccan mosques (with the exception of the Hassan II mosque in Casablanca), Moustafa attended the lecture, and I read a book in the car. Al Kamali wore what he always wore in public: a* jellāba *over a* جبادور (jabādūr), *a long robe with handmade knot-buttons and ornate cotton trim, the* jellaba *hood pulled up on his head, but folded back from his forehead so you couldn't see his hair. He never wore a suit or the* tarbūš lwaṭanī, *the conical red Fez hat, or* alrazza, *the yellow and white Amazigh headwrap, even though other religious chair appointees were known to wear those headcoverings. Moustafa told me the lecture was packed with both men and women, with al Kamali's students surrounding the raised chair on which he sat, the cameras placed in the middle, and any other interested person fanning out through the mosque. The chair was placed next to the* minbar, *the pulpit from which Friday sermons were given each week. His lecture style that evening was to invite one of his students to read a small section of Imam Malik's* hadith *collection (sayings of the Prophet Muhammad) and then ask a question of his students and provide a commentary or story to illustrate something he wanted them to learn. He did so without notes, reciting from books and accounts he had memorized in* fuṣḥā, *with an occasional* darīja *word or phrase. After the lecture, Moustafa tried to speak with him, but again found Professor al Kamali crowded by Moroccans seeking advice, somewhat like a personal* fatwa *or ruling about how to deal with a specific issue religiously. When Moustafa was able to speak with him, al Kamali turned to one of his students, who were trying to manage the crowd, and told him to show Moustafa to the small mosque in his home neighborhood, where they could meet after the evening prayer. We followed some of his students in their car to an old Rabat villa neighborhood about ten minutes away. The mosque was a small building on the backside of the neighborhood, on the edge of a hill and invisible from the road. I sat in the car while Moustafa joined al Kamali for the evening prayer. From where I sat, I noticed that this mosque was different from most of the mosques I had seen in Fez: it had a gated entrance with a coded keypad, security guard, and security cameras. Moustafa described it as a sophisticated mosque, designed for privacy. After praying the evening prayer, al Kamali received him kindly, and they sat in the corner of the mosque for their discussion. Moustafa also affirmed his quiet, calm demeanor, not overly passionate as some religious scholars, which mirrored the way he offered his lectures and Friday sermons recorded and posted on YouTube. He never worked from notes; he quoted extensively from multiple Maliki and Islamic texts and tailored his discussions to the people he was speaking to in that moment, all in his calm yet focused rhythm of speaking.*

Moustafa asked him questions we had prepared together, beginning with how Professor al Kamali felt religious discourse had changed in his lifetime. Both spoke a fuṣḥā*-infused* darīja, *the pace and flow quite relaxed. Professor al Kamali said, "Perhaps what's being said now has always been said. But the difference between the traditional (form of religious speech) and the modern one is in the formation of the lecturer. Beside being* faqīh *(trained in religious sciences), he's now university trained in a secular discipline, and he speaks French. For example, my public university degree was in tourism management, and my doctorate in Islamic studies. But I also studied privately with religious scholars in the traditional way. This is new face of modernity that I see." Moustafa then asked him how he viewed the Moroccan model of Islam. His response linked the model chronotopically to specific times, spaces, and channels: "I personally prefer to call it the Moroccan model of worship. Islam is Islam, but it appears through people and is affected by their appearance and customs and traditions. It also appears through their environment and the way they relate to the land. In the Moroccan model of worship, you grasp civilization, as we inherited the Andalusian civilization. This worship form appears in verbal interaction, and the way* *we treat each other, for example, how we treat our kids, peers, and spouses. These concerns may not appear in other models [of worship] because of civilizational differences." Moustafa and I both noticed how Shaykh al Kamali focused on interaction as central to the Moroccan model of worship and distinguished it from other ways of practicing Islam in other Muslim contexts. He also affirmed a spatiotemporal semiotics of practice: that Islam manifest through clothing and rituals tied to a place.*

Moustafa further questioned him on the apparent absence or "shyness" of Moroccan religious scholars in Muslim media and their lack of influence on religious discourse, both within and without Morocco. Professor al Kamali's reply was immediate: "Media. There are two primary reasons, and the biggest one is media. The second reason is the weakness of those religious scholars who do appear on media; (laughingly) those who do appear deserve to be jailed and many of those hidden from view deserve to be brought to light. Moroccan scholars used to circulate in different royal palaces, like the one in Fez: Moulay Hafid, al Mehdi al Ouazzani, al Kittaniin.[29] *Scholars have always been consultants and those who give specific opinions about public matters. And then (during the colonial period) when they were excluded (from the palace), they were also excluded from the media. Egypt showcases its scholars, Saudi showcases its scholars, all countries showcase their scholars, but (the media) here they don't. Until God provided us with* assādissa, *which at the beginning only presented weak scholars. And then God provided these scholarly chair appointments which they say have some sort of influence, they say. You should not be looking at the quality of religious programming as a black and white issue, if it's not this way it should be that way. There are divergent, branching parties, with many hidden corners, lots of speculations and expectations. You can't just say how can they export such a model? Is this model good for export? The question is not whether it's good for export, you export the whole package: a model of religion with political stability and social tolerance and with it space for differences of opinion. This whole thing. This is the theory, the ideal." After the interview, al-Kamali walked Moustafa out of the mosque and realized that I had been sitting in the car all through the lecture and interview. He apologized to Moustafa for the inconvenience to me, wished us well in our research, and bid him good night.*

*Abu hafs had similar perspectives on the Moroccan model, but a different history of influence and channeling. He too trained through public education and received "traditional" Islamic study memorizing the Qur'an and key texts. His father, a medic who had volunteered with the Red Crescent in Afghanistan during his youth, supplemented Abu hafs' Maliki Moroccan religious education with scholarly training in Saudi Arabia and travel to Afghanistan to experience "*jihad.*" Moustafa first heard about Abu hafs in Fez in the early 2000s, when he* *found a paper notice inviting people to private lectures by Abu hafs at a house in a neighborhood not far from his home. When he asked his friends about this scholar, some had heard that he gave the Friday prayer sermon at a mosque in Sidi Boujida, a crowded neighborhood with a rough reputation near the medina. Abu hafs had already gained a reputation as a* "salafi," *one advocating a different model of Islam than the Moroccan Muslim practices of Fez. The Friday prayers at that mosque in Sidi Boujida were known to attract so many worshippers that the prayer carpets would spill out into the street and cut off traffic through the main western artery of the city. Abu hafs was arrested and imprisoned after the May 16, 2003 bombings, as part of the government's crackdown on "extremism." Some of his supporters spread flyers through Fez, asking for people to demonstrate against his torture. He was not released from prison until 2011, when he issued* مرجعات (murajʿāt), *statements with his intention to reexamine and review his knowledge of Islam because of misunderstandings he had held. He quickly established a Facebook presence to share his new orientation and ideas, left the salafi world and branded himself as* مفكر (mufakkir), *a reformed intellectual trying to find his way into Moroccan public life.*

Moustafa contacted him on his Facebook page, asking for a meeting. Abu hafs suggested Casablanca, but then realized he would be in Fez in a week and agreed to meet near the large Bank al-Maghrib in the heart of the ville nouvelle. *I helped Moustafa prepare questions but did not go with him. When they met, Moustafa suggested they go to the Hotel Merinides for the interview, as it had lovely overlook views of the medina. As he walked in the doors, he realized the hotel served alcohol, immediately apologized to Abu hafs, and offered to go somewhere else. Abu hafs said it was fine, and Moustafa understood this as evidence of his "new" orientation. Abu hafs wore a single, ornately trimmed, loose-fitting robe and a neatly kept goatee-like moustache, short beard, and no head covering, though he appeared at lectures, conferences, and other public events sometimes in a suit, sweater and sports coat,* jellāba, tarbūš lwaṭanī, *or* alrazza. *As they sat sipping juice on the terrace overlooking the medina, Moustafa perceived Abu hafs as more formal and rehearsed in his responses to direct questions than Professor al Kamali. Yet when not in direct interview mode, Abu hafs suggested they take selfie photos to include on his Facebook page.*

When asked about the Moroccan model of Islam, Abu hafs responded, "Islam is one, there is no doubt in this matter in terms of the bases, the widely accepted bases of Islam: belief in God, the prophets, angels, and books. These are not particularly Maghribi or Mashreqi, there is no difference, it is one, but beyond that, I always say that if we set aside the constants, Islam must be affected by time, place, social and political environment. Of course, Islam will be fit to the Moroccan social and political context, its reality, customs, traditions. One of the fundamentals of Islamic jurisprudence means dealing with and respecting the customs of a particular place. Moroccans choose the Maliki tradition, to recite the Qur'an using warš, *to employ the Moroccan cadence call to prayer, to write the Qur'an in Maghribi scriptic style. The Moroccans take pride in their right to cherish their particularity." In his description of the Moroccan model of Islam, Abu hafs sounded much like Shaykh al Kamali, pointing to the semiotic markers of Moroccan practice and tying the particularities to regional differences.*

Moustafa then asked him how effective he felt the media was in communicating the Moroccan model. Abu hafs began apologetically, framing his response as if the lament of media-channeled religious discourse in Morocco was well rehearsed: "First of all, I don't want to be negative. I'm against those who criticize everything. There are points of light in the subject. I was negative about the establishment of Mohammed VI channel, assādissa, *the Moroccan satellite station for religious matters. I saw it as lacking influence, not presenting a good image, unchanging, boring, and lacking technical production and development. But I've recognized a great response to the channel through my tours in various Arab countries—perhaps we've missed the reception outside of Morocco. I was in Saudi Arabia, which considers itself the origin and exporter of religious sciences, and found Saudis who mentioned following the station. I found followers of the channel among people in Libyan cities, especially the broadcast lectures of the religious chairs, such that people knew the names of Moroccan scholars like Moustafa al Behayaoui or Shaykh Said al Kamali or Abderrahim al Nabulsi. These are the forerunners of the channel's influence. If we turn to statistics issued by rating companies, the Mohammed VI radio station has the highest number of listeners, and has for years. This shows that the religious media is having a certain effect. In fact, I would say that Moroccan religious media, although it is developing and needs greater material resources, it contributes positively to marketing the image of a model of moderate Moroccan Islam and is compatible with the religious atmosphere of Sufism,* Maliki fiqh, *and has been appreciated and accepted abroad. Even internally, I think we underestimate the influence of media in the religious field. Not everyone goes to the mosque, but there are televisions in every home, radios in every car, and phones where religious discourse can be accessed in many ways. Every day seven million Moroccans listen to* assādissa. *Media's role is great and growing, and we need to teach people through those mediums. I think the media's presentation of the Moroccan model needs to develop, but it is having a great influence."*

♣

Abu hafs and el Kamali both qualified the Moroccan model as a semiotic expression of Muslim practice within the larger whole of Islam. They employed differences in practice, in terms of their clothing, language styles, and media platforms for their messaging, thus calibrating a Moroccan model of religious discourse that included variability. Both noted the poor production values of *assādissa* as a media channel but felt that it served an important role in disseminating Moroccan religious discourse. While el Kamali didn't clarify what he meant by media hindering the influence of good Moroccan scholars, by singling out the colonial history of separating religious figures who stood in opposition to European influence, as well as the rise of *assādissa*, he made evident the contrast with Morocco's other television stations, such as 2M and even Rabat. He felt the religious scholars who appeared on all those stations were poor examples of Moroccan scholars, purposefully chosen by "the media" to bore Moroccan audiences and keep them from really knowing the depth of Moroccan scholarship. Yet at the same time, he refused to single out a specific party responsible for the lack of Moroccan scholarly influence within Morocco and beyond. The issue was an outcome of colonial or external influences that continued in various forms. What mattered was not the quality of specific religious discourse, but that there was a space for the Moroccan model of worship to tolerate multiple perspectives and modes of practice—even ones he did not agree with. Abu hafs was also concerned about the role of *assādissa* in facilitating *khiṭab addīnī*, but emphasized the poor technical and production quality and initially thinking of it as a source-dependent channel in Kockelman's terms—only those seeking Moroccan religious discourse were phatically connecting to it. In his travels and interactions with Muslims interested in religious discourse outside of Morocco (*liḥtikāk*), he realized that *assādissa* was connecting non-Moroccans to a Moroccan model, but primarily through the scholarly religious chair lectures. Both saw *assādissa* and the Moroccan model of worship as self-channeling channels in Kockelman's terms: paths that would facilitate future social relations, but in slightly different ways. In terms of production values and media ideologies, *assādissa* was a parasite, a troublesome mediator affecting Muslim Moroccanness, yet the broadcasts of Moroccan model religious chair lectures allowed aspects of the channel to be a more influential intermediary of *khiṭab addīnī*.

Phatic Labor of Religious Discourses in Fez

My Fassi colleagues also lamented the poor quality of Moroccan religious media, and many critiqued the state's exemplars of the Moroccan model of Islamic practice. The debates over what constituted appropriate Islam were staples of everyday conversation, but they were not always about the semiotics of the Moroccan model of Islam. Often the calibrations of Muslim Moroccanness entailed more subtle exchanges.

الحلقة ٤: قراء الجميع

Episode 4: Collective Recitation

It was Friday again, and I was eating lunch after the noon prayer with Toufiq's family. He, his father, brother, mother, and aunt had all attended the noon prayer and sermon, though at different mosques. After returning from the mosque, Toufiq set the television to assādissa, *which had just finished a live broadcast of the sermon and prayer at a mosque in Rabat. As we ate, the station began a recording of collective Qur'anic recitation highlighting a mosque group in Settat, Morocco. A group of thirty men sat in a U-shape facing the camera and recited* لحزب (lhizb, *one of 240 recitation divisions) of the Qur'an in unison, with written calligraphic subtitles of the Qur'anic verses included at the bottom of the screen. The father, Mohammed, asked his son to change the station, mumbling that he couldn't stand collective recitation because he couldn't understand the words—it was too difficult when so many were reciting together. Mohammed's other son asked what region was being represented, a specific nod to how the collective recitations were explicit markers of Moroccan regional diversity.*[30]

In this family, assādissa was often on during meals, but really just as background. Sometimes they would have Saudi or Emirati religious stations on as they gathered. They didn't pay attention to the religious programming content, but rather viewed it as an appropriate backdrop for family sociality, as argued in Chapter 3. Mohammed's critique of collective recitation was not an explicit rejection of the state media's embodiment of the Moroccan model of Islam, but rather an ambivalence about representing what the correct relationship of a reciter with sacred text should be. The channel in question was not assādissa, but rather the listening-reciting body (see Kapchan 2015). The next day during lunch assādissa *was on again and broadcasting a collective recitation of a memorized instructional text, a historical poem used to educate religious students in Moroccan Maliki doctrines. Mohammed's younger son asked again where it had been recorded. Mohammed's wife, Meriam, who had been memorizing the Qur'an herself through a women's literacy group at the mosque, identified the text as* alarjūmīya—*she recognized recited religious texts even though she was deemed illiterate by the state.*

♣

As in the next example I present, television viewing events regularly involved multifunctional layering of expressive, referential, and phatic functions but also multifactor layering of communicative channel, language code, and context. Because television viewing/listening of religious programming often occurred in family contexts, psychosocial phatic relationality also involved affective reasoned critique distributed across multiple family members, what I have analyzed elsewhere as a phatic-referential work of affective reason (Schulthies 2013). In Chapter 2 I explored this in more detail: literacy was not viewed as an individually possessed skill set tied to reading/writing, but a collaborative interpretive project. Part of this ideology was a preference for listening over reading. The more important element of learning was sociality of reasoning rather than internal individual labor. Some interlocutors preferred لاحتكاك (*liḥtikāk*),[31] the generative friction of contact—knowledge acquired through effort of interacting with others. In this next example, some family members just wanted to relax rather than discuss morality.

One can see the phatic labor of religious recognition at work in this account of a Fassi viewing event surrounding a Moroccan religious program. I have included the complete transcript in the Appendix. Seven family members, a mother, Meriam, and five children ranging in ages from six to twenty-six were sitting in the smaller of their two salons enjoying tea time together. Toufiq was the eldest, followed by four sisters (Kaltoum, Aicha, Zahra, and Ghita). This was a social event as much as a meal, as described in the previous chapters, and the television was invariably present, sometimes background to conversation (an intermediator) and sometimes capturing the attention of all gathered (mediating). They were watching a weekly Islamic public education program, and the topic was the relationship between predestination and choice, using an account from the life of Moses as an illustration. The program presenter wore a suit with a collared dress shirt and looked like a businessman without a tie. He also had a laptop nearby to which he would refer occasionally. As the first twenty lines demonstrate, it took a while for the family members to orient to the program.

They had all been chatting about the day's events with the television on in the background, when the mother, Meriam, noticed the religious program had started. She and her eldest son, Toufiq, focused the attention of all present to the religious program. While shushing the comings and goings of family members, the mother and other children talked about dinner, moved over onto the couch to make room for a late-arriving sibling, talked about warming water for prayer ablutions, and the program topic: the relationship between destiny and choice (lines 1–28). They watched for about three minutes and then began critiquing the presenter's style. The program and discussion occurred primarily in *darīja*, though the presenter infused more *fuṣḥā* terms throughout, especially when quoting the Qur'an. They responded to the program presenter as a present participant, speaking directly to him (lines 27–28).

Toufiq complained about the shortness of the religious program (lines 31–34). He later explained to me that 2M, the station that they were watching at the moment, only had this one religious program, and it was only half an hour once a week on Fridays. He was always disappointed at how little religious programming this station offered. His mother and sister Kaltoum understood this, as could be seen in their responses to him: what did he expect from that channel? As the presenter related the story, Toufiq continued to engage him directly, facing the television, yet his comments were also intended for his mother and siblings who were present (lines 41–50). Toufiq wished to use a point from the program to raise an issue he had noticed among his siblings—their lack of attention to religious narratives. Notably, they used the conversation to tease each other good-naturedly even as they debated the message of the religious program (lines 51–62). In continuing to bring the discussion back to what he felt were key moral messages of the story and his sisters' lack of attention to them, Toufiq was subtly calibrating appropriate Moroccanness of Islam and critiquing that of the presenter and his siblings. As with most phatic work, his sisters were also adjusting their calibrations of appropriate sociality.

As the program progressed, Toufiq lamented the way the presenter abbreviated the story of Moses and his first meeting with the daughter of Shuaib/Jethro. He then tried to engage his sisters to discuss the moral of the story, but only his sister Kaltoum engaged him initially. She tired of his detailed focus and began jokingly acting like one of the sheep in the story (lines 51–54). She even tried to bring their mother into the topic change by asking her why her son was trying to respond to the question posed by the program presenter. When Toufiq persisted in having her talk about the story of Moses, she joked that she had a pronunciation problem and couldn't speak (lines 59–79). Toufiq began to get frustrated and berated people who presented themselves as one who understood religious matters by using clever talk, but who were really covering up their ignorance. Kaltoum refused to be baited and laughingly told him she understood the moral values of the story quite well (line 60). Toufiq wanted to explain the moral significance of the story to his siblings via a *fuṣḥā* term, التدوداي (*tadudān*), "holding back" (line 80).[32] He used a quote from the "Stories of the Prophets" just recounted in the program to situate the word's meaning and initiate a discussion of its deeper relevance in terms of the kind of respectful gender relations that his sisters should show in public. He wanted them to recognize the ways mixed gender interactions, as a proper Moroccan Muslim, should involve restraint and modesty. However, he had to restart this discussion nine times over the course of twenty minutes because the family's attention was interrupted by a change in the television program or an interruption by a family member. In one instance, he told everyone to be quiet so they could watch a promo for a French language news documentary about an American killed in Gaza protecting Palestinian lands. This precipitated an extended analysis, about five minutes, on Israeli oppression and American support.

An awkward French pronunciation by Kaltoum led to a mocking multilingual riff in French, English, and *darīja* (lines 63–67). These family members often laughingly mocked each other's language skills. Toufiq used a comment about purifying one's intentions to return to the religious discussion in *darīja*-inflected *fuṣḥā* about *tadudān*, the way Shuaib's daughters respectfully held back when Moses approached. Kaltoum deflected his attempts to direct the conversation by using a counter *fuṣḥā* phrase (line 83), and a kind-hearted, half-joking debate ensued about appropriate ways to discuss religion. She paraphrased a *hadīth*, a saying attributed to the Prophet Muhammad, that Islam was not supposed to be a burdensome religion: گالك الإسلام دين يسر ماشي دين عسر (*gālik al'īslām dīn yusr māšī dīn 'usr*), "It is said 'Islam is a religion of ease, not a difficult religion.'" Even as she began, Toufiq overlapped her speech by reciting the same saying in a slightly different way, suggesting that Kaltoum's laughter and joking while discussing religion was inappropriate: يسر ماشي دين تهكم (*yusr māšī dīn tahkm*), "of ease not a religion to mock" (line 84). She continued to banter with him, suggesting she would never mock in the face of a story about the prophets. At the same time, their mother directed the sibling with the remote to change the station so she could follow an Egyptian serial (line 86). This crosstalk led Toufiq to critique fruitless entertainment programming and prompted a rigorous defense by several family members (not included in this transcript). In yet another moment, the Egyptian Arabic of the dramatic serial became fodder for an extended riff on Kaltoum's name and a moral critique about following the serial too intentionally rather than being present socially (as described in Chapter 3). The overlapping of phatic sociality with calibrations of appropriate religious practice was apparent throughout.

In this instance, there was an enormous amount of linguistic labor employed for family members to recognize themselves as interpreters of Islam connected to other signers via channels of channels. The family members critiqued the television channel's screening of the religious account by abbreviating it, discussed the selecting of interlocutors by the choice of *fuṣḥā* phrasing, playfully (and seriously) negotiated appropriate ways to talk religion, engaged media in family settings through multilingual riffs, and furthered some elements of the program content (female demeanor in front of non-kin males) but not the main topic itself (destiny and free-will). They also embedded personal identity alignments in their program critiques and multilingual play. Recognizing models of Islamic practices and principles involved a lot of phatic interactional work, and not all of it was specifically about Islam.

Conclusion

This *liḥtikāk*, rubbing together of interlocutors, channels, and contexts, entailed multiple transductions and multichannel connectivity. Just as energy changes when it travels through a transformer to become electricity, signs can be transduced when traveling via channels—either electronic or human (Silverstein 2003). The friction of interaction was generative of Moroccan Muslim sociality forms (some of which rejected each other, some of which expanded to include each other) as refracted through channels, but not the meaning screened by the electronic channel serving as a signer-directed signer (a sign oriented to interpreters that are supposed to serve as channels to other signers). Subsequent interpreters became channel-directed signers (opening or closing themselves as channels) as they engaged in phatic labor, the real-time unfolding of meaning that involved selection, interruption, displacement, distraction, and redirection. Playing with the metaphor of friction a bit, movement through channels could generate heat and ignite a chain reaction of simmering discontents, as seen by Mohammed when he rejected *assādissa*'s Moroccanness via broadcasts of collective recitation, or Kaltoum when she chose to laugh off Toufiq's efforts to channel 2M's religious program into a discussion about appropriate mixed-gender behavior.

Even though channels try to minimize possibilities for overheating when contact becomes agitated, they cannot contain the meaning flows because the receivers are channels themselves, selecting and screening as they direct connectivity and collectivity. Those managing channels screen, choosing that sign arrays will make the cut to travel via/to a channel. For some this involved religious forms of *darīja* interspersed with *fuṣḥā* interglossing as one strategy for reducing channel friction (even though not used all the time). Collective recitation as collectivity model was another strategy for reducing channel friction (assuming one reciting the Qur'an publicly in a known group would be less likely to secretly engage in extremist acts). But these presupposed certain kinds of interpreters, perceptual channels, and responses. Because channels connect interpreters, who are also potential signers, they cannot constrain the transduction of message that gets channeled to other signers, or even that a channel will connect with an interpreter who will faithfully transmit the message (as a channel) to another interpreter. Religious media channels and programs that presumably connect state addressers/signers with Moroccan addressees/interpreters/public calibrate Islam by allowing ambiguities of channel ideologies and social histories to make a model of Moroccan Islam look unitary. But they are not the only channels or channel ideologies laboring to connect Islam and its Muslims in Fez. Fassis lamented that Muslims were failing to connect appropriately in Morocco, but their laments were constant attempts to reform ways to relate as Muslims, the labor of phatic Moroccanness.

Conclusion

Opening and Closing the Channels

Ideologies about channels, whether media, language forms, or kinds of persons, shaped the ways Fassis understood their social connectedness. So too did the everyday, emergent laments about communicative channel failures that allowed them opportunities to generate productive, often unrecognized social collectivities. As I've tried to argue throughout, laments of communicative failure were Fassi attempts to unify Moroccans. Instead of focusing on instances of "effective communication," Fassis as listening subjects mobilized by differing media and language ideologies and calibrated what appropriate relationality should look like through what they perceived as not happening. In doing so, their laments of communicative failure precipitated Moroccanness, a sense of appropriate relationality. The nonmovements could be named phenomena such as secularist or Islamist, but more often were discursive fields to which Fassis could calibrate their social connectedness personas in specific moments: listening critic, educated and aware, morality advocate, reading public, Moroccan Muslim. Some of those unrecognized political socialities included *liḥtikāk* distributed literacy families as well as *darīja* schooling advocates explored in Chapter 2; *hadra lmizān* gender equity reformers as well as nostalgia consumers who missed the modernizing message in Chapter 3; those who mobilized *darīja* writing for political or commercial projects and those ambivalent to such graphic sensibilities in Chapter 4; those who aligned with and calibrated their Muslim practices to the Moroccan model of Islam and those who debated aspects of the state's channeling of Islam in Chapter 5. I have framed these social groups as binary in the previous sentence, but as the ethnographic examples throughout this book illustrated, these were actually calibrations of a range of perspectives and practices that emerged as Moroccan relationality. Just as a tagine has become a model or emblem of Moroccanness and there are many ways and ingredients to make a tagine recognized as Moroccan, so too are there varied ways of relating language and media to Moroccanness. In the aggregate, laments about communicative failure allowed a range of forms of connection to be recognized as Moroccan and indeed for a quasi-unitary phenomenon of Moroccanness to cohere. Perhaps a final ethnographic story will illustrate the various ways Fassis demonstrated their heightened awareness and concern about medium failures and the relational changes that precipitated.

شهوات شوميشة (*Ch'hiwates Choumicha*) was a culinary program airing daily on 2M,[1] the national television station with the largest daily viewership all through the decade I was working in Fez. Each episode was about fifteen minutes in length, with a focus on how to make healthy contemporary Moroccan and European dishes. The presenter was a woman named Choumicha with a degree in media production who branded the program with her own identity—a modern woman rooted in Moroccan traditions. The program had a website as well as a glossy-cover magazine advertising culinary equipment and products. Choumicha invited Moroccan women, as well as international chefs, to share their regional recipes on the program in a studio-designed "modern" kitchen, replete with shiny electric appliances and bright décor—things lacking in most Fassi kitchens I visited. Most Fassis continued to fuel their stoves from propane (*boutagaz*) tanks they had to replace every so often. Some had propane-fueled ovens, others small electric ovens, and yet others did without an oven. It was a rare Fassi apartment in which the walls of the kitchen were decorated with anything. The primary program was strategically placed during lunchtime (when Fassi families gathered), again at 4 P.M. in the afternoon when women who care for the home had down time, and again around dinner. Some Moroccans recorded episodes and posted them on DailyMotion and YouTube, so that anyone who did not have access to Moroccan television stations could make these dishes. This spawned a whole genre of Moroccan cooking instructional videos by Moroccan women in their own, more modest kitchens, illustrating both بلدي (*beldī*), local, and رومي (*rūmī*), European forms of Moroccan cuisine.

2M created several Choumicha spin-off series: *Diplomatic Appetites*, in which Choumicha interviewed foreign ambassadors to Morocco about how they cooked their regional cuisines in a Moroccan kitchen, and another far more popular program called *National Appetites*, in which she showcased local Moroccan cuisine by traveling around the country to homes and recording women as they prepared their specialty or regional dishes. The program producers, including Choumicha, saw themselves as engaging in public service television, but instead of talking about wearing a seatbelt while driving or not throwing trash into the street, they sought to change perspectives on gender roles through subtle modifications of existing practices. What better medium than food, something already highlighted as a core emblem of Moroccanness? When I interviewed her, Choumicha said, "This was the moment to go back and grab people and return them to our food, because everything is tied to the kitchen even if the Moroccan woman no longer wants it. Why? Because it returns her to the life of her mother and she no longer wants to be like her mother, she wants to get out of those clothes of her mother, she wants to become something else, she wants to be modern." Choumicha admitted to not knowing how to cook much herself, and that was one of the key points of her program—showing Moroccans that a nonspecialist can learn and that Moroccanness entailed a breaking of the tradition-modernity dichotomy. She embodied this through her dress: alternately wearing short-sleeve kaftans (a "modern" variant of the long-sleeved dress Morccan women used to wear at home), jeans or dress pants and a shirt, or a simple *jellāba*. She also spoke in a polite form of *darīja* mingled with French that my Fassi viewers recognized immediately as an educated form of Casawi or Doukaliya (ways of speaking tied to the region around Casablanca, the largest city in Morocco).

I often observed Fassi family members trying to identify the location where a Choumicha *National Appetites* episode was filmed, playing along with 2M's efforts to broaden Moroccans' sense of national diversity. More importantly, I found Fassis regularly talking about something they had seen on the program or referring to someone who had prepared a beautiful table full of Moroccan cuisine as *Choumicha*. I recorded one such interaction that struct me as a calibration of Moroccanness, but one that lamented the media ideologies of the Choumicha program producers. I had spent the morning visiting Hicham's family and observing their everyday media and language practices. As lunchtime approached, they invited me to join them. A few minutes later, Hicham's friend Abdelatif stopped by to say hello and was also invited for lunch. Hicham's sister began bringing out the food, and the following playful critique occurred between Abdelatif and Hicham's siblings.

Abdelatif:	You saw this on Choumicha, on Choumicha (.) observing her. That's what I was going to tell you, Choumicha	*hādī šuftīhā ʿand šūmīšā, ʿand šūmīšā (.) ḥāīn hīyā īllī kunt ghadī ngūlkum šūmīšā*	هادي شفتيها عند شوميشا عند شوميشا (.) حاضين هيا اللّي كنت غدي نگولكم شوميشا	عبد اللطيف
Sanae:	Choumicha am m[	*šūmīšā ām m[*	شوميشا آم م]	سناء:
Abdelatif:	]Wooow! here's the lettuce, here's the cucumber.	*]wāāāw, hā lkhas hā lkhīyar.*	[واااو ، ها الخس ها الخيار.	عبد اللطيف
Nadia:	She is going to teach Moroccans, they say she's the one who's gonna make Moroccans.	*hīya ghatʿallim lmghāribā gālak hīyī īllī ghaṭllʿa lmghāribā.*	هي غتعلّم لمغاربا گالك هيا اللّي غطلّع لمغاربا.	نادية:

Abdelatif teased that Hicham's sisters must have learned how to prepare the meal from watching Choumicha's program. Sanae, Hicham's younger sister, immediately jumped in to correct this idea as Abdelatif continued to mock the simplistic way he saw Choumicha present her cooking show: "Wow, here's the lettuce, here's the cucumber." His elongated vowel on "wooow" was the clue to his not-so-subtle critique. Hicham's other sister, Nadia, added to this lament about the poor attempts at calibrating Moroccanness she observed in Choumicha's cooking program: as if she would be the one to teach them what it meant to become Moroccan. Although Choumicha never explicitly stated her program's goals in the program itself, these Fassi viewers had recognized the channel's attempt to calibrate Moroccanness in ways they themselves found insulting. And yet, they watched the program and debated the merits of the recipes she promoted, as well as the mediums in which she mobilized Moroccans to consume their cuisine.

At the end of that particular fieldwork trip, Toufiq went with me to the medina to buy a few gifts to take back to my family and friends in the U.S. We stopped at a small bookshop stall in Attarin, at the end of one of the main narrow streets that wound through the medina, near the fourteenth-century madrassa from which the sector took its name. I always like to buy Moroccan books at the end of a fieldwork trip, and I wanted to buy Choumicha's cookbook. A couple of Fassi women passing by noticed we were looking at the book, Toufiq showing me the illustrations and recipes. They stopped and said to us, "Oh, you're thinking about buying Choumicha's cookbook? Ah, the influence of the media! Her recipes are too simplistic, the ingredients often expensive or hard to find. Everyone knows that Rachida Amhaouche's cookbook is better, her directions and ingredient measurements more precise." These Fassi women lamented Moroccan electronic media as a communicative channel, even as they encouraged me to purchase another Moroccanness medium—Amhaouche's Moroccan cuisine cookbook.

As I suggested in the introduction, calibrations of Moroccanness as a unitary "thing" among the Fassis I observed often involved laments of communicative channel failures. Those channels could include television, print, and social media, but also linguistic registers (such as *hadra lmizān*, collective Qur'anic recitation) and modalities (moral listening, writing/reading scripts), as well as clothing and prayer beads. This was not a new phenomenon. The idea of renewal or التجديد (*tjaddid*), had often motivated sociality in Morocco's history (Laroui 1977, Miller 2013). In this book, I have described some specifics of what I have called Moroccanness during this period, not to explore the renewing of society, but the subtle calibrations, the forming and reforming, of differentiated social nonmovements that constituted the phatic work of relationality in Fez. Although Fassis often aligned themselves with the public binary of "secularist" vs. "religious" or "educated" vs. "rural" (لعروبي [*l'arūbī*]), a broader range of ideologies and perspectives emerged as they lamented communicative failures in their everyday interactions as a means to relational reform. I look forward to continuing conversations that will shape Moroccan sociality in other ways as Fassis debate what channels, both linguistic and media, do and ought to do in bringing them together.

Appendixes

Transcription Key for:

MA: Moroccan Arabic
FR: French
AM: Amazigh
FA: fusha
[: latching
[]: overlap
FL: disfluency
↓: downward pitch
BC: backchannel cue
EMP: emphasis

Full Transcript for Introduction Episode 2 "We are Not an Arab Country"

Samira Sitail video-recorded Radio Aswat live radio interview with well-known host Rachid al-Idrissi on International Women's Day 2016, in which she stated that Morocco is not an Arab country. Provided as an example of Moroccan communicative failure laments and the calibration of Moroccannness. https://www.youtube.com/watch?v=yRmn7XNTpXY.

Samira	We are not an Arab country	(MA) *ḥnā māšī dūla ʿarabīya*	حنا ماشي دولة عربية	سميرة
Rachid	haaa	*hāāāā*↓	↓هاااااا	رشيد
Samir	I'll say it (.) and I'll say it (.) (*FR*) I assume	*wangūlhā (.) wangūlhā (.)* (FR) *et je l'assume*	ونگولها (.) ونگولها (.) et je l'assume	سميرة
Rachid	We are a country [	(MA) *ḥnā dūla [*	حنا دولة..[	رشيد
Samira	] we are a Maghribi country, we are a [Maghreb] country	*]Nous somme un pays Maghreb. Nous somme un pays [maghrébin]*	]Nous somme un pays maghrébin. Nous somme un pays [maghrébin]	سميرة
Rachid	[Maghrebi]	(MA) *[maghribī]* (FL)	[مغربي]	رشيد
Samira	yes	(MA/AM) *āhāh*	اهاه	سميرة
2nd announcer	Historically	(FA) *tarikhīyan [ḥnā dūla]*	تارخيا [حنا دولة]	المذيع التاني
Samira	Historically	(FA)] *tarikhīyan*	تاريخيا]	سميرة
2nd announcer	Maghribi	*] maghāribīya*	مغاربية]	المذيع التاني
Samira	we look at our origins (.) in terms of our Berber origins, and we see all the confluences, the influences we have received	(FA) *en vois nos origines (.) sur le, nos origines berbères on voit toutes les confluences les influences nous avons reçu, nous somme un pays maghrébin (.)*	en vois nos origines (.) sur le, nos origines berbères on voit toutes les confluences les influences nous avons reçu, nous somme un pays maghrébin (.)	سميرة
Rachid	mmm	(BC) *mmm*	ممم	رشيد
Samira	we are a Maghribi country	(FR) *et il faut que nous assume encore une fois*	et il faut que nous assume encore une fois	سميرة
Rachid	yes	*oui*	oui	رشيد
Samira	and we ought to see it as a tool of power and pride, not an object of totally useless debates today	*il faut que se soit l'objet d'une force (EMP) d'une fierté et non pas l'objet des débats qui sont totalement inutiles aujourd'hui*	il faut que se soit l'objet d'une force (EMP) d'une fierté et non pas l'objet des débats qui sont totalement inutiles aujourd'hui	سميرة

Full Transcript for Chapter 4: *Hearing Written* Darīja *in WhatsApp* Interaction

Group WhatsApp chat collected in 2015 and analyzed in Chapter 4, which occurred between six Fassi friends who were finishing their last year of university studies: three young men (Mehdi, Oussama, Hamza) and three young women (Khadija, Nissrine, Salima). Group chats took place primarily in Romanized, French-based orthography *darīja* mixed with French and some English. In this transcript, the original text formatting with the Moroccan spelling choices is retained in the second column from the left, with an English translation in the third column and my analysis of the orthographic heterogeneity in the fourth column.

	Participant	Text	English Translation	Analysis Comments
1	Khadddijaaa	سؤالنا جميعا ههههه	He asked all of us hhhh	*fuṣḥā* indefinite accusative marker, Arabic script, with Arabic laughter abbreviation (ههههه) signaling ironic formality
2	Mehdi Allem	Hhhh mssab madirouch x)	Hhhh [I] wish they wouldn't [give us the exam] x)	*darīja* in Romanized French orthography, automatic capitalization of initial laughter abbreviation (Hhhh), circumfix negation of modal verb, transitive verb elided, hand-typed mischievous smiley emoticon
3	Nissrine	Wayeeeeh	wayeeeh	*darīja* interjection of ironic exasperation
4	Khadddijaaa	Oui	Yes	French
5	Oussama	Hamza ga rahom biiyno l9oor3a dlmirican had le3chiya	Hamza said they're going to show the American lottery this afternoon	*darīja* in Romanized French orthography, typing error *ga* should be *gal* "said," number substitutions for ق ,ع
6	Nissrine	Hhh feeen	Hhh where	*darīja*
7	Nissrine	Htaa na biit nmxhii	I too want to go	*darīja* elided *a* vowel in *ana* "I," doubling of letters to indicate long vowels (aa, ii), use of xh instead of ch for š (which others in this group chat used), probably from rapid typing on smartphone keyboard
8	Salima	site	Website?	French
9	Nissrine	:3		Cuteness smiley emoticon
10	Oussama	Ana majabch llah	God didn't bring it to me (I didn't get it)	*darīja* free-standing 1SG pronoun for emphasis, transitive gerund with circumfix negation, invoking the name of God as determiner of outcomes is common for Fassis
11	Salima	passe site	Send website	French
12	Oussama	Ook att	Ok, wait	English Ook, French abbreviation *att* for *attends*
13	Oussama	Salima	Salima	*darīja* name
14	Salima	ok	ok	English
15	Nissrine	3laaach majabch laah khaass chii hajaa.	Why didn't God bring it [? Did you miss] something necessary?	*darīja* question word, transitive gerund with circumfix negation, no question punctuation, missing main verb, readers expected to fill in the blank

	Participant	Text	English Translation	Analysis Comments
16	Oussama	https://www.dvlottery.state.gov	https://www.dvlottery.state.gov	copied and pasted weblink
17	Salima	mrc	merci	French abbreviation *mrc* for *merci*
18	Salima	pk mjbch lah	Why didn't God bring it?	French abbreviation *pk* for *pourquoi*, *darīja* transitive gerund with circumfix negation, though written with elided vowels
19	Oussama	Hhh manje7tch fl9or3a	Hhh I didn't win in the lottery	*darīja* circumfix verb negation, 1SG past tense verb, preposition prefix *f* with elided vowels on direct object noun, number substitutions 7, 9, 3 for *darīja* letters ح، ق، ع
20	Oussama	Hhh	Hhh	laughter abbreviation
21	Salima	kayjawbok.dik.saa	Do they answer you instantly?	*darīja* present tense verb markings with suffixed object, proximal demonstrative *dik*, no punctuation but pragmatically inferred by Oussama's response in line 23
22	Oussama	Pourcentage de gagné est 1% aloor!!	The rate of winning is just 1%!!	French sentence for emphasis
23	Oussama	Oui salima	Yes Salima	French response to Salima's question in line 21, with the name not capitalized, personal name marking specific addressee
24	Nissrine	Emmm	Emmm	*darīja* thinking sound used here as an interruption marker
25	Nissrine	Kaydeerulkk chii test wla chi haja??	Do they make you [take] a test or something?	*darīja* capitalized present tense 3PL verb marker with preposition affix *l* and direct object suffix pronoun *k*, indefinite noun marker *chi* with French *test*, vowel duplications
26	Salima	kifach kadir	How do you do [it?]	*darīja* question word with present tense 2SG verb markers, elided question punctuation and direct object
27	Salima	tchrk mafhmtch	[How do] you participate[?] I don't understand.	*darīja* elided question marker, 2SG imperfective verb, past tense 1SG verb with circumfix negation, no punctuation
28	Oussama	Nissrine	Nissrine	Personal name marking change of addressee
29	Oussama	Kifach	How?	*darīja* question word without punctuation
30	Salima	wach kadwz.mtihan	Do you take a test	*darīja* question discourse marker, present tense 2SG verb, no punctuation

	Participant	Text	English Translation	Analysis Comments
31	Salima	bach	in order to	*darīja* discourse conjunction marker with no punctuation
32	Salima	tnjh fhad.9or3a	win that lottery?	*darīja* present tense 2SG verb, preposition prefix with elided vowel on demonstrative, number substitutions for ق، ع
33	Salima	chno kadwz	What [kind of test do] you take?	*darīja* question word, present tense verb marker, vowel elision in verb, no punctuation
34	Nissrine	Waach kaymtahnuuuk	Do they test you?	*darīja* question discourse marker, typing vowel reduplications (*aa, uuu*), present tense 3PL verb with 2SG direct object—*k* "you," no punctuation
35	Nissrine	Ykhraaa 3liik	Curse you	*darīja* curse formula directed to everyone in the group who refused to respond, with typing vowel reduplications (aaa, ii)
36	Nissrine	Chnuu les conditions bach tnjeeh	What can you do to win? (literally, what are the conditions so you can win?)	*darīja* question word, French noun, *darīja* conjunctive with 2SG verb, no punctuation
37	Nissrine	I mean bach y3zluuk	I mean so they can choose you?	English "I mean," possible calque of *darīja* z3ama, *darīja* conjunctive with 3PL verb and 2SG direct object suffix, no punctuation
38	Salima	wa kifach kaydiro hadchi	And how do they do this?	*darīja* question word, present tense 3PL verb marker, merging of demonstrative *had* with indefinite pronoun *chi*, common in everyday Fassi speech
39	Nissrine	Hhhhhhh	Hhhhhh	Laughter abbreviation
40	Salima	kifach 9or3a mafhmtjch	How [does] the lottery, [work]? I don't understand	*darīja* question word with elided main verb, letter substitutions 9 and 3 for ق and ع, circumfix negation on past tense 1SG verb with vowel elisions and typing error *j*
41	Salima	wach ktjwbo.3la.chi haja	Do you answer something	*darīja* question discourse marker, present tense 2PL verb marker with vowel elision, periods used as spaces, number substitution 3 for ع, no punctuation because sentence continued in the next post
42	Salima	bach tnjho	so you can win?	*darīja* conditional conjunctive, 2PL present tense verb, no punctuation

	Participant	Text	English Translation	Analysis Comments
43	Khadddijaaa	Hhh wach ghoir ajii ou sur lmirican	Hhh is it a transnational [lottery], ah, or an American one?	*darīja* laughter abbreviation, question discourse marker, *ghoir* means foreigners, but here used to mean non-American, *ajii* indicates the writer figured out the answer even as she was writing (*ah*), use of French *ou sur* with *darīja* noun *lmirican*, no punctuation
44	Nissrine	Hhhh	Hhhh	*darīja* laughter abbreviation
45	Nissrine	Saafii khliiik fblaaadwek asaalima	Enough! Stay in your country Salima	*darīja* exclamation phrase *Saafii* capitalized by software, vowel duplications and typing error (iii, aaa, w), elided vowel in preposition prefix *f* attached to noun, use of *darīja* vocative *a* with personal name *saalima*, no punctuation
46	Nissrine	Wlaaah matmchiii wtkheelinii	By God, don't go and leave me!	capitalization of *darīja* oath formula *Wlaaah* "by God," vowel duplications (*aaa, iii, ee*) and elisions in oath and verbs, circumfix negation on first verb, no punctuation
47	Salima	la.ndik.maaya	No, I'll take you with me	*darīja* 1SG verb with 2F direct object suffix, vowel duplication on preposition, no punctuation
48	Salima	sqhbfi		Spelling error self-repaired in next line
49	Salima	sahbti	My friend	*darīja* feminine noun with 1SG possessive, no punctuation
50	Salima	maghreb mafih	Morocco doesn't have	*darīja* negation using a preposition, sentence completed on the next line
51	Salima	walo	anything	*darīja* second negation form emphasizing the utter lack of future in Morocco, no punctuation
52	Salima	tal3li frasi	I'm tired of it (literally, It's over my head)	*darīja* idiomatic expression meaning I've had enough, number 3 substitution for ع, no punctuation
53	Nissrine	Laaaa saafii hleeft	No, that's enough, I promised	capitalization of *darīja* word for no, vowel duplications, past tense verb *hleeft* literally means to swear by God, but here it infers Nissrine will support Salima, no punctuation

	Participant	Text	English Translation	Analysis Comments
54	Salima	bghina.n3rfo hadxi kifach whoma	We want to understand how this works, but they are	*darīja* modal 1PL modal verb *bghina* "we want" includes Nissrine against all those in the group who are not responding with information, number substitution 3 for ع, use of *xi* instead of *chi*, sentence completed in next post
55	Salima	mklkhin	grumpy folks	*darīja* vowel elisions in noun meaning the grumpy folks in this group chat, no punctuation
56	Nissrine	Hnaaa lwaaldiiik tb9aaay htaa tmuutii	Here you stay until you die!	capitalization of *darīja* locative *Hnaaa* "here," vowel duplications and letter substitution 9 for ق, use of Moroccan slang about one's parents *lwaaldiik* to show the seriousness of the utterance, reinforcing Salima's post in lines 50–52 that there is no future in Morocco, no punctuation
57	Salima	mafhmonach	They don't understand us	*darīja* circumflex negation on 3PL present tense verb with vowel elisions and 1PL object suffix, no punctuation
58	Salima	hh yeki	Hh right?	*darīja* laughter abbreviation, 2F tag question seeking support, no punctuation
59	Nissrine	9aaleek ghiir kadf3iilhum wkayderio l9or3aa bla test	It's said you apply to them, they do the lottery without a test	*darīja* number substitution for letters ق and ع, vowel duplications and elisions, present tense 2F and 3PL verb markers, no punctuation
60	Mehdi Allem	Matsktounach -_-?	Are you not going to shut up?	capitalization of *darīja* negation *Ma*, 2PL present tense verb with 1PL object suffix, dashes for emphasis
61	Salima	hae	Really?	*darīja* emphatic expression of indignant surprise, *ae* represents an exaggerated glottal stop
62	Salima	wkifach	How	*darīja* question word, no punctuation
63	Salima	hhhh	hhhh	*darīja* laugher abbreviation
64	Salima	kadf3i.wnti.wzhrk	You apply, you and your luck	*darīja* 2SG present tense verb marker, periods representing space between words, vowel elisions, sentence completed in next post

	Participant	Text	English Translation	Analysis Comments
65	Salima	bla.walo	For nothing	*darīja* double negation for emphasis, period representing space between words, no punctuation
66	Salima	hhh	hhh	*darīja* laughter abbreviation
67	Salima	sktna nta wla.khrj mn group	You shut up or leave the group	*darīja* imperative, period representing space between words, use of French word *group*, no punctuation
68	Nissrine	Hhhhh mehdiii mabghaawch yfhmuu rassshum	Hhhh Mehdi they don't want to give us the information (literally, to get it)	*darīja* laughter abbreviation capitalized, personal name not capitalized, vowel and consonant duplications, explaining to Mehdi why they are frustrated, no punctuation
69	Nissrine	Hhhhh	Hhhh	*darīja* use of laughter abbreviation to soften the previous statement that the group members don't get it, no punctuation
70	Salima	khsna.njrbo hdna a nissrin	We should try [our luck] too, Nissrin	*darīja* 1PL modal with 1PL present tense verbs, elided noun of common Fassi phrase *njrbo zharna* "try our luck," narrowing inclusivity to Nissrine, no punctuation

Full Transcript for Chapter 5: *Islam is a Religion of Ease* Family Interaction

This Fassi family viewing event included a mother and her children watching a religious program and discussing key aspects of what appropriate Muslim relations should entail. The analysis for this transcript begins after Episode 4 and provides an example of the phatic labor involved in calibrating *namūdhaj almaghribī*, the Moroccan model of Islamic practice.

1	Meriam:	Turn up, turn up (the sound) a little (.) quiet, [cut out the racket]	*zīd zīdū šwīya fīh (.) skūtū [min aṣṣda']*	زيد زيدو شوية فيه (.) سكوتو[من الصدع]	مريم
2	Toufiq:	[Quiet, cut out the racket] (.) turn up, turn up (THE SOUND) a little	*skūtū [min aṣṣda'] (.) zīdū fīh šwīya*	سكتو]من الصدع](.) زيدو فيه شوية	توفيف
3	(DIRECTIONS TO FAMILY MEMBERS TO HOLD THE PLASTIC TABLECOTH WHILE ONE OF THE DAUGHTERS CLEANS IT FROM THE AFTERNOON TEA CRUMBS)				
4	Mother:	Grab the plastic, (SOMETHING) fell on it (.03)	*tqabtū mīkā ṭayḥā fīhāā*	تقبتو ميكا طيحا فيهاااا	مريم

5	Toufiq:	Come on, hurry up, stop switching the remote enough of . . . (.02) the remote (.03) hey Kaltoum, easy, stop shaking me	*ākhlāṣ daghīya ntā rṣā ʿan iṭṭīlīkūmūnd, barakā mats . . . (.02) iṭṭīlīkūmūnd (.03) ākaltūm ghīr biššwīya bilā matzʿazʿanī*	أخلا ص دغية نتا رصا عن الطيليكوموند بركا متس . . . (.02) الطيليكوموند (.03) أكلتوم غير بالشوية بلا متزعزعني	توفيف
6	Kaltoum:	I'm not shaking you at all! (.06) turn up (THE VOLUME) a little, move over there (to sister) (.02)	*manzʿazʿa ʿakšāy (.06) zīd šwīya lilhīh zīd (.02)*	منزعزعكشاي (.06) زيد شوية للهيه زيد (.02)	كلتوم
7	Toufiq:	This, this, what's it called (.06) this is a big problem, destiny and choice, the world doesn't understand it	*hadā hadā smītū (.06) hadā muškīl kabīr dīyāl ittasīyir wittikhīyar ilʿālam mafahmūš*	هدا هدا سميتو (.06) هدا مشكيل كبير ديال التسيير والتخيرالعالم مفهموش	توفيف
8	Kaltoum:	I understand, thank God (.) God be thanked	*ānā fāhma alḥamdulila allahumalik alḥamd*	انا فاهمة الحمد الله (.) اللهم لك الحمد	كلتوم
9	Toufiq:	(LAUGHTER)	*hhhhhh*	ههههه	توفيف
10	Ghita:	Me too, I [understand, God be thanked][1]	*ḥatā ānā [fāhmāh allahumalik alḥamd]*	حتى انا]فاهماه اللهم لك الحمد]	غيتة
11	Aicha:	[Then explain it to us, O sister]	*[wašarḥūnā ʿukhtī]*	[وشرحونا أختي]	عايشة
12	Kaltoum:	I don't remember anymore	*mābaqaītš ʿāqala*	مابقيتش عاقلة	كلتوم
13	Toufiq:	The most complex issue in religion is destiny and choice (.02)	*āʿaqad masāla fī iddīn hīya ittasīyir wittikhīyar (.02)*	اعقد مسالة في الدين هي التسيير والتخيير(.02)	توفيف
14	Ghita:	(TO SISTER SITTING NEXT TO HER) leave me (ALONE) (.01) my feet, my feet	*āā khalīnī rijlī (.01) ʿārijlī*	آآ خليني رجلي (.01) أرجلي	غيتة
15	Toufiq:	(TONGUE CLICK OF FRUSTRATION) (.04)	(TONGUE CLICK OF FRUSTRATION) (.04)	) (.04) تمطق (	توفيف
16	(ANOTHER SON ENTERS WITH FOOD AND THE MOTHER ADDRESSES HIM)				
17	Meriam:	Straighten your feet in that direction (.01) first, pour a little (tea) for him, and then leave some for your father, the rest for him and Zahra,[2] whatever remains . . . we fight for it	*ṭlaq rijlīk lihād jjīha (.) bʿadā nqibbū lū hūwa wāḥid ššwīya waīllī khalī libāk dīyālū waīllī baqā hūwā wazahra [īllī baqā] n . . . nṭīfū ʿalīh*	طلق رجليك لهاد الجيهة (.) بعدا نقبّو[3] لو هو واحد الشوية واللّي خلي لباك ديالو واللّي بقا هوا وزهرة[اللّي بقا]ن . . . نطيفو عليه	مريم
18	Kaltoum:	Hey mom (.04) (COMPLAINING)	*[āmmī] (.04)*	[أمّي] (.04)	كلتوم
19	Meriam:	Well, we didn't know what to prepare for dinner	*īywā maṣobnā manwajddū filʿašā*	إوا مصبنا منوجدّو فلعشا	مريم
20	Toufiq:	Ok, so are we going to listen now or turn it off?	*īywā dabā wāš ghansmʿaū walā nṭfīyūh*	إوا دبا واش غنسمعو ولا نطفيوه	توفيف
21	Meriam:	No, we . . .	*lā nqad . . .*	. . . لا نقد	مريم
22	Kaltoum:	Turn it off (.04) what's your problem (.02) you're walking weird . . . (LAUGHTER)	*ṭfīyūh (.04) mālak (.02) katbīysṭā . . . hhhhhh*	طفيوه (.04) مالك (.02) كتبيسطا . . . هههههه	كلتوم
23	Toufiq:	Come on (LAUGHING) cut out the noise	*ākhlāṣ hhhh skūtū min ṣṣdʿa*	أخلاص ههhe سكوتو من الصدع	توفيف
24	Kaltoum:	I'm gonna go do ablutions and pray	*ānā ghanimšī ntūwaḍʿā nṣalī*	انا غنمشي نتوضا نصلي	كلتوم

25	Toufiq:	I didn't understand anything (.03)	*ānā mafhimt wālū (.03)*	انا مفهمت والو (.03)	توفيف
26	(ALL LISTEN TO PROGRAM FOR TWO MINUTES)				
27	Toufiq:	(ECHOING THE TELEVISION PRESENTER) "What have you done with what you've learned?"[4] (.09)	*šnū dirtī bidāk ššī īllī t'alimtū (.09)*	شنو درتي بداك الشى اللّي تعلمتو (.09)	توفيف
28	All:	(IN RESPONSE TO A MENTION OF THE PROPHET MOHAMMED ON TELEVISION) Peace Be Upon Him	*ṣalā āllah 'alaīhi wasallam*	صلى الله عليه وسلّم	كلشي
29	(ALL LISTEN TO PROGRAM FOR FOUR MINTUES: SISTER AICHA ENTERS)				
30	Kaltoum:	(CLEARED HER THROAT)	(cleared her throat)	(خلق)	كلتوم
31	Toufiq:	That's it? It's finished (ALREADY)?	*ṣāfī sālā?*	صافي سالا؟	توفيف
32	Meriam:	What do you expect? (.03) hello and goodbye (SARCASTIC USE OF MUSLIM GREETING)	*wašnū sḥābak (.03) 'āssalāmu 'alaīkum wa'alaīkum 'āssalām*	وشنو سحابك (.03) السلام عليكم وعليكم السلام	مريم
33	Aicha:	(TEASINGLY AS IF COMFORTING A BABY) don't cry, it's ok	*waṣāfī matibkīš ṣāfī ṣāfī*	وصافي متبكيش صافي صافي	عايشة
34	Toufiq:	I just began watching and five minutes haven't passed	*tnšūf ānā 'ād bdā makamlāš khams dqā'iq*	تنشوف انا عاد بدا مكملاش خمس دقائق	توفيف
35	Mother:	And what do you expect?	*wašnū ḥsābak*	وشنو حسابك	مريم
36	Toufiq:	No, [they still haven't done the story]	*lā [mā zāl ghīdīrū lqiṣa]*	لا]ما زال غيديرو القصة]	توفيف
37	Zahra:	[They still have to do] the story	*[mā zāl ghīdīr] lqiṣa*	[ما زال غدي يدير]القصة	زهرة
38	Aicha:	ah, ah, ah (SETTLING INTO THE COUCH)	*āḥ āḥ āḥ*	أح أح أح	عايشة
39	Zahra:	(TO HER SISTER) move your feet	*zūwlī rijlīk*	زولي رجليك	زهرة
40	Toufiq:	Listen (ALL LISTEN FOR 30 SECONDS) snakes[5] (.43) you don't know at all who it is that will . . . (.07) (QUOTING FROM THE QUR'AN) the two of them were servants under our righteous master[6] (.48)	*sm'aū (.30) llfā'ī (.43) ma'arftšāy škūn īllī ghadī . . . (.07) kānatā taḥt 'abadīn min 'ibādinā ṣāliḥīn (.48)*	سمعو (.30) اللّفاعي (.43) معرفتشاي شكون اللّي غدي . . . (.07) كانتا تحت عبدين من عبادنا صالحين (.48)	توفيف
41	Ghita:	Kaltoum (.04) Kaltoum (TRYING TO GET HER SISTER'S ATTENTION)	*kaltūm (.04) kaltūm*	كلتوم كلتوم (.04)	غيتة
42	Toufiq:	Listen	*sm'a*	سمع	توفيف
43	Toufiq:	[and our father is a great leader][7](.30)	*[wābūnā šaīkh kabīr] (.30)*	(.30) [وابونا شيخ كبير]	توفيف
44	(ALL LISTEN TO PROGRAM FOR ONE AND A HALF MINTUES)				

45	Kaltoum:	[and our father is a great leader] (.30)	*[wābūnā šaīkh kabīr] (.30)*	[وابونا شيخ كبير] (.30)	كلتوم
46	Toufiq:	"Not watering for us" (TO THE PROGRAPH PRESENTER),[8] not like that. (.04)	*mā saqīt linā. māšī hakāk (.04)*	ما سقيت لنا. ماشي هكاك (.04)	توفيف
47	Kaltoum:	that's it (THE WAY THEY DO IT), he just abbreviates it, he does	*hūwā hadāk ghīr kīkhtaṣirhā hūwā*	هداك غير كيختصرها هوا هوا	كلتوم
48	Toufiq:	No, change it (THE CHANNEL) (.01) this means it is going to have a different meaning, not "watering for us" (REFERRING TO THE QUR'ANIC STORY) (.02) even (.02) because you met and watered for us (.01) wait (.03) "Indeed, my father invites you that he may reward you" then she told him hire him, because when she was walking with him on the road, what did he say to her?[[9]	*lā qalibhā (.01) dabā hīyā ghadī tkūn 'andhā m'anī waḥd ākhūr māšī saqīt linā (.02) ḥattā (.02) litlqā saqīt linā (.01) bilātī (.03) 'in ābī yīd'aūk lyījrīk ājir mā ghād qālatlū 'īstājrū lānā minīn gālat ghādīa hīyā wiyāh fiṭṭrīq šnū galhā?[*	لا قلبها (.01) دبا هيا غدي تكون عندها معني وحتا اخور ماشي سقيت لنا (.02) حتّا (.02) وحتا لّان عندو لتلقا سقيت لنا (.01) بلاتي (.03) إن آبي يدعوك ليجر يك آجر ما غاد قالتلو إستآجره لآنا منين كالت غادية هيا وياه فالطريق شنو]گلها؟	توفيف
49	Kaltoum:	]indeed hire him then	*]īyūwā 'īyā 'īstājrū 'ād*	]ايوا إيه استاجره عاد	كلتوم
50	Toufiq:	then she told him "Hire him. Indeed, the best one you can hire is the strong and the trustworthy." That is why when he (SHUAIB/JETHRO) heard strong and trustworthy, he said "How.. how did you know this guy is strong and the trustworthy?"	*'ād gālatlū 'īstājrū 'īn khaīr min 'ist'ājarat lqūwī alāmīn. bihā minīn sm'a lqūwī alāmīn qāl bāš āā . . . bāš 'ariftī ntī hād ssayīd hūwa lqūwī alāmīn*	عاد گالتلو إستآجره إن خير من إستأجرت القوي الأمين. بها منين سمع القوي الأمين قال باش آآ باش عرفتي نتي هاد السيد هو القوي الأمين!	توفيف
51	Kaltoum:	MMMMAAA (JOKINGLY MAKES A SHEEP SOUND)	*mmmmāāā*	م م ما	كلتوم
52	Toufiq:	You are a pig, I'm talking with an ignorant person	*īwā ntī ghīr ḥalūf kanhadr m'a binādm makllikh*	13 وان تي غير حلوف كنهدر مع بنادم مكلّخ	توفيف
53	Ghita:	(LAUGHTER)	*hhhhhh*	هههه	غيتة
54	Kaltoum:	BAA BAA BAA (TO HER MOTHER) this is your son, responding to the question in the program	*bā'bā'bā' hadā hadā hād wildik hād nnās y'anī jūwāb 'iss'ūāl fīlbarnāmij*	باع باع باع هدا هدا هاد ولدك هدا الناس يعني جواب السؤال في البرنامج	كلتوم
55	Toufiq:	Why? Tell us, you know, about the story of our Sayyid Moses and, you know, the two daughters of Shuaib/Jethro[10]	*'alāš? 'awdnā 'alā smītū lqiṣa dīyāl sayīdnā mūsā wsmītū bintī šu'īb*	علاش؟ عودنا علا سميتو القصة ديال سيدنا موسى وسميتو بنتي شعيب	توفيف
56	Kaltoum:	I am, I, I have a problem, a pronunciation problem	*ānā mā ānā dabā lmuškīl 'andī muškīl nnuṭq*	انا ما انا دبا المشكيل عندي مشكيل النطق	كلتوم
57	Toufiq:	No, you can speak	*lā 'andik nnuṭq*	لا عندك النطق	توفيف
58	Kaltoum:	fluency	*ssilāsā*	السلاسة	كلتوم

59	Toufiq:	Impudence, saucy talk and misunderstanding, these are the worst characters in people. A person who doesn't understanding anything and is yet impudent	*ddsārā waṣlābā waqalit mafhāmā wahadī ākhbat ṣifā fibinādm hīyā hadī. mafāhm wālū wakīdasr*	الدسارا والصلابا وقلت مفهاما و هدي آخبت صفا فبنادم هيا هدي. مفاهم والو وكيدسر	توفيف
60	Kaltoum:	I understand, by God, I understand (LAUGHTER) I understand more than that!	*kanfahm āllah 'īlā kanfahm hhhh ānā 'ād kanfahm ktar min lqīyās*	كنفهم الله إلا كنفهم هههه. كنفهم كتر من لقياس انا عاد	كلتوم
61	Toufiq:	You shouldn't take and talk about it just like that (.) you need to see the value of the morals.	*māšī tqabṭ wathadr 'alīhā ghīr hakāk (.) katšūf lqīma dīyāl l'ākhlāq*	ماشي تقبط وتهدر عليها غير هكاك (.) كتشوف القيمة ديال الأخلاق	توفيق
62	Kaltoum:	Well, we know them	*'īwā hinā 'arfīnhā*	إوا حنا عرفينها	كلتوم
63	Kaltoum:	Foreigners (.) of course foreigners	*French: Des Ètrangers (.) bien sur Des Ètranger*	Des Ètrangers (.) bien sur Des Ètranger	كلتوم
64	Aicha:	(MOCKING HER SISTER'S FRENCH) Foreigners (.) of course foreigners	*French: Des Ètrangers (.) bien sur Des Ètranger*	Des Ètrangers (.) bien sur Des Ètranger	عايشة
65	Kaltoum:	(IN ENGLISH) yes or no	*English: yes or no*	yes or no	كلتوم
66	Toufiq:	Poor thing, try, just try	*mskīna ḥawlī, ghī ḥawlī*	مسكينة حولي غي حولي	توفيق
67	Aicha:	Some day you'll succeed by the grace of God, don't worry, just try	*wāḥid nnhār yiqadr yifūqik āllah māšī muškil ghī ḥawlī*	واحد النهار يقدر يفوقك الله ماشي مشكل غي حولي	عايشة
68	Kaltoum:	I'm accepted by God!	*ānā mūwfaqnī āllah*	انا موفقني الله	كلتوم
69	Toufiq:	But you have to purify your intentions	*wlakin khāṣkī tṣafī nītik*	خاصكي تصفي نيتك ولكن	توفيق
70	Kaltoum:	Look, with this intention I'm totally fine before God	*štī bihād nnīya, alḥamdulillah āllahmalikalḥamd*	شتي بهاد النية، الحمد الله اللهم لك الحمد	كلتوم
71	Toufiq:	With what intention?!!	*bāš bihād nnīya*	باش بهاد النية	توفيق
72	Kaltoum:	Fiiiiine	*bīīīkhīr*	بييخير	كلتوم
73	Toufiq:	He's telling a story about Sayidna Moses	*hūwa kihadr 'alā qiṣa dīyāl sīyidnā mūsā*	هو كيهدر على قصة ديال سيدنا موسى	توفيق
74	Kaltoum:	Better than Figuig[11]	*fūq figīg*	فوق فگيگ	كلتوم
75	Toufiq:	and you're sitting kikiki[12]	*wnītī gālsa kī kī kī*	ونتي گالسة كي كي كي	توفيق
76	Kaltoum:	What's wrong with that? Did I say something haram?	*mālī gālsa gūlt šī ḥāja ḥarām?*	مالي گالسة گولت شي حاجة حرام؟	كلتوم
77	Toufiq:	No, not at all	*lā wālū*	لا والو	توفيق
78	Kaltoum:	Well then	*'īwā ṣāfī*	إيوا صافي	كلتوم
79	Meriam:	Leave it, leave it, it's about to start	*khalīh khalīh hadā yīlāh bdā*	خليه خليه هدا يلاه بدا	مريم
80	Toufiq:	Explain to me (to Kaltoum) what is *tadudan*	*šarḥ lī 'īntayā šnū hīya tadūdān*	شرح لي انتيا شنو هي تدودان	توفيق
81	Kaltoum:	He told you	*gālik*	گالك	كلتوم
82	Toufiq:	And he found two women *tadudan*	*wawakhad min dūnahumā 'īmr'ātān tadūdān*	ووخد من دونهما إمرأتان تدودان	توفيق
83	Kaltoum:	It is said ["Islam is a religion of ease]	*gālik [al'īslām dīn yusr]*	گالك]الإسلام دين يسر[	كلتوم

84	Toufiq:	[of ease not a religion] to mock	*[yusr māšī dīn] tahkm*	[يسر ماشي دين تهكم]	توفيق
85	Kaltoum:	[not a difficult religion"]	*[māšī dīn 'usr]*	[ماشي دين عسر]	كلتوم
86	Meriam:	(TELEVISION CHANNEL CHANGED (change it	*qalib*	قلب	مريم
87	Kaltoum:	I'm not mocking, shame, shame (LAUGHINGLY)	*mātantahkmš ḥāša ḥāša*	ماتتهكمش حاشة حاشة	كلتوم
88	Meriam:	change it (REFFERRING TO THE TELEVISION CHANNEL)	*waqalib*	وقلب	مريم
89	Kaltoum:	Would I mock in the face of the prophets?	*wāš ntahkm ānā 'alā wijh al'ānbīyā'*	واش نتهكم انا على وجه الأنبياء	كلتوم
90	Toufiq:	Is religion laughing at everything?	*dīnū ḍahk f'ay ḥāja*	دينو ضحك فأي حاجة	توفيق
91	Mother:	change it	*waqalib*	وقلب	مريم
92	Toufiq:	What's this? What's wrong that you're making this babel (.) it's just an Egyptian serial	*šnū hūwa? mālik dīr lbalbāla (.) ghīr musalsal maṣrī*	شنو هو؟ مالك دير البلبالة (.)غير مسلسل مصري	توفيق

Acknowledgments

Books are multi-year projects that involve research, writing, revising, seeking out a publisher whose interests align with the book's topics, waiting for external reviews, revising again, and waiting patiently for the final product. As an anthropologist, the research element also entails ethnography, a time-intensive investment in the lived experiences of the people among whom one chooses to work. For me, the ethnographic work extended over a decade. In the process, I have accrued a debt of gratitude to so many who have supported and inspired me along the way. I could never have accomplished this without the Moroccan families who generously allowed me to interview, observe, and record their interactions. Although I cannot name them, I continue to be blessed by my associations with them: they opened homes and hearts to me, separated people from politics, challenged my assumptions, and grounded me through the sharing of food and friendship. I hope I have done something worthwhile with the richness they offered me.

I appreciate the research support provided by the U.S. Fulbright Program and the Moroccan-American Commission for Educational and Cultural Exchange, the American Institute for Maghrib Studies, the Wenner-Gren Foundation, the Council for American Overseas Research Centers, the American Council of Learned Societies, and the Rutgers University Research Council.

Learning the multiple varieties of Arabic that contributed to this project was a collaborative task as well. Paul Hoskisson's scholarly tutelage and encouragement sent me to Syria; Donna Lee Bowen introduced me to Morocco and fostered my academic propensities; Van and Elizabeth Gessel modeled what the life of the mind could be. I had so many interlocutors who enriched my understanding of Arabic and Arabs in all their diversity: Dilworth Parkinson,

Kirk Belnap, Samira Farwaneh, Sulaf al-Zoubi, Halima Mjahed, Abdelhafid, Mohamed Zawahiri, Abdessalam, Mohammed Barakat, Wafa El Abdi, Lubna Boakraa, Fatiha Faraoun, Siham Oubry, Zoubida Rami, Lhoucine and Zahra Boum, Mirella, Denise Badawi, Razan al-Salah, Nermine al-Horr, Fouad Shehabeddine, Margo Akoury, Antoinette Khazan, Kassem Aina, and Georges Farra. I also must include the numerous Moroccan family members, students, and random folks who challenged and encouraged my Arabic skills.

Norma Mendoza-Denton's generous mentoring and training, Jane Hill's brilliance and wit, Leila Hudson's keen theoretical insights, and Tad Park's timely advice can all be found interdiscursively woven throughout my thought and writing. The following have all shaped this book and my ethnographic sensibilities through myriad interactions: Diane Riskedahl, Amahl Bishara, Paja Faudree, Marcy Brink-Danan, Sherine Hamdy, Jessaca Leinaweaver, Saida Hodzic, Aomar Boum, Nicole Taylor, Mourad Mjahed, Kate Goldage, Ari Amand, Ana Preto-Bay, Andrea DenBoer, Jenn Neves, Natalie Jensen, Kristin Monroe, Anne Bennett, Muhammad Ali Khalidi, Abdellatif Hakim, Hassan Rachik, Mohamed Dhabi, Khalid Bekkaoui, Abdelmajid Hajji, Bouazza Bagui, Abdellatif Bencherifa, Michael Silverstein, Asif Agha, Marco Jacquemet, Charles Briggs, Paul Kockelman, Greg Urban, Laura Ahearn, Janet McIntosh, Kate Riley, Nada El-Kouny, Ahmed AlMaazmi, Alan Chen, Kayla Chisholm, Sophie Darbaidze, Zahra Khetani, as well as many others.

Last but not least, I express appreciation to my family. It's a long way from dairyman's daughter to doctorate, from plow to professor. The work ethic, passion to know, and shared humanity I learned in rural Oregon formed the base for all I am and do. Mohammed has walked me through all the times I didn't think I could finish this project: his vision exceeded my own. Zeineb made it all worthwhile.

Notes

Introduction: Moroccan Channels, Channeling Moroccanness

1. "Fassi" is the Arabic identity adjective for someone (or something) who affiliates with the Moroccan city of Fez (English spelling), known as Fès in French and فاس (*fās*) in Arabic. These events often included neighbors, guests, visiting family members, and in my case an observing anthropologist.

2. French for "snack-time," which had become part of everyday speech in Fez.

3. After transcribing this interaction, I asked the family to help me understand what they were doing. My thoughts thus emerged through multiple interactions with my Moroccan friends, triangulated with writings and concepts of other scholars and my own ethnographic observations.

4. Their co-constructed critique in this interaction highlighted an interpretive practice that relied on familiar embodied actions (continuously moving the beads/remote buttons through one's fingers), repetitive linguistic phrases (expressing glory to God as the beads circle), evaluative cues (breathy intakes, tongue clicks, falling pitch contours, mimicry, cooperative affirmations), and explanatory content (the mother's comments about mindless Moroccans worshipping both television and God).

5. Tamazight was added as an official language in 2011, but not well implemented during my fieldwork. A law passed in 2019 sought to rectify this but was not a substantive part of discussions among my Fassi interlocutors.

6. Others have made a similar claim for the development of language sciences (Bauman and Briggs 2003).

7. These were metapragmatic moments of defining what kinds of interactions were appropriate for Moroccanness. Metapragmatics is the study of how speaker awareness of what interaction can or should do emerges and shapes interaction (Silverstein 1993; Bublitz and Hübler 2007). It also extends to semiotic systems

coordinated with language, such as gesture, clothing, bodily comportment, and artifacts, and how interaction and social relations emerge through these multimodal bundles (Agha 2007; Keane 2003).

8. Among linguistic anthropologists, genres like laments are not a discourse classification tool that focuses on identifying formal linguistic features (Briggs and Bauman 1992) mobilized to create hierarchies by colonial and postcolonial scholars (Irvine and Gal 2000). Genres, instead, are orienting frameworks by which listeners, speakers, readers, and writers relate to and use language (Hanks 1987). Scholars have thus analyzed the ways in which speakers linked or distanced linguistic features from previous instances of a genre to do specific social acts (Gal 2018).

9. I have used pseudonyms for all participants in this book, except for Moroccan public figures mentioned by my interlocutors. A transcript of this interaction is included in Appendix I.

10. See the YouTube clip titled, "Benkirane, Tiiini Is Unprofessional and Samira Sitail Has No Shame," https://www.youtube.com/watch?v=wg46Z_2Xsz8, accessed June 2016.

11. See the clip posted on the Radio Aswat YouTube channel: https://www.youtube.com/watch?v=yRmn7XNTpXY, accessed March 2016. In an instance of media navel-gazing, other news networks reported the viral response: https://arabic.cnn.com/world/2016/03/11/samira-sitayl-talks-about-arabic-and-morocco, accessed March 2016.

12. Moroccan phonology drops word-initial vowels; I represent this in my Arabic writing of the term for Moroccan Arabic: الدريجة ("*ad-darīja*") in formal Arabic grammar becomes *darīja* (with a stress on the dental stop sun-letter assimilation of the definite article /l/ into [dd]). See Chapter 4 on ideologies of writing.

13. Fassis referred to formal Arabic as الفصحى (*fuṣḥā*), short for اللغة العربية الفصحى (*allugha alʿarabīya alfuṣḥā*, "the pure/eloquent Arabic"). They included the Arabic of the Qurʿan and the classical literary works, as well as the spoken Arabic of news broadcasts and the written Arabic of books and newspapers within this term. Some scholars have differentiated classical Arabic as separate from the formal Arabic of contemporary states (which they call "modern standard Arabic," or MSA—see Ennaji 1991), but my Moroccan interlocutors never did. They only contrasted *fuṣḥā* with Moroccan *darīja*.

14. Egyptian serials were most often in Cairene Arabic, though they sometimes included serials in Saʿidi Arabics of upper Egypt (Armbrust 1996; Abu-Lughod 2005; Bassiouney 2018).

15. The plural form used here indexes all the North African countries, not just Morocco.

16. In Tamazight, feminine nouns are marked with circumfix /t/, meaning the noun begins and ends with /t/. In this instance, the Arabic word *maghrib* has a denominal noun marker /ī/ and Tamazight circumfix /t/, indexing the mixed linguistic and cultural heritage of Morocco/Maghrib.

17. As Dominic Boyer has stated, "Nostalgia always carries with it a politics of the future" (2012, 25). Ethnographies of nostalgia talk have emphasized it as a reaction to

accelerated temporality of "modernity" (Angé and Berliner 2014) and explored the role of nostalgia by conservative elements of society seeking to legitimate their privileges (Natali 2004), as well as nostalgia as moral critique (Parla 2009), a homeland of the future (Bryant 2008; Hoffman 2006), and as ideological work designed to conceal feelings of guilt by elites and as deceive subordinate groups about class interests (Rosaldo 1989). In this Moroccan case, nostalgic laments of connective failure can be doing several of these things, depending on the context and speakers. Both "conservatives" and "progressives" engaged in nostalgic longing for idealized mediums of social connectedness, whether plurilingualism, multiculturalism, Islam, sartorial expression, respect registers, educational paths, or social media platforms.

18. He had worked alongside opposition journalists Ali Anouzla and Rachid Ninni, all jailed by the Moroccan government for crossing red lines in their newspaper writings (or in Bouachrine's 2018 highly public arrest for sexual harassment). See http://www.alyaoum24.com/539261.html, accessed March 2016, and https://www.hespress.com/opinions/298528.html, accessed March 2016.

19. I appreciate an anonymous reviewer pointing out that the wandering media-attuned shepherd is a recurring trope: see Lacouture and Lacouture 1958.

20. The word meant "beloved" in Arabic, and its use as a kinship term was primarily associated with Fez. It indexed a form of polite cosmopolitanism for Fassi families and could also point to affectation for those who did not identify with Fez.

21. I did not audio- or video-record interactions with Selma's family, but recorded these interactions in my fieldnotes.

22. Most families in Fez lived in multi-residence apartment buildings. "Villas" was the term used for single-family stand-alone dwellings and was associated with wealth and prestige for almost everyone I met.

23. Moroccan national television broadcast the call to prayer according to the schedule in Rabat, which was about five minutes delayed from sunset in Fez.

24. Moroccan stew named for the pottery in which it was made.

25. This was an organic scholarly perspective mirroring Frankfurt School critiques of media, see Horkheimer and Adorno 2002 [1944].

26. I recorded this interaction in my fieldnotes.

27. For other accounts of moments when forms of Arabic become mediator channels of specific kinds of phatic connection, see McIntosh 2010 (Arabic as mediator of madness among the Giriama and piety among the Swahili of Kenya); in Senegal and Morocco (Qur'anic Arabic as healing mediator), see Perrino 2002 and Pandolfo 2018.

28. My thanks to the Center for Middle East Studies at the University of Arizona for granting me the Title VI Foreign Language and Area Studies Fellowship.

29. I found an irony in the mismatch between these readings of a Moroccan representation and Crapanzano's aims, one telling of the power participant frameworks have on interpretative communities (Fish 1980, 335) and the power

dimensions of texts and representations (Fabian 1983). Anthropologists of the 1980s heralded Crapanzano's *Tuhami* as transformative in early postmodern experimental ethnography (Tyler 1986, 136; Fischer 1986, 208, 212). He himself challenged previous ideas about objective knowledge transfer, arguing that interlocutors in an interview setting could create different interactional roles and expectations than the anthropologist assumed (Crapanzano 1981; see also Briggs 1986); *Tuhami* was his response. He wanted *Tuhami*'s voice and framing of Moroccanness to dominate the narrative. Despite this, the Moroccan students in Fes viewed Crapanzano's descriptions as part of familiar otherizing processes they encountered when reading English works about Islam, Arabs, Berbers, Morocco, and the Middle East more generally. They would agree with E. Anne Beal: "An acute sensitivity to one level of the ethnographic encounter—the interaction between the anthropologist and his or her informant—does not translate into the liberation of the works from Orientalist self-other dichotomies, and from the stereotyping of Islamic others as essentially irrational and passive. How is it that Orientalist stereotypes persist despite the explicit sensitivity of these authors to the nuances of the field encounter?" (Beal 1995, 299).

30. Spadola, another ethnographer who worked in Fez, noticed a similar distinction among his interlocutors, but used the Arab premodern literary divisions known as elites (*khassa*) and underclass (*'amma*) commoners (2014:15).

2. Literate Listening: Broadcast News and Ideologies of Reasoning

1. This definition did not foreground literate ways of hearing, though it could be included in the idea of basic skills.

2. In practice, the primary broadcasts of the Moroccan public television news narratives were in *fuṣḥā* or French, with interviews in many ways of speaking. Moroccan Arabics were not translated into *fuṣḥā* or French, but French (or English, Spanish, Japanese, or any other language) interviews on the *fuṣḥā* broadcast were translated to *fuṣḥā*. All forms of Arabic, the Tamazight languages, and foreign languages were dubbed during French language news. From 1994 there was a daily news broadcast in Tamazight, Tarafit, and Tashelhit on Rabat (*al'ūlā*, the first national station), though it only broadcast for ten minutes, once every afternoon, in each language. In 2010, the state created a Tamazight station as a part of its expanded satellite bouquet of channels. The majority of families I worked with in Fez did not speak Tamazight, Tarafit, or Tashelhit, though some did identify as Amazigh. I thus focus my interest on the *fuṣḥā* and French news programming.

3. Notice the national adjective applied to the word "dialect": *darījā* has been nationalized as Moroccan Arabic, even though there are many regional and class-related ways of speaking.

4. I found it significant that many Fassis continued to reproduce the idea that the state should provide jobs for those they educate. Despite three decades of structural adjustment programs in which outside entities like the World Bank directed the

Moroccan state to reduce the number of state employees, I consistently heard the following lament: the state no longer had positions for the educated, so they purposefully made the high school baccalaureate exams so difficult that most students would fail them. They then could not enter university, and the state would not need to worry about their obligations to provide jobs for them. As one Fassi told me, "Why would an educated person want to work in a company?," which for him meant unstable factory work unrelated to the university education received (see also Newcomb 2017, 93).

5. Medi1 started in 1980 as a Tangier-based French-Moroccan radio station at the request of Hassan II, previous king of Morocco. Medi1 marketed itself as a North African station; its programming included news, music, and social and political talk shows in both French and Arabic (news and documentaries in *fuṣḥā* and most of the other programming in *darīja*). Some Moroccans felt Medi1 covered international issues and events more than Moroccan ones, but I heard far more Fassis who enjoyed the station's programming when listening to their car radios. In 2006, after the 2004 communications law opened opportunities for private channel licensing, Medi1 launched an Arabic (*fuṣḥā*) news and documentary television station.

6. How does one learn how to think like a modern citizen through language? Partly through the venues and curriculum where literacy is acquired in Morocco—public schools—and partly through the discipline of repeating grammar rules and uses. However, this assumes a neat transmission among literacy pedagogy, content, ideologies, and minds, which goes against the experiences of almost all Arabic educational studies (Adely 2009; Boutieri 2016; García-Sánchez 2014; Boyle 2004; Wagner 1993).

7. This has certainly been the case in postcolonial Morocco, where the state inherited colonial French assumptions about literacy-as-citizen-control at the same time it mobilized Qur'anically trained educators into the public education system.

8. See chapter 5 for a more detailed description.

9. In attestation to the perduring French influence on communications technology, many Fassis used the French term *numérique* for domicile digital satellite receivers, *télécommande* for television remote control, *ordinateur* for computer, and *portable* for mobile phones.

10. The Mohammed VI Foundation, named after the current king, was created to support Moroccans living abroad.

11. Vacancier + ين = *vacanciin*, or ڤاكونسيّين: Moroccan Arabic speakers regularly attach Arabic plural forms, diminutive markers, or verb tense markers onto French words as a part of plurilingual play and cosmopolitan identity-marking.

12. See Lynch 2006, 35, on Yemeni qat chews and Kuwaiti men's salons.

13. For a detailed ethnographic view of *fuṣḥā* ideologies tied to Moroccanness projects in formal schooling contexts, I recommend the Boyle (2004), Boutieri (2016), and García-Sánchez (2014) studies mentioned previously.

3. Reregistering Media and Remediating a Register: Moroccan Morality Tales

1. I wish to suggest ways we might analyze implicit and explicit media ideologies of producers and viewers when a "lost" commodified register changes mediums and participant frameworks. By paying attention to the ways that different sensorial qualities get linked to possible meanings when embodied in specific contexts (Keane 2003; Hoffman 2006), we can come to understand how implicit and explicit media ideologies can be mobilized in Moroccanness connections. I'm drawing on Webb Keane's elaboration of Charles Sanders Peirce's semiotic theory, in which a particular quality, such as redness, gets linked with other indexical qualities, such as crispness, roundness, sweetness when embodied in a specific manifestation of an apple.

2. http://www.aawsat.com/details.asp?section=24&article=45632&issueno=8252, accessed April 15, 2011.

3. http://aflcine.ahlamontada.com/t378-topic, accessed August 31, 2010.

4. I also heard it called كلام منضومة: *klām mandouma*, "ordered speech."

5. http://www.unesco.org/culture/ich/index.php?pg=00011, accessed October 31, 2010.

6. Thomas Ladenburger and Hannes Nehls created a multimedia presentation/preservation of Moroccan street performers that involved an ethnographic film, storytelling CDs with translational layers, and a visual ethnography website "translating" the contexts and traditions of Moroccan storytelling in Marrakesh: www.alhalqa.com. They entextually and indexically connected street storytelling to Moroccanness: "The Halqa is more than just entertainment and show. It also is an appropriate instrument for the construction of cultural identity. The immediate aesthetic appeal, the agile playing and the almost osmotic exchange between artist and audience are used to pass on information and news, to lecture and to instruct people through moral stories and parables."

7. Shaherarzade and Shahrayar, Said Bouyid Souda, Lalla Aicha La'bou.

8. She reiterated this repeatedly in journalistic interviews: "Producer Fatema Boubekdi Shoots Berber Fable 'The Pillar' in Fifteen Episodes with CGI," *Asharq al Awsat*, July 2, 2004, http://www.aawsat.com/details.asp?section=25&article=210571&issueno=9166; "Boubekdi Renews Contacts with 2M Fans with Hadidan," *Almaghribiya*, accessed March 26, 2010, http://www.almaghribia.ma/paper/Article.asp?idr=14&idrs=14&id=106111; "Fatema Boubekdi: Dramatic Recuperation of Popular Heritage," *Al Hayat*, accessed October 30, 2010, http://www.daralhayat.com/portalarticlendah/197168.

9. Joha is a well-known, slightly ridiculous comedic figure in folk wisdom literature throughout the Arabic-speaking world.

10. The most important Muslim religious feast day in Morocco, in which each family ritually slaughters a sheep and shares portions with the poor, neighbors, and family.

11. Storytellers in Morocco are called لحلاقي (*lḥlāyqī*), the one who creates.

12. دقة مراكشية (*diqqa marrakešīya*): a musical style in which twenty to forty men led by a caller use differently sized drums and a range of off-set beats to create intense rhythms and calls.

13. VCD players' first Moroccan appearance was in 1999, but they were too costly for broad acceptance, starting at 2,500 MAD (about $250 USD). These players were out of the range of most families for reasons other than the player's price. This included the unfamiliarity of the technology, which seemed complicated for many people, and the cost of purchasing CDs in comparison with the initial cost, simplicity, and entertainment variety of satellite dishes. While satellite television continued as the primary and preferred source of entertainment through the 2000s, VCD players began to take off in 2002 with the flood of cheap Vietnamese and Korean players within the range of most family's purchasing power—250–600 MAD ($30–70 USD)—and the option of VCD rentals from sidewalk vendors. VCD players were multifunctional, offering to play CDs, MP3s, and MPEGAVs using one's television—an accessory found in most Moroccan households regardless of economic conditions. In 2004, a merchant in Bab Ftouh Fez who sold VCDs, DVDs, and TVs told me that he sold up to 100 VCD players a day. In that early period, VCDs relied on the contraband circulation infrastructures of migration and trade to connect pirated films with consumer markets. By the late 2000s, the better quality of pirated DVDs cornered the market, and by 2013 online streaming shifted film/series viewing practices.

14. *Bāb alḥāra* was one of the longest-running and most successful Ramadan television series, produced in Syria but broadcast on the Saudi entertainment channel MBC (Middle East Broadcasting Company).

15. These programs were no longer prominent as of 2014.

4. Scripting Sounds and Sounding Scripts: Senses, Channels, and Their Discontents

The epigraph beginning "The national debate . . ." was taken from Abu Zayd al-Muqriʿ, مناقشة دعاة الدارجة, "Debating the Call of darīja," YouTube lecture, https://www.youtube.com/watch?v=_gxOpg74rJo, accessed January 2014.

1. I too am casting myself as a listening subject in this book and writing for an English reading audience.

2. This chapter arose from several presentations: at the Middle East Studies Association Meeting in 2013, at the Writing in the Visual/Virtual Conference at Rutgers University in 2014, and at the American Anthropological Association Meeting in 2015. My thanks to panel coparticipants and discussants for providing a rich environment in which to think about scriptic sensibilities.

3. See the official state website: www.maroc.ma, accessed March 2014.

4. This episode is a composite of interactions I recorded in my fieldnotes over a decade.

5. *Bīp-ī ʻala-yā*: French verb + Moroccan Arabic 2SF imperative suffix, Moroccan Arabic phrasal verb preposition + 1S pronoun suffix.

6. See this graphic design and public debate summarized on http://www.blafrancia.com/node/630, accessed December 15, 2015.

7. Most of the Fassis among whom I worked referred to both Classical Arabic and Modern Standard Arabic (MSA) as *fuṣḥā*. The use of MSA was an English-language educational shibboleth.

8. "Meditel Facebook," modified on October 1, 2011, accessed June 28, 2014, https://mbasic.facebook.com/meditel/photos/a.10150201299391256.307120.315483546255/10150298327266256/?type=1&source=46&refid=17.

9. Many Moroccan advertising companies wrote some Arabic forms in *fuṣḥā* even when Moroccan *darīja* is phonologically distinct, yet most Fassis would read them out loud with the *darīja* pronunciation.

10. Benchemsi transliterated the brand title into French *as Nichane*, *darīja* for "direct" or into street register as "Straight Up."

5. Mediating Moroccan Muslims

Scholarly lecture delivered by Doctor Muhammad al-Ta'wil, professor of religious jurisprudence at Qarawiyyin University during Ramadan 2011 as part of the Hassan lectures (*durus ḥassanīya*). These are state-invited and broadcast religious lectures during the holy month of Ramadan given to an audience of the king, and his brother and son, his advisors, and a contingent of other invited religious scholars of diverse nationalities; http://www.lamppostproductions.com/the-special-characteristics-of-the-maliki-madhhab-shaykh-muhammad-al-tawil/, accessed May 2015.

1. As described in Episode 3 of the introduction to this book.

2. Notably, Moroccans use the Gregorian date (2003) as the reference term, rather than the Muslim *hijri* calendar date (1424), both in media and everyday discussions of the event. Moroccan Muslim historical reference normally uses the *hijri* dates (beginning from the time the Prophet Muhammad fled persecution in Mecca) followed by the Gregorian dates (which they call التاريخ الميلادي ["birth (of Jesus) history"]). In this instance, the event has not been included in Muslim historical time, but rather Europeanized Moroccan national time.

3. Muslim Spain from the fourth to ninth centuries in the Muslim calendar, tenth to fifteenth centuries Gregorian.

4. The radio station began by broadcasting primarily to the urban centers for ten hours a day during Ramadan of that year, but as of 2014 broadcast twenty-four hours a day throughout the country. The television station was available transnationally as well as terrestrially beginning in 2005.

5. الإذاعة والقناة المحمد السادس للقرآن الكريم (http://www.assadissatv.ma/presentation.php?lang=ar).

6. The female leaders have been the subject of great European and American interest, with many documentaries and special news reports about the program.

7. Spadola identified the relationship to *jinn* as the differentiating tool of Islam in Morocco: commoner Muslim practices and beliefs dealt with *jinn* possession while elite Muslims decried possession rituals as sorcery, filled with impurity dangers. Lots of authorities clamored for recognition of effective Islam: the state, *jinn*, *fuqaha* (local healers who employed religious talismans), medical doctors, *shuwafa* (female exorcists), Islamists all claimed knowledge of the unseen. "National discourses of *jinns* often emphasize the dangers of indiscriminate communication across mass fields, rather than within older hierarchical distinctions and channels . . . the anxiety of the reception of the *jinns*—always mediated by material ritual—is thus an anxiety over the call itself at the point where hierarchy is uncertain and does not manage the connections between people" (Spadola 2014, 27).

8. Fassis called this mark a *dirham* because of its iconic resemblance in size to the silver coin of the Moroccan currency.

9. In reference to their practice of wearing long beards with a slightly shaved mustache, as the prophet Muhammad reportedly did.

10. https://www.youtube.com/watch?v=qyiMbKDM1NU.

11. Notice that they did not broadcast information about the American report until El Omari made his claim about the channel indoctrinating extremism. Arabic report found here: http://www.alyaoum24.com/545822.html; English report, http://americaabroadmedia.org/documentary-or-newsroom/examining-religious-television-channels-middle-east.

12. Plural of *murshīda*.

13. At least according to the law. In practice, the king's coterie would interfere in government appointments.

14. It is important to note that religious education has been described as far more informal during pre-independence eras (Eickelman 1985) and even pre-2003 religious education (Spadola 2014).

15. One way for Muslims to accrue good deeds even after they die is to establish an Islamic endowment: "From 750 C.E., perhaps even earlier, an increasingly popular vehicle for the provision of public goods was the *waqf*, known in English also as an "Islamic trust" or a "pious foundation." A *waqf* is an unincorporated trust established under Islamic law by a living man or woman for the provision of a designated social service in perpetuity. Its activities are financed by revenue-bearing assets that have been rendered forever inalienable" (Kuran 2001, 842). Importantly for Morocco, once privately administered, these endowments were taken over by the state after independence (and French colonial legal discussions about whether these endowments were considered property; see Shatzmiller 2001, 49).

16. For those unfamiliar with these terms, "Sufi" is used in English to refer to religious groups organized around a set of practices that are supposed to help devotees have more personal, transcendent experiences with God. These groups are often named for pious individuals who set a devotional path that others follow.

"Sunni" is the English term for Muslims who believe that the leadership of Islam should fall to pious individuals approved by consensus of the community (rather than descendants of the Prophet Muhammad) and be governed by a specific textual tradition (known as the Sunnah). Shi'a is a term used by Sunnis to label those who follow a different leadership and textual tradition.

17. http://www.hespress.com/orbites/267978.html.

18. http://hidayamosque.free.fr/Shari3a/5a9a2e9.php; see English translation at http://www.lamppostproductions.com/the-special-characteristics-of-the-maliki-madhhab-shaykh-muhammad-al-tawil/. See also http://www.mestaoui.com/%D8%B9%D9%82%D8%AF-%D8%A7%D9%84%D8%A7%D8%B4%D8%B9%D8%B1%D9%8A-%D9%88%D9%81%D9%82%D9%87?lang=ar.

19. Ali has argued that Salafi pragmatics are much different from the ones explained here. His understanding of Ibn Taymiyyah's interpretive model (a key source for current Salafi scholarship) suggests that textual interpretation needs to be contextualized to the historical context of Qur'anic revelation rather than construed as analogous to other events (Ali 2000, 87).

20. http://www.moroccoworldnews.com/2015/02/151976/understanding-salafism-part-ii-specificities-salafist-doctrine/.

21. A specific form is even called الجلابة المخزانية (the *Makhzen jellaba*), meaning the one worn by the government employees.

22. Departure from the red Fez and *jellaba* was seen as an opposition move, as occurred in October 2016, when two newly elected parliamentarians, Omar Belafrej and Moustapha Shenaoui, chose to appear at the opening session of parliament in a white *tarbūš lwaṭanī* instead of the standard red Fez. Belafrej said he did so to honor a previous Moroccan politician and national independence leader, Abderrahim Bouabid.

23. Al-Fasi also wore the red Fez and *alrazza* as part of his move to include many Moroccan groups in the independence movement.

24. An example of this recognized index can be found in this Qur'anic recitation instructional episode on Iqra' satellite station, which explicitly addresses viewers in "بلاد المغرب العربي" Arab Maghreb, West Africa, and North Africans in Europe (minute 3:30, and again at 28:15); https://www.youtube.com/watch?v=wcddeaaSdYg, accessed March 2016.

25. Notably, collective recitation used to be the primarily form of learning the Qur'an for children in كتاب (*kuttab*), schools designed for children to orally acquire Qur'anic speech for worship purposes.

26. Most of the Fassis I moved among could immediately identify the difference between Moroccan-style *warš 'an annāf'a* recitations and the more widely known *hafs 'an 'āsim* style. *Hafs* recitation style was used throughout most of the Muslim world, but Moroccans called it the *Mashreqi* or Saudi style. Those Fassis who did not align with the Moroccan model preferred the *hafs* style.

27. Butler explored the ways in which racist utterances by state officials were accepted in "exceptional time" and permitted the legalizing and legitimizing of

detentions and torture of Muslims and noncitizens in Guantanamo Prison. She drew on Austin's speech act to argue that 9/11 created the felicity conditions of "exceptional time." Morocco's situation was different, in that state speech could never demonize Islam, but "May 16" did create "exceptional time" in which specific forms of Islamic practice were screened by the state.

28. Other sciences chairs, named after important scholars in the Maliki tradition, included that of Imam Shatabi for the science of recitation styles; Imam Zaqaq for the science of *fiqh* rules and norms (Islamic law); Imam Ibn Rushd for the science of *fiqh* practices; Imam Sahali for the science of Prophetic biographies; Imam Ibn Atiya for the science of *tafsir*, Qur'anic commentaries; Imam Qarfi for the science of *fiqh* sources; Imam Junayd for the science of Sunni Sufism; Imam Ibn Ajroum for the science of grammar as outlined in the *alarjūmīya* poetic text of Maliki tenets; Imam Naf'a for the science of Qur'anic recitation styles; Imam Warsh for the science of *warš 'an annāf'a* recitation style; Imam Qadi 'Ayyad for the science of Prophetic Merits; and Imam Ibn Hassan Ash'ari for the science of Ash'ari doctrines. Each of these chairs was housed in a large mosque in the city where the scholar resided, so the recording of their lectures took place in cities throughout Morocco. The scholars also had "day jobs"—these appointments were not paid but held significant prestige. Only one chair was held by a female scholar during my fieldwork, that of Imam Warsh for the science of *warš 'an annāf'a* recitation style.

29. These are names of religious scholars or families that produced many scholars in precolonial Morocco of the nineteenth and early twentieth centuries. Those al Kamali named were Qarawiyyin-trained, took oppositional stances to European influence, and were connected to a Sufi *zāwīya*.

30. Another Fassi family made a game of guessing from which regional mosque the collective recitation was being broadcast.

31. Notice the lovely iconic rubbing of phonetic reduplication.

32. This was transcribed by a Fassi with Moroccan Arabic pronunciation of the voiced interdental ذ /ð/ as a dental /d/. The word is recited in connection with the Qur'anic account of Jethro's daughters encountering Moses at the well. The brother sought to focus on the moral implications of "holding back" when in the presence of non-kin males, foregrounding his role as moral teacher to his younger sisters.

Conclusion: Opening and Closing the Channels

1. The transliteration of the Arabic program title is her own and indexes her French educational background (in the /ch/ for ش and /es/ for ات: see her website, www.choumicha.ma.

Appendix

1. Brackets indicate overlapping talk, demonstrating how they anticipated each other's responses.

2. Another sister.

3. Pour from pot to teacup.

4. In his echoing of the presenter's words, Toufiq was intending his siblings and mother as the overhearers of his emphasized statement: what were they doing with the things they were learning from this program?

5. Derogatory term for women, in response to story introduced by the speaker about two unfaithful women, the wives of Lot and Noah.

6. Co-constructed with TV preacher, from Qur'an.

7. Simultaneous co-construction between Toufiq and Kaltoum and TV preacher.

8. Co-constructed with TV preacher, then critiqued.

9. This bracket indicates latching, in which there was no break between Toufiq and Kaltoum's exchange.

10. "Sayid" is a title of respect given to prophets, descendants of Muhammed, and righteous individuals. Shuaib is a prophet mentioned in the Qur'an who becomes Moses' father-in-law, Jethro/Reuel/Hobab.

11. Figuig is the most westerly town in Morocco; this expression is used as a mocking intensification.

12. *Kikiki* = iconic sound of giggling.

Bibliography

'Abed al-Jabri, Mohammed. 1999. *Arab-Islamic Philosophy: A Contemporary Critique*. Austin: Center for Middle Eastern Studies, University of Texas at Austin.

Abu-Lughod, Lila. 1997. "The Interpretation of Culture(s) after Television." *Representations* 59:109–34.

———. 2005. *Dramas of Nationhood: The Politics of Television in Egypt*. Cairo: University of Cairo Press.

Adely, Fida J. 2009. "Educating Women for Development: The Arab Human Development Report 2005 and the Problem with Women's Choices." *International Journal of Middle East Studies* 41 (1): 105–22.

Agha, Asif. 2004. "Registers of Language." In *A Companion to Linguistic Anthropology*, edited by Alessandro Duranti, 23–45. Malden, Mass.: Blackwell.

———. 2005. "Voice, Footing, Enregisterment." *Journal of Linguistic Anthropology* 15 (1): 38–59.

———. 2007. *Language and Social Relations*. Cambridge: Cambridge University Press.

———. 2011. "Meet Mediatization." *Language & Communication* 31:163–70.

Agrama, Hussein Ali. 2010. "Ethics, Tradition, Authority: Toward an Anthropology of the Fatwa." *American Ethnologist* 37 (1): 2–18.

Aguadé, Jorge. 2006. "Writing Dialect in Morocco." *Estudios de Dialectología Norteafricana y Andalusí* 10:253–74.

Al-Batal, Mahmoud. 2002. "Identity and Language Tension in Lebanon: The Arabic of Local News at LBCI." In *Language Contact and Language Conflict in Arabic: Variations on a Sociolinguistic Theme*, edited by Aleya Rouchdy, 91–115. London: Curzon.

Ali, Muhammad M. Yunis. 2000. *Medieval Islamic Pragmatics: Sunni Legal Theorists' Models of Textual Communication*. New York: Routledge.

Alomary, Shaban. 2011. "Conative Utterances: A Qur'anic Perspective." Ph.D. dissertation. Salford, UK: University of Salford.

Amine, Khalid. 2001. "Crossing Borders: Al-halqa Performance in Morocco from the Open Space to the Theatre Building." *Drama Review* 45 (2): 55–69.

Amine, Khalid, and Marvin Carlson. 2008. "Al-halqa in Arabic Theatre: An Emerging Site of Hybridity." *Theater Journal* 10 (1): 71–85.

Androutsopoulos, Jannis. 2010. "Localizing the Global on the Participatory Web." In *The Handbook of Language and Globalization*, edited by Nikolas Coupland, 203–26. New York: Routledge.

Angé, Olivia, and David Berliner, eds. 2014. *Anthropology and Nostalgia*. Berghahn.

Angermeyer, Philipp Sebastian. 2005. "Spelling Bilingualism: Script Choice in Russian American Classified Ads and Signage." *Language in Society* 34 (4): 493–531.

Armbrust, Walter. 1996. *Mass Culture and Modernism in Egypt*. Cambridge: Cambridge University Press.

Asad, Talal. 2009. "Free Speech, Blasphemy, and Secular Criticism." In *Is Critique Secular? Blasphemy, Injury, and Free Speech*, 2:20–63. Townsend Papers in the Humanities. Berkeley: University of California Press.

Bakhtin, Mikhael. 1981. *The Dialogic Imagination: Four Essays*. Edited by Michael Holquist. Austin: University of Texas Press.

"Barbero, Jesús Martín. 1987. *De los medios a las medaciones: Comunicación, cultura y hegemonía*. Ediciones G. Gili.

Bassiouney, Reem. 2009. *Arabic Sociolinguistics*. Edinburgh: Edinburgh University Press.

———. 2010. "Identity and Code-Choice in the Speech of Educated Women and Men in Egypt: Evidence from Talk Shows." In *Arabic and the Media: Linguistic Analyses and Applications*, edited by Reem Bassiouney, 97–121. Leiden: Brill.

———. 2012. "Women and Politeness on Egyptian Talk Shows." In *Arabic Language and Linguistics*, edited by Reem Bassiouney and E. Graham Katz, 129–36. Washington, D.C.: Georgetown University Press.

———. 2018. "Constructing the Stereotype: Indexes and Performance of a Stigmatised Local Dialect in Egypt." *Multilingua* 37 (3): 225–53.

Bate, Bernard. 2009. *Tamil Oratory and the Dravidian Aesthetic: Democratic Practice in South India*. New York: Columbia University Press.

Bayat, Asif. 2010. *Life as Politics: How Ordinary People Change the Middle East*. Stanford, Calif.: University of Stanford Press.

Bazzaz, Sahar. 2010. *Forgotten Saints: History, Power, and Politics in the Making of Modern Morocco*. Cambridge, Mass.: Harvard University Press.

Bauman, Richard. 2004. *A World of Others' Words: Cross-Cultural Perspectives on Intertextuality*. Malden, Mass.: Blackwell.

Bauman, Richard, and Charles L. Briggs. 2003. *Voices of Modernity: Language Ideologies and the Politics of Inequality*. New York: Cambridge University Press.

Beal, Anne. 1995. "Reflections on Ethnography in Morocco: A Critical Reading of Three Seminal Texts. *Critique of Anthropology* 15 (3): 289–304.

Benmamoun, Elabbas. 2001. "Language Identities in Morocco: A Historical Overview." *Studies in the Linguistic Sciences* 31 (1): 95–106.

Bishara, Amahl. 2013. *Back Stories: US News Production and Palestinian Politics.* Stanford, Calif.: Stanford University Press.

Blommaert, Jan. 2005. *Discourse: A Critical Introduction.* New York: Cambridge University Press.

———. 2008. *Grassroots Literacy: Writing, Identity and Voice in Central Africa.* New York: Routledge.

———. 2010. *The Sociolinguistics of Globalization.* Cambridge: Cambridge University Press.

———. 2013. *Ethnography, Superdiversity and Linguistic Landscapes: Chronicles of Complexity.* Tonawanda N.Y.: Multilingual Matters.

Bouasria, Abdelilah 2012. "The Second Coming of Morocco's 'Commander of the Faithful': Mohammed VI and Morocco's Religious Policy." In *Contemporary Morocco: State, Politics and Society under Mohammed VI*, edited by Bruce Maddy-Weitzman and Daniel Zizenwine, 49–68. New York: Routledge.

Boum, Aomar. 2008. "The Political Coherence of Educational Incoherence: The Consequences of Educational Specialization in a Southern Moroccan Community." *Anthropology and Education Quarterly* 39 (2): 205–23.

———. 2012. "Festivalizing Dissent in Morocco." *Middle East Report* 263:22–25.

———. 2013. *Memories of Absence: How Muslims Remember Jews in Morocco.* Stanford, Calif.: Stanford University Press.

Bourdieu, Pierre. 1986. *Distinction: A Social Critique of the Judgment of Taste.* London: Routledge.

Boutieri, Charis. 2012. "In Two Speeds (A deux vitesses): Linguistic Pluralism and Educational Anxiety in Contemporary Morocco." *International Journal of Middle East Studies* 44 (3): 443–64.

———. 2013. "Inheritance, Heritage and the Disinherited: Ambiguities of Religious Pedagogy in the Moroccan Public School." *Anthropology and Education Quarterly* 44 (4): 363–80.

———. 2016. *Learning in Morocco: Language Politics and the Abandoned Educational Dream.* Bloomington: Indiana University Press.

Boyarin, Jonathan. 1993. *The Ethnography of Reading.* Berkeley: University of California Press.

Boyer, Dominic. 2012. "From Algos to Autonomos: Nostalgia Eastern Europe as Postimperial Mania." In *Post-Communist Nostalgia*, edited by Maria Todorova and Zsuzsa Gille, 17–28. Oxford: Berghahn.

Boyle, Helen N. 2004. *Quranic Schools: Agents of Preservation and Change.* New York: Routledge.

Briggs, Charles. 1986. *Learning How to Ask: A Sociolinguistic Appraisal of the Role of the Interview in Social Science Research.* Cambridge: Cambridge University Press.

Briggs, Charles L., and Richard Bauman. 1992. "Genre, Intertextuality, and Social Power." *Journal of Linguistic Anthropology* 2 (2): 131–72.

Briggs, Charles, and Daniel C. Hallin. 2007. "Biocommunicability: The Neoliberal Subject and Its Contradictions in News Coverage of Health Issues." *Social Text* 25 (4): 43–68.

Brown, Wendy. 2009. "Introduction." In *Is Critique Secular? Blasphemy, Injury, and Free Speech*, Townsend Papers in the Humanities, 2:7–18. Berkeley: University of California Press.

Brustad, Kristin. 2017. "Diglossia as Ideology." In *The Politics of Written Language in the Arab World: Writing Change*, edited by Jacob Hoigilt and Gunvor Mejdell, 41–67. Leiden: Brill.

Bryant, Rachel. 2008. "Writing the Catastrophe: Nostalgia and Its Histories in Cyprus." *Journal of Greek Modern Studies* 26:399–422.

Bublitz, Wolfram, and Axel Hübler. 2007. *Metapragmatics in Use*. Philadelphia: John Benjamins.

Burke, Edmond. 2014. *The Ethnographic State: France and the Invention of Moroccan Islam*. Oakland: University of California Press.

Butler, Judith. 2004. *Precarious Life: The Powers of Mourning and Violence*. New York: Verso.

Cairoli, M. Laetitia. 1998. "Factory as Home and Family: Female Workers in the Moroccan Garment Industry." *Human Organization* 57 (2): 181–89.

Campaiola, Jill. 2014. "The Moroccan Media Field: An Analysis of Elite Hybridity in Television and Film Institutions." *Communication, Culture and Critique* 7 (4): 487–505.

Carr, Summerson. 2011. *Scripting Addiction: The Politics of Therapeutic Talk and American Sobriety*. Princeton. N.J.: Princeton University Press.

Caubet, Dominique. 1993. *L'arabe marocain: Phonologie et morphosyntaxe*. Vol. 1. Paris-Louvain: Éditions Peeters.

———. 2005. "Génération Darija!" *Estudios de Dialectología Norteafricana y Andalusí* 9:233–43.

———. 2017. "Morocco: An Informal Passage to Literacy in *Dārija* (Moroccan Arabic)." In *The Politics of Written Language in the Arab World: Writing Change*, edited by Jacob Hoigilt and Gunvor Mejdell, 117–41. Leiden: Brill.

Cherribi, Sam. 2017. *Fridays of Rage: Al Jazeera, the Arab Spring, and Political Islam*. New York: Oxford University Press.

Clarke, Morgan. 2010. "Neo-Calligraphy: Religious Authority and Media Technology in Contemporary Shiite Islam." *Comparative Studies in Society and History* 52 (2): 351–83.

Cody, Francis. 2011. "Echoes of a Teashop in a Tamil Newspaper." *Language and Communication* 31:243–54.

———. 2013. *The Light of Knowledge, Literacy Activism and the Politics of Writing in South India*. Ithaca, N.Y.: Cornell University Press.

Colla, Elliott. 2015. "Dragomen and Checkpoints." *Translator* 21 (2): 132–53.

Combs-Schilling, Margaret Elaine. 1989. *Sacred Performances: Islam, Sexuality, and Sacrifice*. New York: Columbia University Press.

Crapanzano, Vincent. 1980. *Tuhami: Portrait of a Moroccan*. Chicago: University of Chicago Press.

———. 1981. "Text, Transference, and Indexicality." *Ethos* 9 (2): 122–48.

Crawford, David. 2014. *Nostalgia for the Present: Ethnography and Photography in a Moroccan Berber Village*. Amsterdam: Amsterdam University Press

Crawford, David, and Katherine Hoffman. 2000. "Essentially Amazigh." In *The Arab-African and Islamic Worlds*, edited by Kevin Lacey and Ralph M. Coury, 117–33. New York: Peter Lang.

Curtis, Bruce. 2008. "On Distributed Literacy: Textually Mediated Politics in Colonial Canada." *Paedagogica Historica: International Journal of Education* 44 (1–2): 233–44.

Darwish, Ali. 2009. *Social Semiotics of Arabic Satellite Television: Beyond the Glamour*. Victoria, Australia: Writescope Pty.

Davis, Natalie Zemon. 2006. *Trickster Travels: A Sixteenth-Century Muslim Traveler between Worlds*. New York: Hill and Wang.

Davis, Susan, and Douglas Davis. 1995. "'The Mosque and the Satellite': Media and Adolescence in a Moroccan Town." *Journal of Youth and Adolescence* 24:577–93.

De Saussure, Ferdinand. 1959. *Course in General Linguistics*. Edited by Charles Bally and Albert Sechehaye. Translated by Wade Baskin. New York: Philosophical Library.

Dickinson, Jennifer. 2015. "Plastic Letters: Alphabetic Mixing and Ideologies of Print in Ukranian Shop Signs." *Pragmatics* 25 (4): 517–34.

Dwyer, Kevin. 2004. *Beyond Casablanca: M. A. Tazi and the Adventure of Moroccan Cinema*. Bloomington: Indiana University Press.

Eckert, Penelope, and Sally McConnell-Ginet. 1995. "Constructing Meaning, Constructing Selves: Snapshots of Language, Gender, and Class from Belten High." In *Gender Articulated*, edited by Kira Hall and Mary Bucholtz, 469–507. New York: Routledge.

Eickelman, Dale. 1976. *Moroccan Islam: Tradition and Society in a Pilgrimage Center*. Austin: University of Texas Press.

———. 1985. *Knowledge and Power in Morocco: The Education of a Twentieth-Century Notable*. Princeton, N.J.: Princeton University Press.

Eickelman, Dale, and Jon Anderson, eds. 2003. *New Media and the Muslim World: The Emerging Public Sphere*. 2nd ed. Bloomington: Indiana University Press.

Eisenberg, Andrew. 2013. "Islam, Sound and Space: Acoustemology and Muslim Citizenship on the Kenyan Coast." In *Music, Sound, and Space: Transformations of Public and Private Experience*, edited by Georgina Born, 186–202. New York: Cambridge University Press.

Eisenlohr, Patrick. 2011. "Media Authenticity and Authority in Mauritius: On the Mediality of Language in Religion." *Language & Communication* 31 (3): 266–73.

Elinson, Alexander. 2013. "Dārija and Changing Writing Practices in Morocco." *International Journal of Middle East Studies* 45 (4): 715–30.

———. 2017. "Writing Oral and Literary Culture: The Case of Contemporary Moroccan *Zajal*." In *The Politics of Written Language in the Arab World: Writing Change*, edited by Jacob Hoigilt and Gunvor Mejdell, 191–211. Leiden: Brill.

El-Katiri, Mohammed. 2013. "The Institutionalisation of Religious Affairs: Religious Reform in Morocco." *Journal of North African Studies* 18 (1): 53–69.

El Mansour, Mohamed. 2004. "Moroccan Islam Observed." *Maghreb Review* 29 (1–4): 208–18.

El-Nawawy, Mohammed, and Adel Iskandar. 2003. *Al-jazeera: The Story of the Network That Is Rattling Governments and Redefining Modern Journalism*. Cambridge, Mass.: Westview.

El Ouardani, Christine. 2014. "Childhood and Development in Rural Morocco: Cultivating Reason and Strength." In *Everyday Life in the Muslim Middle East*, edited by Donna Lee Bowen, Evelyn Early, and Becky Schulthies, 24–38. 3rd ed. Bloomington: Indiana University Press.

Elyachar, Julia. 2010. "Phatic Labor, Infrastructure, and the Question of Empowerment in Cairo. *American Ethnologist* 37 (3): 452–64.

Ennahid, Said. 2007. "The Archaeology of Space in Moroccan Oral Tradition: The Case of 'Malhun' Poetry." *Quaderni di studi arabi* 2:71–84.

Ennaji, Moha. 1991. "Aspects of Multilingualism in Morocco." *International Journal on the Sociology of Language* 87:7–25.

———. 1995. "A Syntactico-Semantic Study of the Language of the News in Morocco." *International Journal on the Sociology of Language* 112:97–111.

———. 1999. "Language and Ideology: Evidence from Media Discourse in Morocco." *Social Dynamics* 25 (1): 150–61.

———. 2005. *Multilingualism, Cultural Identity and Education in Morocco*. New York: Springer Media.

Ennaji, Moha, and Fatima Sadiqi. 2008. "Morocco: Language, Nationalism and Gender." In *Language and National Identity in Africa*, edited by Andrew Simpson, 44–60. Oxford University Press.

Erguig, Reddad. 2005. "Conceptions of Literacy in Morocco from the 1960s to the 1990s." *Languages and Linguistics* 15/16:133–50.

Errington, Joseph. 2001. "His Master's Voice: Listening to Power in Suharto's Indonesia." *Crossroads: An Interdisciplinary Journal in Southeast Asian Studies* 15 (1): 1–10.

Fabian, Johannes. 1983. *Time and the Other: How Anthropology Makes Its Object*. New York: Columbia University Press.

Faudree, Paja. 2013. *Singing for the Dead: The Politics of Indigenous Revival in Mexico*. Durham, N.C.: Duke University Press.

Ferguson, Charles. 1959. "Diglossia." *Word* 15:325–40.

Fernea, Elizabeth Warnock. 1975. *A Street in Marrakech: A Personal View of Urban Women in Morocco*. Long Grove, Ill.: Waveland.

Fischer, Michael M. 1986. "Ethnicity and the Arts of Memory." In *Writing Culture: The Poetics and Politics of Ethnography*, edited by James Clifford and George E. Marcus, 194–233. Berkeley: University of California Press.

Fish, Stanley. 1980. *Is There a Text in This Class?: The Authority of Interpretive Communities*. Cambridge, Mass.: Harvard University Press.

Foucault, Michel. 1975. *Discipline and Punish: The Birth of the Prison*. New York: Random House.

Gal, Susan. 2018. "Registers in Circulation: The Social Organization of Interdiscursivity." *Signs and Society* 6 (1): 1–24.

García-Sánchez, Inmaculada. 2014. *Language and Muslim Immigrant Childhoods: The Politics of Belonging*. Malden, Mass.: Wiley-Blackwell.

Geertz, Clifford. 1971. *Islam Observed: Religious Development in Morocco and Indonesia*. Chicago: University of Chicago Press.

———. 1973. *The Interpretation of Cultures*. New York: Basic Books.

Gershon, Ilana. 2010a. *The Breakup 2.0: Disconnecting over New Media*. Ithaca, N.Y.: Cornell University Press.

———. 2010b. "Media Ideologies: An Introduction." *Journal of Linguistic Anthropology* 20 (2): 283–93.

Gershon, Ilana, and Paul Manning. 2014. "Language and Media." In *The Cambridge Handbook of Linguistic Anthropology*, edited by N. J. Enfield, Paul Kockelman, and Jack Sidnell, 559–76. New York: Cambridge University Press.

Gillespie, Marie. 1995. *Television, Ethnicity and Cultural Change*. New York: Routledge.

Glasser, Jonathan. 2016. *The Lost Paradise: Andalusi Music in Urban North Africa*. Chicago: University of Chicago Press.

Goodman, Jane. 2005. *Berber Culture on the World Stage: From Village to Video*. Bloomington: Indiana University Press.

Goodwin, Charles, and Marjorie Harness Goodwin. 2006. "Participation." In *A Companion to Linguistic Anthropology*, edited by Alessandro Duranti, 222–44. Malden, Mass.: Blackwell.

Goody, Jack. 1977. *Domestication of the Savage Mind*. New York: Cambridge University Pres.

Graiouid, Said. 2007. "A Place on the Terrace: Café Culture and the Public Sphere in Morocco." *Journal of North African Studies* 12:531–50.

Grandguillaume, Gilbert. 1983. *Arabisation et politique linguistique au Maghreb*. Paris: Editions G.-P. Maisonneuve et Larose.

Haeri, Niloofar. 1997. "The Reproduction of Symbolic Capital: Language, State, and Class in Egypt." *Current Anthropology* 38 (5): 795–805.

———. 2003. *Sacred Language, Ordinary People: Dilemmas of Culture and Politics in Egypt*. New York: Palgrave Macmillan.

———. 2009. "The Elephant in the Room: Language and Literacy in the Arab World." In *The Cambridge Handbook of Literacy*, edited by David R. Olson and Nancy Torrence, 418–30. New York: Cambridge University Press.

Hachimi, Atiqa. 2005. "Dialect Leveling, Maintenance, and Urban Identity in Morocco: Fessi Immigrants in Casablanca." Ph.D. dissertation. University of Hawaii.

———. 2007. "Becoming Casablancan: Fessis in Casablanca as a Case Study." In *Arabic in the City: Issues in Dialect Contact and Language Variation*, edited by Catherine Miller, Enam El-Wer, Dominique Caubet, and Janet Watson, 97–122. New York: Routledge.

———. 2012. "The Urban and the Urbane: Identities, Language Ideologies, and Arabic Dialects in Morocco." *Language in Society* 41 (3): 321–41.

———. 2013. "The Maghreb-Mashreq Language Ideology and the Politics of Identity in a Globalized Arab World." *Journal of Sociolinguistics* 17 (3): 269–96.

———. 2017. "Moralizing Stances: Discursive Play and Ideologies of Language and Gender in Moroccan Digital Discourse." In *The Politics of Written Language in the Arab World: Writing Change*, edited by Jacob Hoigilt and Gunvor Mejdell, 239–65. Leiden: Brill.

Hafez, Kai. 2008. *Arab Media: Power and Weakness*. New York: Continuum.

Hammoudi, Abdellah. 1997. *Master and Disciple: The Cultural Foundations of Moroccan Authoritarianism*. Chicago: University of Chicago Press.

Hankins, Joseph D. 2012. "Semiotics of Organizations." In *A Companion to Organizational Anthropology*, edited by D. Douglas Caulkins and Ann T. Jordan, 204–18. Malden Mass.: Blackwell.

Hanks, William. 1987. "Discourse Genres in a Theory of Practice. *American Ethnologist* 14 (4): 668–92.

———. 1996. *Language and Communicative Practices*. Boulder, Colo.: Westview.

Haute-commissariat au Plan. 2018. *Données du Recensement general de la population et de l'habitat de 2014—Niveau national*. Rabat.

Hawkins, Simon. 2014. "'Madam, You Drive a Hard Bargain': Selling to Tourists in Tunis' Medina." In *Everyday Life in the Muslim Middle East*, edited by Donna Lee Bowen, Evelyn Early, and Becky Schulthies, 262–73. Bloomington: Indiana University Press.

Hirschkind, Charles. 2006. *The Ethical Soundscape: Cassette Sermons and Islamic Counterpublics*. New York: Columbia University Press.

Hoffman, Katherine. 2006. *We Share Walls: Language, Land and Gender in Berber Morocco*. Malden, Mass.: Blackwell.

Holes, Clive. 2004. *Modern Arabic: Structures, Functions, and Varieties*. Washington, D.C.: Georgetown University Press.

Horkheimer, Max, and Theodor W. Adorno. 2002 [1944]. Dialectic of Enlightenment. Stanford, Calif.: Stanford University Press.

Hutchins, Edwin. 1995. *Cognition in the Wild*. Cambridge, Mass.: MIT Press.

Hymes, Dell H. 1962. "The Ethnography of Speaking." In *Anthropology and Human Behavior*, edited by Thomas Gladwin and W. C. Sturtevant, 13–53. Washington, D.C.: Anthropological Society of Washington.

Ingold, Tim. 2007. *Lines: A Brief History*. New York: Routledge.

Inoue, Miyako. 2006. *Vicarious Language: Gender and Linguistic Modernity in Japan.* Berkeley: University of California Press.
Irvine, Judith. 1989. "When Talk Isn't Cheap: Language and Political Economy." *American Ethnologist* 16 (2): 248–67.
Irvine, Judith, and Susan Gal. 2000. "Language Ideology and Linguistic Differentiation." In *Regimes of Language: Ideologies, Polities, Identities*, edited by Paul Kroskrity, 35–84. Santa Fe: School of American Research Press.
Jackson, Michael. 1998. *Minima Ethnographica: Intersubjectivity and the Anthropological Project.* Chicago: University of Chicago Press.
Jacquemet, Marco. 2000. "Conflict." In *Key Terms in Language and Culture*, edited by Alessandro Duranti, 37–40. Malden, Mass.: Blackwell.
Jakobson, Roman. 1960. "Linguistics and Poetics." In *Style in Language*, edited by Thomas A. Sebeok, 350–77. Cambridge, Mass.: MIT Press.
———. 1990. "Shifters and Verbal Categories." In *On Language*, edited by Linda R. Waugh and Monique Monville-Burston, 386–92. Cambridge, Mass.: Harvard University Press.
Kapchan, Deborah. 1996. *Gender on the Market: Moroccan Women and the Revoicing of Tradition.* Philadelphia: University of Pennsylvania Press.
———. 2015. "Body." In *Keywords in Sound*, edited by David Novak and Matt Sakakeeny, 33–44. Durham, N.C.: Duke University Press.
Keane, Webb. 1995. "The Spoken House: Text, Act and Object in Eastern Indonesia." *American Anthropologist* 22 (1): 102–24.
———. 2003. "Semiotics and the Social Analysis of Material Things." *Language & Communication* 23:409–25.
Khalil, Joe, and Marwan Kraidy. 2009. *Arab Television Industries.* New York: Palgrave Macmillan.
Khatibi, Abdelkebir. 1990. *Love in Two Languages.* Translated by Richard Howard. Minneapolis: University of Minnesota Press.
Kockelman, Paul. 2010. "Enemies, Parasites, and Noise: How to Take Up Residence in a System without Becoming a Term in It." *Journal of Linguistic Anthropology* 20 (2): 406–21.
———. 2011. "Biosemiosis, Technocognition, and Sociogenesis: Selection and Significance in a Multiverse of Sieving and Serendipity." *Current Anthropology* 52 (5): 711–39.
Kraidy, Marwan. 2009. *Reality Television and Arab Politics: Contention in Public Life.* Cambridge: Cambridge University Press.
———. 2016. *The Naked Blogger of Cairo: Creative Insurgency in the Arab World.* Cambridge, Mass.: Harvard University Press.
Kroskrity, Paul. 2010. "Language Ideologies." In *Society and Language Use*, edited by Jürgen Jaspers, Jef Verschueren, and Jan-Ola Östman, 192–211. Philadelphia: John Benjamins.
Kuran, Timur. 2001. "The Provision of Public Goods under Islamic Law: Origins, Impact, and Limitations of the Waqf System." *Law & Society Review* 35 (4): 841–98.

Lacouture, Jean, and Simonne Lacouture. 1958. *Le Maroc à l'épreuve*. Éditions du Seuil.
Laroui, Abdallah. 1973. "Cultural Problems and Social Structure: The Campaign for Arabization in Morocco." *Humaniora Islamica* 1:33–46
——. 1977. *The History of the Maghrib: An Interpretive Essay*. Translated by Ralph Manheim. Princeton, N.J.: Princeton University Press.
Laroui, Fouad. 2011. *Le drame linguistique marocain*. Léchelle, France: Zellige.
Latour, Bruno. 2005. *Reassembling the Social: An Introduction to Actor-Network-Theory*. Oxford: Oxford University Press.
Lavy, Victor, Jennifer Spratt, and Natalie Leboucher. 1995. "Changing Patterns of Illiteracy in Morocco: Assessment Methods Compared." *Living Standards Measurement Study Working Paper* 115. Washington D.C.: World Bank.
Lemon, Alaina. 2017. *Technologies for Intuition: Cold War Circles and Telepathic Rays*. Berkeley: University of California Press.
Lerner, Daniel. 1958. *The Passing of Traditional Society: Modernizing the Middle East*. Glencoe Ill.: Free Press.
Levy, Andre. 2015. *Return to Casablanca: Jews, Muslims and an Israeli Anthropologist*. Chicago: University of Chicago Press.
Lynch, Marc. 2006. *Voices of the New Arab Public: Iraq, Al-Jazeera, and Middle East Politics*. New York: Columbia University Press.
MacPhee, Marybeth. 2004. "The Weight of the Past in the Experience of Health: Time, Embodiment, and Cultural Change in Morocco." *Ethnos* 32 (2): 374–96.
Malinowski, Bronislaw. 1936 [1923]. "The Problem of Meaning in Primitive Languages." In *The Meaning of Meaning*, edited by C. K. Ogden and A. I. Richards, 296–336. New York: Harcourt, Brace.
Mardam-Bey, Farouk. 2002. *Ziryab: Authentic Arab Cuisine*. Woodbury Conn.: Ici La Press.
Mattelart, Armand. 1996. *The Invention of Communication*. Translated by Susan Emanuel. Minneapolis: University of Minnesota Press.
Mateo Dieste, Joseph Luis. 2013. *Health and Ritual in Morocco: Conceptions of the Body and Healing Practices*. Boston: Brill.
McIntosh, Janet. 2010. *The Edge of Islam: Power, Personhood, and Ethnoreligious Boundaries on the Kenya Coast*. Chapel Hill, N.C.: Duke University Press.
McMurray, David. 2001. *In and Out of Morocco: Smuggling and Migration in a Frontier Boomtown*. Minneapolis: University of Minnesota Press.
Mendoza-Denton, Norma. 2007. *Homegirls: Language and Cultural Practice among Latina Youth Gangs*. Malden, Mass.: Wiley-Blackwell.
Mernissi, Fatima. 1994. *Dreams of Trespass: Tales of a Harem Girlhood*. New York: Perseus.
Messick, Brinkley. 1993. *The Calligraphic State: Textual Domination and History in a Muslim Society*. Berkeley: University of California Press.
Messier, Ronald, and James A. Miller. 2015. *The Last Civilized Place: Sijilmasa and Its Saharan Destiny*. Austin: University of Texas Press.

Miles, Hugh. 2006. *Al-Jazeera: The Inside Story of the Arab News Channel That Is Challenging the West.* New York: Grove.

Miller, Catherine. 2012. "Mexicans Speaking in *Dariia* (Moroccan Arabic): Media, Urbanization, and Language Changes in Morocco." In *Arabic Language and Linguistics*, edited by Reem Bassiouney and E. Graham Katz, 169–88. Washington, D.C.: Georgetown University Press.

——. 2017. "Contemporary *Darija* Writings in Morocco." In *The Politics of Written Language in the Arab World: Writing Change*, edited by Jacob Hoigilt and Gunvor Mejdell, 90–115. Leiden: Brill.

Miller, Catherine, Enam El-Wer, Dominique Caubet, and Janet Watson. 2007. *Arabic in the City: Issues in Dialect Contact and Language Variation.* New York: Routledge.

Miller, James. 2001. "Trading though Islam: The interconnections of Sijilmasa, Ghana, and the Almoravid Movement." *Journal of North African Studies* 6 (1): 29–58.

Miller, Susan Gilson. 2013. *A History of Modern Morocco.* New York: Cambridge University Press.

Miller, W. Flagg. 2007. *The Moral Resonance of Arab Media: Audiocassette Poetry and Culture in Yemen.* Cambridge Mass.: Harvard University Middle East Monographs.

Mitchell, Timothy. 1988. *Colonizing Egypt.* Berkeley: University of California Press.

Munson, Henry Jr. 1993. "The Political Role of Islam in Morocco (1970–90)." In *North Africa: Nation, State and Region*, edited by Geoge Joffe, 187–202. New York: Routledge.

Natali, Marcos. 2004. "History and the Politics of Nostalgia." *Iowa Journal of Cultural Studies* 4:10–25.

Newcomb, Rachel. 2009. *Women of Fes: Ambiguities of Urban Life in Morocco.* Philadelphia: University of Pennsylvania Press.

——. 2017. *Everyday Life in Global Morocco.* Bloomington: Indiana University Press.

Nevins, M. Eleanor. 2004. "Learning to Listen: Confronting Two Meanings of Language Loss in the Contemporary White Mountain Apache Speech Community." *Journal of Linguistic Anthropology* 14 (2): 269–88.

Nozawa, Shunsuke. 2015. "Phatic Traces: Sociality in Contemporary Japan." *Anthropological Quarterly* 88 (2): 373–400.

Ong, Walter. 1982. *Orality and Literacy: The Technologizing of the Word.* New York: Methuen.

Ortner, Sherry. 2005. "Subjectivity and Cultural Critique." *Anthropological Theory* 5 (1): 31–52.

Pandolfo, Stefania. 1997. *Impasse of the Angels: Scenes from a Moroccan Space of Memory.* Chicago: University of Chicago Press.

——. 2018. *Knot of the Soul: Madness, Psychoanalysis, Islam.* Chicago: University of Chicago Press.

Parla, Ayse. 2009. "Remembering Across the Border: Postsocialist Nostalgia among Turkish Immigrants from Bulgaria." *American Ethnologist* 36 (4): 750–67.

Peirce, Charles Sanders. 1955 [1897–1910]. "Logic as Semiotic: The Theory of Signs." In *The Philosophical Writings of Peirce*, edited by Justus Buchler, 98–115. New York: Dover.

Pennell, Charles. 2013. *Morocco: From Empire to Independence.* Oxford: Oneworld.

Perrino, Sabina. 2002. "Intimate Hierarchies and Qur'anic Saliva (Tefli): Textuality in a Senegalese Ethnomedical Encounter." *Journal of Linguistic Anthropology* 12 (2): 225–59.

Phillips, Susan U. 2000. "Power." In *Key Terms in Language and Culture*, edited by Alessandro Duranti, 190–92. Malden, Mass.: Blackwell.

Porter, Geoff D. 2003. "Unwitting Actors: The Preservation of Fez's Cultural Heritage." *Radical History Review* 86 (1): 123–48.

Rausch, Margaret. 2000. *Bodies, Boundaries, and Spirit Possession: Moroccan Women and the Revision of Tradition.* New York: Columbia University Press.

Rinnawi, Khalil. 2006. *Instant Nationalism: McArabism, Al-Jazeera, and Transnational Media in the Arab World.* New York: University Press of America.

Rouighi, Ramzi. 2012. "Why Are There No Middle Easterners in the Maghrib?" In *Is There a Middle East? The Evolution of a Geopolitical Concept*, edited by Michael E. Bonine, Abbas Amanat, and Michael Ezekiel Gasper, 100–116. Stanford, Calif.: Stanford University Press.

Rosaldo, Renato. 1989. "Imperialist Nostalgia." *Representations* 26:107–22.

Rugh, William. 2004. *Arab Mass Media: Newspapers, Radio and Television in Arab Politics.* Westport, Conn.: Praeger.

Sadiqi, Fatima. 2003. *Women, Gender and Language in Morocco.* Leiden: Brill.

Salamandra, Christa. 2008. "Creative Compromise: Syrian Television Makers between Secularism and Islamism." *Contemporary Islam* 2 (3): 177–89.

Schulthies, Becky. 2013. "Reasonable Affects: Moroccan Family Responses to Mediated Violence." In *The Language of War and Peace*, edited by Adam Hodges. Oxford: Oxford University Press, 193–221.

———. 2014a. "Reviving Official Language Debates in Morocco: The Language of Instruction or the Instruction of Language?" Society of Linguistic Anthropology section column, *Anthropology News*, March 2014.

———. 2014b. "Orthographic Diversity in a World of Standards: Graphic Representations of Vernacular Arabics in Morocco." In *Writing Through the Visual and Virtual: Inscribing Language, Literature, and Culture in Francophone Africa and the Caribbean*, edited by Ousseina Alidou and Renee Larrier, 187–202. Lanham, Md.: Lexington.

———. 2015. "Do You Speak Arabic? Axes of Adequation and Difference in Pan-Arab Talent Programs." *Language and Communication* 44:59–71.

Sebba, Mark. 2012. "Orthography as Social Action: Scripts, Spelling, Identity, and Power." In *Orthography as Social Action: Scripts, Spelling, Identity and Power*, edited by Alexandra Jaffe, Janis Androustopoulos, Mark Sebba, and Sally Johnson, 1–20. Boston, Mass.: Walter de Gruyter.

Seckinger, Beverly. 1988. "Implementing Morocco's Arabization Policy: Two Problems of Classification." In *With Forked Tongues: What Are National Languages Good For?*, edited by Florian Coulmas, 68–90. Ann Arbor: Karoma.

Segalla, Spencer. 2009. *The Moroccan Soul: French Education, Colonial Ethnology, and Muslim Resistance, 1912–1956*. Lincoln: University of Nebraska Press.

Sells, Michael. 1999. *Approaching the Quran: The Early Revelations*. Eugene, Ore.: White Cloud.

Serres, Michel. 2007 [1980]. *The Parasite*. Minneapolis: University of Minnesota Press.

Shannon, Jonathan Holt. 2015. *Performing al-Andalus: Music and Nostalgia across the Mediterranean*. Bloomington: Indiana University Press.

Shatzmiller, Maya. 2001. "Islamic Institutions and Property Rights: The Case of the 'Public Good' Waqf." *Journal of the Economic and Social History of the Orient* 44 (1): 44–74.

Silverstein, Michael. 1976. "Shifters, Linguistic Categories, and Cultural Description." In *Meaning and Anthropology*, edited by Keith H. Basso and Henry A. Selby, 11–54. New York: Harper & Row.

——. 1993. "Metapragmatic Discourse and Metapragmatic Function." In *Reflexive Language: Reported Speech and Metapragmatics*, edited by John Lucy, 33–57. Cambridge: Cambridge University Press.

——. 1996. "Monoglot 'Standard' in America: Standardization and Metaphors of Linguistic Hegemony." In *The Matrix of Language: Contemporary Linguistic Anthropology*, edited by Donald Brenneis and Ronald H. S. Macaulay, 284–306. Boulder, Colo.: Westview.

——. 2003. "Translation, Transduction, Transformation: Skating 'Glossando' on Thin Semiotic Ice." In *Translating Cultures: Perspectives on Translation and Anthropology*, edited by Paula J. Reubel and Abraham Rosman, 75–105. New York: Berg.

Silverstein, Michael, and Greg Urban, eds. 1996. *Natural Histories of Discourse*. Chicago: University of Chicago Press.

Spadola, Emilio. 2008. "The Scandal of Ecstasy: Communication, Sufi Rites, and Social Reform in 1930s Morocco." *Contemporary Islam* 2:119–38.

——. 2014. *The Calls of Islam: Sufis, Islamists, and Mass Mediation in Urban Morocco*. Bloomington: Indiana University Press.

Spitulnik, Debra. 2000. "Media." *Journal of Linguistic Anthropology* 9 (1–2): 148–51.

Spratt, Jennifer, Beverly Seckinger, and Daniel Wagner. 1991. "Functional Literacy in Moroccan School Children." *Reading Research Quarterly* 26 (2): 178–95.

Street, Brian. 1984. *Literacy Theory and Practice*. Cambridge: Cambridge University Press.

Suleiman, Yasir, 2003. *Arabic Language and National Identity*. Washington, D.C.: Georgetown University Press.

——. 2004. *A War of Words: Language and Conflict in the Middle East*. Cambridge: Cambridge University Press.
——. 2006. "Charting the Nation: Arabic and the Politics of Identity." *Annual Review Applied Linguistics* 26:125–48.
Suleiman, Yasir. 2011. *Arabic, Self and Identity: A Study in Conflict and Displacement*. Oxford: Oxford University Press.
Tambar, Kabir. 2012. "Islamic Reflexivity and the Uncritical Subject." *Journal of the Royal Anthropological Institute* 18:652–72.
Theodoropoulou, Irene, and Joseph Tyler, 2014. "Perceptual Dialectology of the Arab World: A Principal Analysis." *Al-Arabi* 47:21–40.
Tyler, Stephen. 1986. "Post-Modern Ethnography: From Document of the Occult to Occult Document." In *Writing Culture: The Poetics and Politics of Ethnography*, edited by James Clifford and George E. Marcus, 122–40. Berkeley: University of California Press.
Urban, Greg. 2001. *Metaculture: How Culture Moves through the World*. Minneapolis: University of Minnesota Press.
van den Boogert, Nico. 1989. "Some Notes on Maghribi Script." *Manuscripts of the Middle East* 4:30–43.
Viveiros de Castro, Eduardo. 1998. "Cosmological Deixis and Amerindian Perspectivism." *Journal of the Royal Anthropological Institute* 4 (3): 469–88.
——. 2004. "Exchanging Perspectives: The Transformation of Objects into Subjects in Amerindian Ontologies." *Common Knowledge* 10 (3): 463–84.
Wagner, Daniel. 1993. *Literacy, Culture, and Development: Becoming Literate in Morocco*. Cambridge: Cambridge University Press.
Wagner, Daniel, Brinkley Messick, and Jennifer Spratt. 1986. "Studying Literacy in Morocco." In *The Acquisition of Literacy: Ethnographic Perspectives*, edited by Bambi Schieffelin and Perry Gilmore, 233–60. Norwood, N.J.: Ablex.
Walters, Keith. 1990. "Language, Logic, Literacy." In *The Right to Literacy*, edited by Andrea Lunsford, Helene Moglen, and James Slevin, 173–88. New York: Modern Languages Association.
——. 1994. "Diglossia, Linguistic Variation and Language Change in Arabic." In *Perspectives on Arabic Linguistics*, edited by Mushira Eid, 8:157–200. Philadelphia: John Benjamins.
——. 1999. "Opening the Door of Paradise a Cubit." In *Reinventing Identities: The Gendered Self in Discourse*, edited by Mary Bucholtz, A. C. Liang, and Laurel A. Sutton, 200–217. New York: Oxford University Press.
Warner, Michael. 2004. "Uncritical Reading." In *Polemic: Critical or Uncritical*, edited by Jane Gallop, 21–46. New York: Routledge.
Warschauer, Mark, Ghada El Said, and Ayman Zohry. 2002. "Language Choice Online: Globalization and Identity in Egypt." *Journal of Computer-Mediated Communication* 7 (4). http://jcmc.indiana.edu/vol7/issue4/warschauer.html#use.
Waterbury, John. 1972. *North for the Trade: The Life & Times of a Berber Merchant*. Berkeley: University of California Press.

Webber, Sabra. 1991. *Romancing the Real: Folklore and Ethnographic Representation in North Africa*. Philadelphia: University of Pennsylvania Press.

Wedeen, Lisa. 1999. *Ambiguities of Domination: Politics, Rhetoric and Symbols in Contemporary Syria*. Chicago: University of Chicago Press.

Wenger, Étienne. 1999. *Communities of Practice: Learning, Meaning, and Identity*. Cambridge: Cambridge University Press.

Wilce, James. 2007. Narrative Transformations. In A *Companion to Psychological Anthropology: Modernity and Psychocultural Change*, edited by Conerly Casey and Robert B. Edgerton, 123–39. Malden, Mass.: Blackwell.

——. 2009. *Crying Shame: Metaculture, Modernity, and the Exaggerated Death of Lament*. Malden, Mass.: Wiley Blackwell.

Willis, Michael J. 2002. "Political Parties in the Maghrib: Ideology and Identification; A Suggested Typology." *Journal of North African Studies* 7 (3): 1–28.

——. 2014. *Politics and Power in the Maghreb: Algeria, Tunisia and Morocco from Independence to the Arab Spring*. New York: Oxford University Press.

Wortham, Stanton, and Angela Reyes. 2015. *Discourse Analysis beyond the Speech Event*. New York: Routledge.

Youssi, Abderrahim. 1995. "The Moroccan Triglossia: Facts and Implications." *International Journal on the Sociology of Language* 112:29–43.

Zaid, Bouziane. 2010. *Public Service Television and National Development in Morocco: Contents, Production, and Audiences*. Riga, Latvia: VDM Verlag Dr. Müller.

——2013. "Quantitative Content Analysis of Moroccan Public Service Television." *Global Media Journal* 3 (1–2): 3–19.

——. 2015. "State-Administered Public Service Broadcasting in Morocco." In *Crossing Borders and Boundaries in Public Service Media*, edited by Gregory Ferrell Lowe and Nobuto Yamamoto, 153–70. Goteborg, Sweden: Nordicom.

Zaid, Bouziane, and Ibrahine Mohamed. 2011. "Mapping Digital Media: Morocco." A *Report by the Open Society Foundations*. https://www.opensocietyfoundations.org/sites/default/files/mapping-digital-media-morocco-20130805.pdf.

Zaouali, Lilia. 2007. *Medieval Cuisine of the Islamic World: A Concise History with 174 Recipes*. Translated by M. B. DeBevoise. Berkeley: University of California Press.

Zhiri, Oumelbanine. 2001. "Leo Africanus's Description of Africa." In *Travel Knowledge*, edited by Ivo Kamps and Jyvotsna G. Singh. New York: Palgrave Macmillan, 258–66.

Index

Becky Schulthies is an Associate Professor of Anthropology at Rutgers, the State University of New Jersey. She is trained as a linguistic anthropologist, with areas of interest including Arabic language ideologies, graphic sensibilities, social media discourse, and, more recently, human-plant semiotic ideologies. She has previously coedited, with Donna Lee Bowen and Evelyn Early, the third edition of *Everyday Life in the Muslim Middle East* (Bloomington: Indiana University Press, 2014).

www.ingramcontent.com/pod-product-compliance
Lightning Source LLC
Chambersburg PA
CBHW032133020426
42334CB00016B/1140
* 9 7 8 0 8 2 3 2 8 9 7 2 1 *